With twenty years' work in Fleet Street behind him, William Moore brings a challenging and perceptive eye to bear on military history. His own military experience includes specialist duties at the Staff College, Camberley, after the war and a period with the intelligence section of a Territorial infantry brigade. Mr Moore now writes full-time and has completed a series of novels, 'The Soldiers', for Sphere. His other non-fiction titles are *Accidental Agent* which was written for John Goldsmith, S.O.E. agent, *The Thin Yellow Line* and *The Durham Light Infantry* for the 'Famous Regiments' series.

Also by William Moore and available from Sphere Books

THE SOLDIERS: BAYONETS IN THE SUN

THE SOLDIERS: AGAINST THE ASSEGAIS

See How They Ran

WILLIAM MOORE

SPHERE BOOKS LIMITED
30/32 Gray's Inn Road, London WC1X 8JL

First published in Great Britain by Leo Cooper Ltd 1970

Published by Sphere Books 1975

TRADE
MARK

Set in Linotype Times

Printed in Great Britain by
Hazell Watson & Viney Ltd
Aylesbury, Bucks

ISBN 0 7221 6151 4

CONTENTS

MAPS

LINE ILLUSTRATIONS

PLATES

TABLES

ACKNOWLEDGEMENTS TO THE ILLUSTRATIONS

Plates nos. 1, 4 and 16: captured propaganda postcards. Nos. 2, 12, 13 and 14: Ullstein. Nos. 3 and 6: London News Agency. No. 5: I.W.M. Nos. 7 and 8: official French photographs. Nos. 9, 10 and 11: Keystone. No. 15: World Wide Photos. Nos. 17 and 18: Mr David Heneker.

The illustrations on pages 74 and 201 are reproduced by permission of *The People*. The Divisional signs on pages 201 and 242 were prepared by Terry Rand and Simon Allen; the maps through the book were drawn by Pat Leeson.

'I congratulate you on your running. I hope you will run as well in the presence of the enemy'

—attributed to Sir Douglas Haig in a speech to Aldershot cross-country teams

PROLOGUE

The drab industrial towns dotting the green face of England were home to thousands of working-class men – men sketchily educated, often ill-nourished, and unacquainted with the world beyond their immediate district. It was a slow-moving world, dominated by steam railways and the horse, where motor transport was a rarity, gas lights more common than electricity, where radio was in its uncertain infancy, and television not even a dream in the unimagined future. For the men of the towns life was often unutterably humdrum – work, early marriage, children, football, boiled cabbage, Saturday night at the pub, and early death. Soldiering was despised and the savage struggle to keep large families on low wages was fought in deadly earnest, for the cheapest raw material in fast developing industrial Britain was the human being. Yet, when the time came, these men were forged into one of the most remarkable armies the world has ever seen.

Why? What is it that holds any army together when according to all experience it should crumble? In the spring of 1918 the British Army had to find a practical answer to that question for General Ludendorff, the most fanatical and powerful of Germany's warlords, had decided on a new course of action. This time he would attack not a city, or a river, or a province, but the British Army itself. Ludendorff would destroy the flesh and blood of Britain in the field; he would smash it, harry it, drain it, until it was beaten to the ground. Crush Britain and the rest would fall of their own accord. On 21 March 1918, he launched his offensive, an overwhelming juggernaut that changed the nature of the war in France and Flanders, and ended the era of trench warfare for good.

Suddenly the British public, its politicians, and some of its generals learned that British troops, after all, were not immovable in defence. After years of marking gains in hundreds of yards they had to swallow the unpalatable truth that the Germans were measuring theirs in miles. Strongholds were overrun in a matter of hours; whole divisions were driven hither and thither at will. The government and GHQ did their best to clamp down on the details of the German successes – with the result that rumour soon blew them out of their already outsize proportions. Quite unfairly the British Fifth Army was made whipping boy for the debacle and its commander, General Sir Hubert Gough, was cast to the wolves. There was talk of an inquiry, but within a matter of days yet another great German offensive sent the British reeling again and the whole matter was precipitately swept to one side. No inquiry was ever held.

Gradually, during the post-war years, the truth was accumulated and it was tacitly admitted that Gough had been wronged. He was belatedly awarded the GCB by the King in person with the, perhaps, ambiguous words: 'I suppose you can take this as a recognition of the gratitude of your country.' (A more significant reward came at the beginning of the Second World War when Churchill picked Gough to command the Home Guard to defend London in the event of an invasion. For a man who had once been blamed for the worst British defeat since Yorktown this was balm indeed.) Gough regretted at the end of his long life that there had been no inquiry, if not for his sake, at least for the sake of the brave men who had been slandered at the same time. Few people outside his own circle of friends realized that this diminutive Irishman lived on to see the start of the 1960s comfortably ensconced in a flat high in St Mary Abbots, Kensington. Ironically visitors to his study-cum-sitting room could see from the window a prominent advertisement: 'Don't be vague. Ask for Haig.'

'The truth of the matter is that I was too loyal to Haig,' he once told me, 'far too loyal.' Gough held Haig responsible for his exposed position on the right wing of the British front and believed that an inquiry would at least have made it plain that he was obeying orders. Gough believed also that, had he been given the troops, he could have dealt the Germans a severe riposte. 'We were counter-attacking with what we had by the end of March,' he said. 'If I'd been given the proper reinforcements there would have been a much different story.' Perhaps. In the event he was sent home in disgrace and even the name of the Fifth Army was obliterated for a time.

Crippled with arthritis in his declining years, Gough would sit in his shapeless, well-stuffed armchair studying articles on ancient Roman coins with the aid of a specially shaped magnifying glass. In a case on the wall beside his bookcase hung a cabinet containing all the brassards he had worn during the war; there was one he had worn commanding the 3rd Cavalry Brigade at Mons, another for the 7th Division he led at Festubert; there was the brassard of I Corps which had been under him at Loos and, of course, his Fifth Army insignia. Alongside these mementos were the medals, including the Victoria Cross, won by his brother John who died of wounds in 1915 while on Haig's staff. Sitting on a gloomy autumn day amid relics, one could not have blamed the old soldier for losing himself in memories and regrets. But Gough would have none of it. He was more likely to discuss the difficulty of getting his wracked frame 'backside first' into a car for some outing or to advise on the real way to take a fence on a good horse . . . 'sit well forrard, well forrard.' When visitors left he insisted on escorting them to the lift despite his infirmity; with his scarlet waistcoat bearing the 'Flying Fox' buttons of the Fifth Army, he would stand at attention until the lift doors closed.

It would be imprudent to be dogmatic in passing judgement on Gough or on the conduct of the British troops who fought in the great defensive battles of 1918 – on the Somme in March, on the Lys in April, and on the Aisne in May. What I have attempted to do is to give some idea of *how* they fought, basing much of my material on contemporary letters and eye-witness reports although, where it has been possible to establish that a veteran's memory is correct, I have used such information as well. In particular I have drawn on the original war diaries of the 6th, 7th, and 8th Battalions, The Durham Light

Infantry, which I was able to study in detail thanks to the good offices of Colonel Leslie Lohan who found time to help me despite his own exacting role at the Ministry of Defence during a difficult period. Sir John Russell, president of the Fifth Army Association, has given me every encouragement and assistance and no one has been kinder than Major-General Hubert Essame, a veteran of The Great Retreat who was later wounded at Villers Bretonneux. (More than twenty-five years later he also took part in The Great Advance and fought with the famous 43rd Wessex Division through Normandy to the Baltic.) As a regular soldier, adjutant of an infantry regiment, General Essame was shocked by much of what he saw at the height of the March retreat. A member of the Institute of Strategic Studies, he has been a forthright critic of the higher command during the First World War. But, as has been said, we shall leave it to readers to judge for themselves. We shall watch how our soldiers fought; we shall see how they ran, and we shall see how they turned to fight again that grim, sullen spring of 1918, the spring after Passchendaele.

CHAPTER ONE

THE VETERANS GATHER

France, January 1918. A howling blizzard whips across the plain of Picardy. Thick, wet snow filters into shell holes, obscures lonely graves, stings the red faces of the living; it soaks greatcoats and chills already numbed feet. A small convoy of staff cars bumps and slides along the road leadings to the small town of Nesle. The ice-encrusted pennant fluttering on the bonnet of the leading car bears a racing red fox with a white-tipped tail – the personal insignia of General Sir Hubert de La Poer Gough, Commander of the British Fifth Army. With his sharp eyes and neat movements, Sir Hubert, a dapper Irish Cavalryman, does not look unlike the fox he has taken as his emblem.

In Nesle, Gough dismounts briskly, brushes the snow from his gleaming boots, exchanges salutes, and turns to the ranks drawn up for his inspection. They are a draft destined for a Midlands regiment and, like Gough himself, are mostly old soldiers with stained and worn uniforms. Time and again in his inspection, Gough's quick eyes register the small gold stripe that denotes the wearer has been wounded. Some men have two stripes. Some three. Gough notes also that a considerable proportion of the men are below average height, and most are far from young. Years later, Gough said, 'I thought to myself, how on earth am I going to win a battle if all they will send me is men like this? As it turned out those chaps did very well, but I couldn't help being worried at the time.'

Gough might well have worried, for hundreds of miles away snow was falling on other, fresher, and larger drafts of men. Amid scenes even more wintry than those at Nesle ranks of soldiers were forming up in Russia, in Poland, and in Romania. Other generals in spiked Prussian helmets and jackboots were dismounting from their staff cars and strutting up and down ranks of young men wearing field grey.

A month before, in December 1917, the Russian Army – its might recklessly squandered in the name of the Czar, and its soul now tormented in the name of the Revolution – had quit the field. An armistice was signed on 15 December and soon afterwards peace negotiations opened at Brest Litovsk. For more than three years Germany had fought on two fronts but now her vast war machine could concentrate its attentions on the British and French. Before the ink was dry on the armistice agreement, the first battalions of German troops were marching to entraining points – 80,000 picked officers and men were on their way to the Western Front, their morale high as one would expect of a victorious army.

All too accurately British intelligence calculated that ten divisions a month could be transferred from east to west on Germany's highly developed railway system and that by the end of February the German Army in France and Belgium would total 185 divisions. Another fifteen divisions could be expected before the end of May. For the first time since the war began, the Allies would be heavily outnumbered. True, the Americans were coming but, considering that the United States had entered the war in April 1917, it was taking an inordinately long time for her troops to arrive in significant numbers. Eight American divisions might be expected by the end of March and thirty-five by midsummer. By then it might be too late.

General Erich Ludendorff, First Quartermaster General of the German Army by title, and its controller in actual fact, was planning a massive new attack. He had demanded the best available troops for his great victory offensive and his wishes had been granted. The troops from the east were blooded veterans still in their prime – most were under thirty-five. The cream of German military might was on its way to a rendezvous with the shabby veterans from Nesle. To understand that meeting in its full context we must first travel back to July 1917 and to Ypres Salient; the Ypres Salient, that awkward bulge jabbing its way so stubbornly into the German lines.

CHAPTER TWO

PASSCHENDAELE'S LEGACY

There was no compelling strategic necessity for maintaining the Ypres Salient. It was held mainly to satisfy the nation's pride; the pride, that is, of that part of the nation not obliged to do the holding. The Salient was perhaps nine miles across the base and as much as four miles deep but there was not a single inch of that shellswept wilderness that could not be reached by German guns, and much of it was under direct enemy observation.

There can have been few more unlikely bases from which to launch a major offensive, yet this is precisely what Haig chose to do. He planned to burst through from the Salient, free the Flanders coast, and put the enemy submarine bases there out of action. Moreover, Haig felt that he had to retain the offensive in order to bolster the uncertain morale of the French Army, stricken by mutinies after its shattering casualties in General Nivelle's offensive the previous April.

There were other ways of helping the French Army, but Haig did not seriously consider them and certainly did not adopt them. He never wavered in his belief that the only way to win the war was to defeat the German Army in the field and he devoted himself singlemindedly to that goal, sometimes to the exclusion of other reasoning. (There was, for example, no real reason to suppose that freeing the Belgian coast would materially affect the war at sea,[12] the U-boats would simply move to other ports.)[12] A more likely explanation of his choice of Flanders was the fascination Ypres held for the whole of the British Empire, and for the survivors of the old Regular Army in particular. It was in Flanders in 1914 that the highly trained riflemen of the original British Expeditionary Force had shattered the legend of German invincibility. It was in

Flanders in 1915 that Canadians, Indian, and British regulars and Territorials had closed the breach ripped in the front by the first gas-attack. Ypres seemed to bring out the best in British troops. Surely, Haig may have reasoned, it would do so again. And there *were* practical advantages in Haig's choice. The British Army had been operational in the Ypres area longer than anywhere else on the Western Front (the cafés even sold egg and chips) and here was already collected much of the paraphernalia needed to sustain battle. There were gun parks, RE stores, rest camps, delousing centres, hospitals, laundries, roads, and railways all run by British for British. Nearby were the ports through which replacements and reinforcements could reach their units from England with remarkable speed. (There is on record the case of a wife who received news of her husband's death in action only forty-eight hours after he had set off on his return from leave in Birmingham.)[54]

But emotional and logistical reasons aside, the Ypres sector had one more virtue in the eyes of Haig – the French had nothing to do with choosing it. Throughout 1915, 1916, and the early months of 1917, Haig had loyally co-ordinated the offensive actions of his own troops with the plans of our allies. For despite their enormous losses up to that time, it was the French Army that the vast majority of people (including Britain's political leaders) expected to provide victory. This expectation had never burned so brightly as before Nivelle's ill-fated offensive against the German position on the Aisne. When that failed, so faith in the French Army withered too – in the hearts of Frenchmen as well as their allies. As far as Haig was concerned it was now up to him. And after his near-success in breaking through at Arras in April 1917, and the mighty mine blast at Messines in June of that year, he was confident. But Haig did not deny, to himself at least, the possibility that the offensive might fall short of expectation.

> If we have a really good success in our forthcoming operations, the value of the French troops will be much

> increased, and while their re-awakened enthusiasm lasts [he had been impressed by General Pétain's appearance at a meeting the week previously] we should concentrate our endeavours on developing this success.
>
> If we do not have a really good success our most urgent and serious care will be to nurse France through the winter without impairing our offensive power for next year's campaign, which is practically certain to be the last campaign we shall induce France or Russia to face (even if we can get them to face that which is doubtful).*

Only a week later Haig complained in a letter to Lord Derby, Secretary of State for War, that he had received no word from the government that it was really determined to concentrate its resources at 'this decisive point at this decisive moment!'

Nevertheless, whatever his reasons and whatever his doubts, Haig was awakened at 0415 on the cool, grey morning of 31 July 1917 by a massive artillery barrage that literally shook the earth. Twenty-five minutes earlier the British infantry had gone over the top taking the first steps on the long, deadly trail to a village called Passchendaele.

The divisions in the attack had been trained after a fashion. The infantry, for instance, had been given blood-curdling lectures in bayonet fighting by a certain Colonel Campbell (who was reputed to drink a pint of bull's blood every morning to keep up his offensive spirit). It was wasteful, the Colonel explained, to plunge a bayonet straight through the body of an opponent. Three inches of cold steel was enough for any man. You jabbed him [the enemy] in the guts, stirred around briefly, swung the butt of your rifle to stun the German next to him while kicking a third gentleman in field grey in the stomach. The troops also solemnly engaged in practice attacks – an unlikely process that consisted of walking behind lines of soldiers carrying flags to represent the barrage which (the powers-that-be swore) would 'obliterate' the German positions.

*From notes dated 22 July 1917, found among Haig's papers.

The paper war grew too. Operation orders, movement orders, appendices, sketches, amendments, and maps poured out, followed by appendices to appendices and amendments to amendments. One infantry battalion* calculated that it had a file of orders a foot thick by the time it took its place in the line for the attack.

Having thus trained them, reinforced them, directed them, and inspected them, the commanders then sent the assault troops into the Salient for what was euphemistically termed a 'familiarization period'. The troops went up singing, at least on the first stretches of their journey, in columns four abreast. Each battalion had four companies, theoretically 136 men strong, of four platoons. Somewhere in the columns there were mules or ponies loaded with reserve small arms ammunition and, more important (to the men at any rate), there were four steaming, seething, horsedrawn vehicles known as cookers. These peculiar vehicles could do two things. They could make tea or they could make stew. The result, of course, was that the stew contained tea leaves and the flavour of onions was never absent from the tea. Not that these small discomforts were apt to trouble the marching warriors, for a man who had humped his equipment miles over the uneven roads of Flanders was unlikely to have a delicate palate at the end of the journey.

As a battalion drew near Ypres, the solid khaki columns gradually split up, first into platoons, then into sections. There were only two main exits towards the line and no one lingered near them very long and lived. Troops left Ypres either by the Menin Gate via Hellfire Corner to one sector, or to the other sectors by the Lille Gate and a forlorn plank road called the Warrington Track. As the troops marched from Ypres, that brooding, crumbling medieval city with its ruined tower, they entered a wasteland. In the low-lying fields from which the attack was to be launched, lay all the awful litter of three years of war. Splintered trees. Shellholes. Shattered trenches. Ruptured sandbags. Broken gas masks. Helmets. Webbing belts. Rusting small arms and ordnance. Shell cases. Sodden fragments of paper and unidentifiable bits of cloth. The

*2nd Northants.

blackened skeleton of a gun limber. Anonymous, gnarled pieces of metal. The variously decayed corpses of men thrust hurriedly in shallow graves (some in 1914, some in 1915, some the previous week) rising from the slime. Other corpses still strung on fragments of barbed wire. Abandoned dumps looming up like the derelict remains of lost civilizations. And everywhere was the smell – a combination of the sweet cloying odour of rotting flesh, and the acrid stink of burnt animal hair and cordite, the mustiness of stale gas. It was a smell that clung to the clothing; a smell that made the teeth ache and the eyes water. A smell that once smelled was never forgotten.

In the ramparts and along the banks of the Yser Canal, which flows through Ypres, conditions grew worse as more troops were crowded into tunnels and caves. All the exits had been registered by German gunners and, though proof against direct hits, leaving and entering these underground havens was a matter of gamble, scramble, flash and bang. A constant stream of traffic through these tunnels did not make life easier for the waiting troops, nor did it improve the efficiency of harassed officers battling vainly with the never-ending stream of orders and counter-orders. Some men looked on the coming assault as almost a deliverance from these intolerable conditions. Thus, when it was announced that the attack had been postponed, hearts sank.

The French First Army had a subsidiary task to play on Haig's left flank and it wasn't quite ready. This was not unanticipated. As early as the beginning of July, Haig had written in his diary after a meeting with General Antoine, the French Army Commander:

> He seemed anxious about the state of morale of his gunners, because many of his guns had come straight from the battle on the Aisne and they [the gunners] must be sent on leave and given "repos". This being so, I arranged to send a brigade of infantry to make the emplacements for the French guns; and also some labour battalions to move the ammunition from the broad to the narrow gauge railways. . . .

While the French were completing their preparations the congestion in the Salient reached its peak. An officer whose battalion was waiting in a vast dugout recalled:

> The atmosphere was mephitic . . . a compound of the stink of marshes, sewage and human sweat. . . . For four days . . . we remained in the tunnel. The sewers of any large city, today, offer more salubrious accommodation, and the rush hour on the London Underground has more room to move. The supply of candles ran out. The casualties to the signal line parties worried me a lot. With these running at the rate of fifty per cent per twenty-four hours it appeared we were likely to start the battle with the reserves of signallers exhausted.[17]

Under constant German fire the casualties in and around Ypres averaged 500 a day even though all troops not on duty were ordered to remain under cover. Men of all arms wondered at the courage and endurance of the Army Service Corps drivers who, night after night, guided their horse-drawn limbers or primitive motor vehicles through the lurid frenzy of the bottlenecks and traffic jams of the streets of Ypres. (Haig himself was moved to pay tribute to these humble heroes in the last entry in his diary before Zero hour on 31 July.)

Fourteen divisions altogether were involved in the initial attack made by the Fifth and Second Armies. All had been involved in severe fighting in the previous eighteen months and three of them, the 8th, 18th, and 30th Divisions had taken part in the assault on 1 July 1916, when 57,500 troops in the eleven attacking divisions were killed or wounded. This time the casualties were not in the same proportion as on that fatal day but it takes a man of formidable insensitivity to accept the Official Historian's comment that, 'The losses, 31,850 for the three days 31 July–2 August were moderate, although in themselves severe.' This ambiguous statement acknowledges that the first attack on the Somme achieved only minor gains whereas the British were able to advance 3,000 yards in the opening of the Ypres offensive.

More artillery support was needed to sustain the attack. The guns had to be brought forward. But the way ahead was torn and blasted, pulverized by the very gunners who would now have to establish themselves there. Across this lunar wilderness the horse-drawn limbers of the ammunition columns would have to plod their perilous way each night. In this riven earth, firm and level gunpits would have to be constructed. All this might have been just possible in dry weather but, in the afternoon of the first day of Haig's cherished offensive, it began to rain. It cleared briefly and then rained harder than ever early next morning. Gradually the shellholes filled with water, the battered trenches started to cave in, and mists hung dankly in the splintered woods. The carefully engineered drainage system in Flanders had been shattered and every crater now added to the horror of the swampland. Philip Gibbs, the most experienced of war correspondents, visiting the battlefield on 3 August wrote:

> The weather is still frightful. It is difficult to believe that we are in August. Rather it is like the foulest weather of a Flemish winter, and all the conditions which we knew through so many dreary months during three winters of war up here in the Ypres Salient are with us again. The fields are quagmires and in the shell-crater land which is miles deep round Ypres, the pits have filled with water. . . . It is hard luck on our fighting men.[21]

(Just how unlucky they were to be was mercifully withheld, but from past experience the troops involved in the initial assault knew better than to expect it to be called off within a few days. Still, even the hardiest would have found it difficult to believe that they would be attacking in the same vicinity more than three months later.)

August 10th saw the resumption of the attacks, designed in this case to clear out strong points along the Westhoek Ridge. No less than ten German counter-attacks had to be dealt with that day and in one place the Germans drove the British back to the start-line of 31 July. Six days later the men of the Fifth Army went forward again, slightly more optimistically because there had been no rain for a few days, but the sodden ground was as implacable as before. Tanks ordered to support the infantry were helpless. Even foot soldiers could make only the slowest progress. Six weighty German counter-thrusts brought the attack to a standstill.

The 8th Division, which had lost 160 officers – including nine battalion commanders – and more than 3,000 men on 31 July was again badly mauled in a vain attempt to take an objective which should have been captured on the first day of the offensive. The cost this time was eighty-nine officers and 2,074 men. Major-General Hubert Essame, who went through both attacks as the adjutant of an infantry battalion, later commented: 'After the middle of August 1917 there was a growing distrust of the staff. It would not be too much to say that we hated them.' Coming from an officer who had led a highly successful brigade through Normandy and into Germany in 1944–45 it is an opinion that cannot be disregarded lightly. Fortunately, not every senior staff officer was unaware of the difficulties facing the troops.

General Gough bluntly informed the Commander-in-Chief that the campaign should be abandoned. Referring to Haig's project of clearing the Belgian coast he said that, 'We would not get through and we ought to stop now.' Haig thought otherwise. Pointedly Haig transferred the major part of the embattled front from Gough's Fifth Army to Sir Herbert Plumer's Second Army.

It was not, alas, in Haig's power so easily to transfer the powers that ordained the weather, nor could he at will change the texture of the saturated soil of Flanders. Throughout September the ground dried out slightly but when the offensive was reopened on the night of the 20th, it again rained heavily. Nearly all the objectives were taken but this general advance of three-quarters of a mile at its deepest point was far removed from the heady ambitions of 31 July.

By 26 September, after another dry spell, the ground was so powdery that Australian troops had to use compasses to keep their bearings in the dust cloud raised by the barrage.[13] Polygon Wood, now a featureless mass of stumps, holes, withered foliage, barbed wire, and shattered pillboxes, was finally taken. Part of it at least was to have been captured, when the battle opened six weeks earlier, as a minor side operation, but by 26 September it had become so important that it gave its name to the battle. And in retrospect, Polygon Wood was probably the most successful of all the Ypres operations. All the limited objectives of the attack were taken (they lay about 400 yards ahead of the start-line), the artillery was able to crush the predictable German counter-attacks, and not a yard of the captured ground was retaken. Flushed by this somewhat overstated success Haig decided to seize, as his next step, the ridge or plateau on which lay the village of Passchendaele.

All other operations would be shelved for the time being and the troops earmarked for them brought to Flanders. Cavalry divisions were allotted to the Second and Fifth Armies, 'pursuit' brigades of infantry were to stand by, and armoured units were warned that they might soon have the opportunity to deploy on firmer terrain. The operation would be initiated on 4 October, in preparation for the main attack about 10 October.

It began to rain at dusk on 3 October. It rained on the tall Australians marching out of Ypres by the Menin Gate. It rained on the New Zealanders moving into positions near the remains of soldiers killed in 1915, buried and exhumed by the shells of countless guns. The rain gleamed too on the helmets and waterproof capes of the British straggling clumsily forward on greasy duckboard tracks beside the swollen streams of the Lekkerboterbeek (Little Bugger Beek the troops called it), and through the pulverized glades of Glencorse Wood. The right of the attack lay in a sector which had been drained by the Reutelbeek and Polygonbeek in more peaceful days. 'Normally a few feet wide and a few inches deep the beds of these brooks, broken by shell craters, had become belts of oozing mud of uncertain depth; joining near the objective, they formed a muddy valley of well over half a mile wide. . . .' So says the Official History. There was worse to come.

As they struggled back with their wounded the next day the survivors of the 21st Division were unaware that they had taken part in a 'great victory'. There were over 4,600 prisoners and more German dead had been seen than on any previous occasion, but the men who took the prisoners and killed the Germans were too busy tending their bleeding comrades and counting their own dead to find time for enthusiasm. The 21st Division, foundering on hidden pillboxes, alone had 2,616 casualties. The Second Army total was 12,000 casualties; the Fifth Army nearly 5,000. About eleven divisions had been shattered in this 'great victory' and yet, let it be repeated, the worst was yet to come. For it had not stopped raining. Until 6 October meteorologists classified it as drizzle with heavy showers but then came squalls of 'cold, drenching rain'.

About the only thing not quenched by this downpour was Haig's ardour. His two army commanders, Gough and Plumer, wanted to call it a day. Plumer had commanded in the Salient longer than any other general and no one knew better than he the terrors of winter there. Gough had seen enough for himself. But Haig insisted that they should continue. There was the necessity of keeping the Germans away from the French. There was the collapse of Russia. Certainly there were plenty of reasons for keeping the battle going but why it should have been in the Ypres Salient Haig did not explain. And so the battle went on, involving division after division, until the best part of the British Army had been plunged into that evil, featureless bog that grew ever deeper and more dismal.

The final attempt to seize Passchendaele village and the surrounding slopes started on 9 October. It was a grim, confused debacle. The 6th Green Howards record that it was so stormy and exceptionally dark that runners sent out with orders for assaulting companies lost their way. Tapes laid out to guide the battalion into position were submerged and unrecognizable. Some units marched for fourteen hours through the mud and reached their positions far too exhausted and too late to keep pace with the barrage. Men of the 49th Division found themselves waist deep in the flooded Ravebeek at the end of their night march. Beyond lay German pillboxes guarded by new-laid barbed wire. The exhausted men of the 66th Division, in their first serious action, were mown down by machine guns from another group of pillboxes. Even the experienced Australians suffered severely. At the end of the day the 66th and 49th Divisions and the 2nd Australian Division had lost nearly 7,000 men between them.

Furthermore, losses of artillery pieces (which had always been heavy in the Salient) were becoming prohibitive. Guns were sinking not to their axles but to their muzzles. The Salient became dotted with red flags where guns had sunk and vanished from sight.

Nevertheless, three days after the disaster of 9 October, the 3rd Australian Division and the New Zealand Division attacked over the same ground. They marched up in darkness, each man clinging to the equipment of the man in front, through an uncomfortable but ineffective counter-bombardment. The New Zealanders attacked behind a weak, inaccurate barrage and were massacred on a wide belt of uncut wire. The Australians were taken in enfilade while struggling through the morass and eventually fell back to their start-line. A few survivors of the 66th Division, who had been hiding in shellholes since the 9th, staggered back with them.

Then it was the turn of the Canadians. They went over for the first time on 26 October drenched by heavy rain and scourged by high explosive and machine gun barrages. They were stopped 400 yards short of their objective. To their right, the 7th and 5th Divisions made a heroic attempt to capture two strongly held spurs of the Gheluvelt plateau, but more than one hundred officers and 3,000 other ranks fell in the attempt and all the ground taken during the day was given up.

On the northern flank the veteran 63rd, 50th and 58th Divisions, plus the relatively inexperienced 57th Division, tried to advance up the valley of the Lekkerboterbeek. The attack merited seventeen lines from the Official

Historian; 'The mud, knee-deep, checked progress to a crawl of rather less than a yard a minute. The barrage was lost, rifles became quickly clogged, and the men fell back, if they could, to the starting-line, or were cut off. . . .' A mild enough epitaph for the 900 dead, the 1,700 missing, the 3,000 wounded.

Strategy, tactics, and morale were gradually submerged together in the muck and squalor. The Poor Bloody Infantry now knew they had no hope. From Ypres it was a nine-hour march across the network of duckboards to the front lines. When the duckboards ended, men were forced to grope around under the slime for the tapes that led to the forward posts – generally rain-filled shellholes without overhead cover. The objectives of an attack became not the ruins of the villages, as they had been in the past, but single blockhouses, or fortified farmhouses. Teal Cottages, Sourd Farm, Varlet Farm, Banff Houses, all held by the Kaiser's faithful machine gunners, absorbed the attention of sections, platoons, and companies plodding slowly up Passchendaele Ridge. To fall wounded meant almost certain death by suffocation or drowning. Even unwounded men stuck in the mud and had to be abandoned. If they were lucky, and their comrades could find the courage, they might be put out of their misery rather than left to slow death.

Service in the Salient was made still more horrible by the Germans' introduction of new gas shells, all neatly marked with crosses so the gunners could identify them. (Apart from tear gas to blind you, there was Green Cross to choke you, Blue Cross to poison you, and Yellow Cross – mustard gas – to burn you.) The latter was first used by the Germans (the Allies did not have mustard gas until the summer of 1918) on the night of 12 July in the Ypres area and was known to the French henceforth as Yperite. Hardly a night passed in the three weeks before the opening of the offensive without some part of the Ypres area hearing the unmistakable belching burst of mustard gas shells. Throughout the months that followed the barrage was steadily intensified. Ugly greenish-yellow splashes marked where the shells had fallen to earth and the liquid took its toll of all who had the misfortune to come into contact with it. It evaporated from splashed clothing and was breathed into the lungs. If it touched the skin great blisters arose. Many men suffered temporary blindness. In the Fifth Army area alone, nearly 8,000 men were gas casualties in the period 21 July to 4 August. By the end of December 1917, more than 48,000 gas casualties had been treated. Deaths numbered 1,500.

The increased gas menace often struck when least expected. Five men of the 2nd Oxfordshire and Buckinghamshires suffered severe vomiting and pain after drinking tea made from a shellhole containing water contaminated by a Blue Cross shell. Thirty-two men of the 18th London Regiment received blistered faces and gums after washing and shaving with water taken from a mustard gas shellhole. The very earth seemed to have turned against the attackers. Only discipline of the highest order can keep an army in action under such conditions. But discipline cannot make a man smile, nor can it hide self-evident truth. As Philip Gibbs put it, the British Army for the first time lost its 'spirit of optimism'.[21]

Passchendaele was finally taken on 6 November by the Canadian Corps and four days later the Canadians attacked again in heavy rain to consolidate their gains. Officially the Third Battle of Ypres was over. Ironically the date was 11 November.

The Official History gives the casualties for 31 July–3 October as 138,787. For 4 October–12 November the figure is 106,110. The Official History concludes vaguely that the Germans must have lost even more men than the British. Whatever the German casualties were, the fact remains that overwhelming damage was done to the British Army for negligible gain. What had been achieved? The Flanders coast had not been cleared; in most places the attackers had reached positions only three or four unimportant miles beyond the objective set for the first day; nor had the offensive diverted German divisions from Italy where their impetus brought about the disaster at Caporetto. No, the outstanding achievement of Passchendaele was to shake what had been until then the British

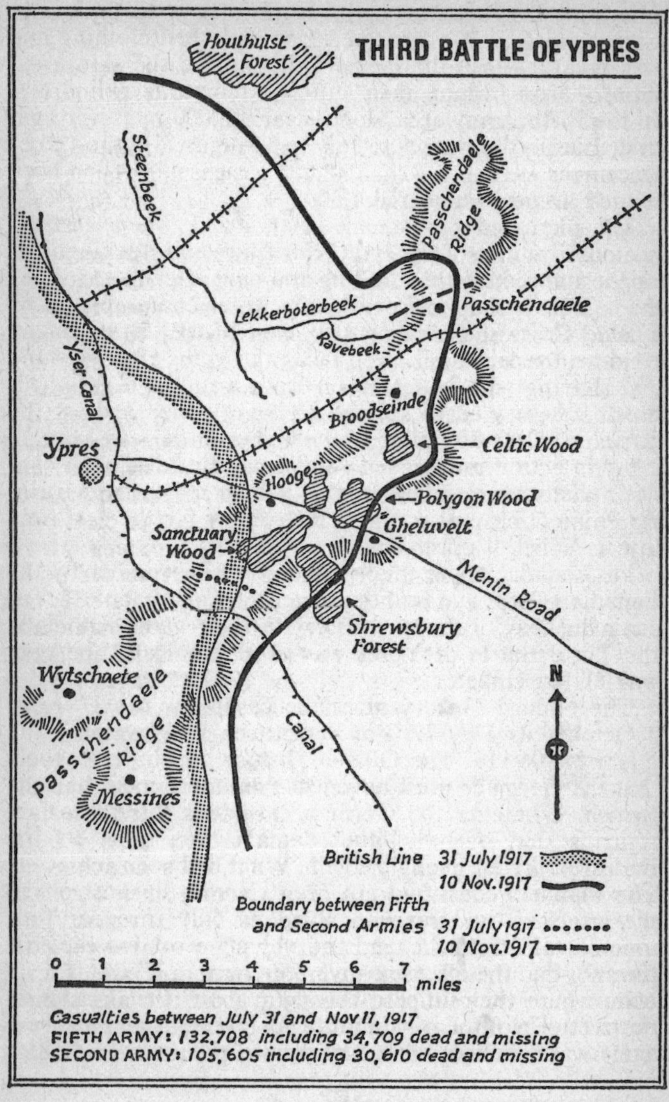

THIRD BATTLE OF YPRES
Houthulst Forest
Steenbeek
Passchendaele Ridge
Passchendaele
Lekkerboterbeek
Ravebeek
Yser Canal
Broodseinde
Celtic Wood
Ypres
Hooge
Polygon Wood
Gheluvelt
Sanctuary Wood
Menin Road
Shrewsbury Forest
Wytschaete
Passchendaele Ridge
Messines
Canal
N
British Line 31 July 1917
10 Nov. 1917
Boundary between Fifth and Second Armies 31 July 1917
10 Nov. 1917
0 1 2 3 4 5 6 7 miles
Casualties between July 31 and Nov 11, 1917
FIFTH ARMY: 132,708 including 34,709 dead and missing
SECOND ARMY: 105,605 including 30,610 dead and missing

Army's greatest asset – its belief in itself and the strength of its regimental system.

As Major-General Essame wrote, 'Every accepted canon of man management of troops in battle had been violated. The turnover of men in the infantry . . . was so rapid that the junior officers seldom had time to learn all their men's names. As I look back on my experiences, I see only a large mass of shapeless, nameless and faceless figures in the ranks.'

Another serious factor which affected British morale was the knowledge that anyone who was wounded would have to wait perhaps twenty-four hours (or longer) before he could could be evacuated, and that the trip to the rear would be made across tracks swept regularly by storms of gunfire. At the beginning of the battle, the wounded were dealt with by RAMC stretcher bearers and regimental aid men. Later two platoons of infantry were seconded to each battalion to act as stretcher bearers during attacks. It was then taking eight men up to four hours to carry stretcher cases shoulder high through the mud to clearing stations. When the mud reached its worst, sixteen men (four teams of four to relieve each other) were needed and whole companies were taken from the infantry battalions in support to do the job. Even the German machine gunners seemed to take pity on the men engaged in this thankless task. After an attack on Teal Cottages on 2 December (note the date) the Germans allowed the wounded to be brought in 'so long as the stretcher bearers did not go too near the post'.[32]

Although officially ended on 10 November, the battle nevertheless spluttered on in a series of savage and bloody encounters. On 2 December elements of the attacking 8th Division reported many gaps blown in the duckboard tracks and subsequently a number of men stuck fast in the mud. Bright moonlight enabled the German machine gunners to see groups of men at about 200 yards range and although the British captured 150 prisoners and four machine guns they suffered heavily and did not take their objectives. The 8th Division's attacks on these meaningless fragments of trench, barbed wire, and pillboxes cost 186 officers and 2,444 men; the 32nd Division suffered equally heavy casualties – casualties that the Official History does not include in the final figures for Passchendaele.

Why had these terrible encounters suddenly become of so little consequence? Because all eyes had been switched to the south where on 20 November the Tank Corps, operating on good ground for the first time, had burst the enemy's line at Cambrai. Ten thousand prisoners and 100 guns were taken, but there was no one to exploit the success. The troops who might have been used to 'go through' the gap were either still engaged at Passchendaele – or they were dead. On 30 November the Germans counter-attacked and took 6,000 prisoners and 100 guns.

Sixteen of the British infantry divisions involved at Cambrai had already been through the slaughter of Passchendaele (the 29th Division had lost 6,000 men at Arras, 4,500 men at Ypres, and a further 4,000 at Cambrai) and yet the generals could not understand 'what went wrong'. A court of inquiry finally absolved the 'higher commanders' and virtually blamed the troops themselves for the Cambrai debacle. The junior NCOs had not been sufficiently trained; machine gunners had not held their ground; there had been confusion, almost panic. None of this (of course) was held to be the fault of the generals; the generals remained as determined as ever to hold their positions to the last private soldier. Sir Douglas Haig certainly thought that the brasshats had been let down. 'I saw General Pulteney, III Corps,' he wrote in his diary for 4 December. 'He looked tired and had evidently passed through an anxious time. . . . The position rushed is immensely strong but the defenders seem to have put up little or no fight at all.'[6]

It is a pity that the court of inquiry could not call as witness Lt Ernst Junger of the 73rd Hanoverian Fusilier Regiment who wrote that his storm company had to deal with machine gun after machine gun at Cambrai adding, 'The English resisted valiantly. Every traverse was contested. Mills bombs and stick-bombs [the German grenade] crossed and recrossed. Behind each traverse we found dead or still quivering bodies.' His unit took 200 prisoners, he records, but 'unhappily, we too had a casualty list of fifty per cent in which was a large proportion of officers and NCOs'.[40]

The simple truth of the situation at the end of 1917 was that the bulk of the fighting troops were exhausted – physically, mentally, and emotionally. Nothing shows more vividly the nerve-wrenching strain on the men who endured the horrors of Ypres and Passchendaele than the findings of the doctors who compiled the Official Medical History of the War. The Official History gives a number of uncompromising accounts of individual patients in the NYD(N) – Not Yet Diagnosed (Nervous) – Centre No. 62 at Haringhe, some twelve miles behind the lines.

> The patient, aged about 27 years, was a man with very inferior physique. He lay with his head under the blankets. When his head was uncovered, his gaze became fixed and he had the appearance of witnessing some terrifying spectacle. This lasted for a few minutes, and then he broke into loud weeping. He appreciated questions only when shouted at loudly. He could not speak, sit up or walk. When placed on his feet he collapsed limply. . . .[46]

Miraculously this patient made some sort of recovery.

NYD(N) Centre No. 62 was opened in July 1917 and served the Fifth Army. From then until the end of the war 8,000 patients suffering from shell-shock, war neuroses, and various mental disorders passed through it. Of this number 5,000, be it noted, were treated during August, September, and October 1917. Some men were admitted suffering from what was termed, 'Exhaustion psychosis'. Describing a typical patient, wildly excited and unwilling to remain in bed, the Official History records:

> He kept up a constant low muttering, snatches of which were intelligible and were found to refer to his later experiences in the line. . . . He appeared to be

living again and again through his recent experiences . . . and interpreted anything occurring near him from this point of view. Those next to him he thought were comrades in his unit whom he addressed by name and talked to continually; or they were German snipers and so on. Frequently he would sit up in bed with a terrified look on his face, shout "Look, look!" after which he would sink back in bed moaning a friend's name.

Any noise occurring near was thought to be from bombs, shells, machine guns or other weapons, and was liable to bring on one of these brief outbursts.

There were a number of men who suffered total amnesia. A man of twenty-five, in the prime of life, did not know why he was in the NYD(N) Centre. He explained in a puzzled way, 'I was assisting Lieutenant "X" in looking after some wounded. We had several bombardments. I went outside the dug-out for fresh air, and I remember climbing the stairs to get out. The next thing I knew, I found myself in bed . . . and wondered why they would not give me my clothes.'

A large group of nervous cases consisted of men suffering from an 'incipient breakdown'. Men who to all intents and purposes were perfectly well but, when suddenly 'faced with an experience of inexpressible horror,' lost their self control. The prolonged and constant subjection to bombardment, sometimes for hours, sometimes for days, accounted for another group of casualties. Doctors observed that during the waiting period before an assault nerves were kept on edge. After an attack came the poignant experience of the roll call which so many comrades failed to answer. Worse still was the repetition of the experience, frequently with nothing to compensate for the horror they had undergone. 'Little by little, men became worn down by such experience,' wrote a medical observer, 'and despite their best efforts, the time would come when it was impossible to keep their minds from preying on the ordeals and sights of the battlefield.' Such men would decline slowly and often reached hospitals tagged with the report that they had become 'quite useless in the line'. The wonder of it was that slightly more than half the 'nerve cases' were returned to their units after treatment.

Sometimes apparently callous decisions were taken, as in the case of the tunnelling officer who, having been trapped and gassed when the enemy blew a counter mine which wrecked the underground gallery he was in, suffered a complete retrograde amnesia. Gradually deteriorating, he was evacuated to England where it was recorded that 'his aspect and regard have those of extreme mental defect'. He was unable to perform the simplest toilet act without supervision. Six months after the incident he was improving although he 'still had days when his memory was very poor'. This did not prevent the medical board some weeks later passing this wreck fit for further service and returning him to a tunnelling unit in France. 'It was found, however, that his memory was not reliable, and he could not be trusted with any important work.' If officers could be treated in such a ruthless way, what hope was there for other ranks?

To make things even more difficult, sheer physical hardship can cause what appear to be 'mental' symptoms. Basically, the majority of cases treated at No. 62 NYD(N) Centre were suffering from 'simple exhaustion'. Unlike the neurasthenia and anxiety cases, unlike the hysterical cases and those in a confusional state, the exhaustion cases did not have exaggerated symptoms or need specialist treatment. They were given plenty of good, hot food, as much sleep as they wanted, night or day, and eventually transferred to a convalescent block where their recovery was normally rapid. To put it simply, they had gone beyond the limits of endurance and were unable to continue without rest. No one was immune from such a possible collapse. In fact, the incidence of officers treated at No. 62 NYD(N) Centre was proportionately higher than that of other ranks during the Ypres battle.

The real point about these shell-shock cases is that they were only the extreme visible symptoms of a condition which afflicted, in varying degrees, all troops who spent any time in the nightmare trenches between Ypres and the Passchendaele Ridge. This included most of the

British Army. The mere fact that many more men were not in hospital from mental breakdown did not mean that they were untouched by their experiences.

An officer of the 1/5th Royal Warwickshire who won the Military Cross commanding a company during the attack of 4 October, and whose battalion was in the front line for four days following the attack, wrote subsequently, 'During the last two days of this affair my mind was so numbed and my body so exhausted that I was utterly useless.' When the division was sent to a quiet part of the line to recuperate (the word is his) he found himself, 'so low in spirits, so nervously exhausted that I could hardly apply myself to reconstructing the company, the first task being to write twenty-two letters to the wives and mothers of men killed under my command'.[61]

Fear – monstrous, unremitting fear – was the constant, nerve-fretting companion of any soldier at Passchendaele. Guy Chapman remembers when the 13th Royal Fusiliers were relieved by a battalion of the East Lancashires during a barrage. 'We fled away with orders to rendezvous at Shrapnel Corner, an unknown place of unhealthy name, where lorries would pick us up. The enemy was dropping 5.9s about the Bassevillebeek, but not the footbridges, fortunately, for the duckboards were crowded with dazed and desperate men from our own and the 5th Division; they were tumbling over one another in their anxiety to escape from the pit.'[11]

E. Norman Gladden had a similar experience,

> As a line of khaki figures appeared along the horizon from the rear, pandemonium seemed to be let loose. Coloured lights dropped from the plane, while in front fearful red rockets shot into the sky. The relief was in but the enemy no doubt thought that another attack was developing. 'Clear out' and 'Every man for himself' were shouted along the line. Panic took command. In a mad stampede we passed through the relieving company. Undoubtedly we had lost our nerve. . . .
>
> I saw men crying and I would have cried myself had I the tears. The company that night was in the grip of

a sort of communal terror, a hundred men running like rabbits.[25]

The most impressive thing about Gladden and his comrades is not that they fled in fear, but that despite the terrors which pursued them and surrounded them, these ordinary soldiers ('I never saw our officers') dutifully made their way back to Ypres in small groups and the whole company was present at roll call the next morning.

Simply to occupy a stretch of the line in the Ypres Salient during the winter of 1917–18 was enough to test the nerves of the strongest and bravest. German artillery barrages continually swept the area and were considered by experts to be among the heaviest shelling of forward positions ever experienced. The mud and water grew deeper and corpses slowly dissolved and became at one with the elements.

Relief was a word to dream about. Those for whom the dream did come true could hardly believe it. When the 23rd Division was transferred from Ypres to the Italian front, it went by rail from the Salient down the Rhone Valley and through the south of France. The effect of such beauty after the horrors of Flanders was considerable. 'Our morale has increased 50 per cent today; the Riviera has revived our battered spirits as much as a tot of rum would have done. I feel quite tired with rushing from one side of the carriage to the other to see some new and wonderful sight,' an officer recorded in his diary.[56]

The 23rd Division was among the lucky ones, only five divisions in all being sent to Italy. For the others it meant another winter in France or Flanders. For the unluckiest of all it meant freezing in the slush of Passchendaele Ridge. Even the redoubtable Haig confided to his diary, 'All British divisions were very weak and tired after a year's fighting.'

In the NYD(N) wards in No. 62 casualty clearing station the 'simple exhaustion' cases tossed, moaned, and murmured in their sleep. No one would have dreamed of telling them to get well quickly because they would be needed the following spring. But it was true for all that.

CHAPTER THREE

THE MANPOWER PROBLEM

The early weeks of 1918 were, for most British soldiers on the Western Front, the slack tide of the war. The non-stop Allied attack was over. Now it was the turn of the Germans, but everyone knew they wouldn't attack until they had received enough reinforcements from Russia. Until that day arrived, apart from holding the line and sampling the dubious joys of winter in the trenches, there would be time for very necessary training, there would be time for sport. There was even a chance of home leave.

In the meanwhile, in Britain itself, the search for replacements for the depleted battalions in France continued but it was hardly prosecuted with great vigour. After the fervour of the volunteers early in the war, disillusionment had set in and potential conscripts did not hesitate to find excuses no matter how extravagant.

Pleading for the deferment of a cemetery superintendent, a Bath town councillor stated the man was no good for the army because he suffered from rheumatism. The chairman of the tribunal remarked shrewdly that if that was so the cemetery was no place for him. The councillor was not deterred and returned to the attack; the superintendent knew every grave and it would be very awkward if someone put a deceased wife in with the wrong husband. Result: three months' exemption.

In the years that followed the war, an acrimonious argument flourished in which the generals blamed the politicians for holding in England troops that should have been sent to France; the politicians replied that the generals were given enough men but did not use them properly. A more realistic argument is that by 1918 the war had become too big and complex for anyone to prosecute it confidently and with skill. Never before in Britain's history had the demand for manpower come from so many sources. The vastly extended Royal Navy had to be kept up to strength yet skilled men had to be held back for the vital work of building and repairing merchant ships after the terrible ravages of the almost successful 1917 U-boat campaign. Our chemical industry, which had been practically non-existent before the war (we depended on Germany!), had been built up from scratch and was now a thriving and demanding section of the war economy. Similarly our expanding armaments factories needed labour, as did the mines, and the land, and the public services. It had become a question of priorities which was never satisfactorily answered. Apart from the shortage of manpower, there was an even greater shortage of confidence in the leaders whose task it was to win the war.

Haig was ordered to remain on the defensive (he had earlier been talking of resuming the offensive in Flanders in the spring) and a strict clamp was placed on the number of reinforcements. Instead of more manpower, Haig would have to rely upon increased fire power – more Lewis guns per battalion, more Vickers guns per division, more tanks and planes per Corps and Army. There would be no cut in the number of divisions but, as in the French and German armies, the number of infantry battalions would be reduced and the surplus units used to reinforce existing divisions. At the same time, after discussions involving the Allied Supreme War Council at Versailles, Haig was ordered to take over twenty-eight miles of the front then held by the French on his immediate right. With his resources thus stretched to the limit there was no possibility of Haig trying to persuade the government to let him try another grand assault.

At this juncture another man might have felt that it was his duty to offer his resignation. Haig believed in little or nothing that he was being asked to do; in fact, he was certain that it was wrong. But he stayed – for what reasons we can only guess. Had he resigned (as did Sir William Robertson over the proposal to create a general reserve for the

French, British, and Italian armies), the subsequent conduct of the war might well have been altered by a new Commander-in-Chief. Instead Haig obeyed orders. Relations between Sir Douglas and the Prime Minister, Mr David Lloyd George, were now extraordinarily delicate. The latter had made it clear to Haig before the start of the Ypres offensive that if it looked like turning into another Somme it would have to be called off. His criticism behind the scenes was scathing and unceasing, but Lloyd George shrank from confrontation. He even sent a hypocritical message of congratulations to Sir Douglas at one of the blackest periods in the Passchendaele campaign. Conversely, Sir Douglas had regularly assured the Prime Minister and the Cabinet that his attacks were gradually smashing the German will to fight. The stunning German riposte at Cambrai had destroyed that illusion. Now neither Prime Minister nor Commander-in-Chief had faith in one another but neither was willing to force an end to the psychological stalemate between them. Lloyd George could not bring himself to sack Haig (and thereby admit that he had not been strong enough to dismiss him during the Ypres battles); Haig was not prepared to tempt the government by offering his resignation. In the end both men compromised, with disastrous consequences for the soldiers at the front.

And the officers and men in the line already had worries enough. The decision to disband the New Army battalions before any others in order to provide reinforcements for the reorganized divisions may have made sense militarily, but it caused bitter resentment.

Kitchener's New Armies, it has been said, contained the cream of the nation's manhood and this is probably for the most part true. To a man they were volunteers, hand-picked for fitness (standards were to fall later), and were inspired with a Victorian idealism, ambition, and faith that seems naive today but which proved singularly effective and powerful at that time. They did not take kindly this veiled criticism of their efficiency. The transfer of battalions caused unrest too. It was widely believed that most brigadiers would use the new structure to rid themselves of their problem children but in the event they did not. A number of reliable battalions had to be transferred to the 16th Irish and 36th Ulster Divisions to maintain their strength. There was no conscription in Ireland and the recruiting – depressed as much by the bungling at Passchendaele as by the Easter Rising – had fallen to rock bottom. As a result, a crack formation like the Inniskilling Fusiliers was posted from the 29th Division to the 36th Division. Other English battalions were posted to regional formations; e.g., the 5th King's Shropshire Light Infantry was transferred from the 63rd Division to the 19th Division, a West Country unit. Happiest of all the soldiers in France at the prospect of a transfer were the men of the 2nd Battalion, Royal Welch Fusiliers, for they would at last be leaving the accursed 33rd Division whose commander had forbidden the issue of rum and substituted tea and cocoa in its place.

The tactical efficiency of the new divisional structure was the most difficult problem of all. The British Army's peacetime training had been based on divisions comprised of three brigades with four battalions each. For three years the British Army had fought in this formation and now, on the eve of the impending German offensive, they had to reorganize their thinking. No longer could a division with two brigades in the line risk relieving both at once; nor could a brigade with two battalions in the line do likewise. The long-suffering Pioneer battalions, reduced from four companies to three, were now seen by their commanders more and more as a potential emergency reserve.

The tactical handling of machine guns was another issue the reorganized army had to deal with. At the beginning of the war all infantry battalions had two obsolete Maxim guns which were gradually replaced by the Vickers gun. In peacetime one of these guns was kept carefully tucked away for special occasions and the other was used for training and exercises. The result was that stress was inevitably laid on the role of a single gun generally in a colonial and minor context.

The German system was better suited to a European

war.* Their regiments were similar to our brigades, but the commanders of regiments looked upon the machine gunners as belonging to the formation as a whole. A German regiment's machine gunners trained together on exercises and as there were many more machine guns in a German regiment than in a British brigade, they were more effective. Increasing the number of machine guns in British battalions during the war, first to four, then to sixteen and even more, did not fundamentally change the approach, despite the formation of the Machine Gun Corps.†

Only in February 1918 did machine gun battalions combine the four machine gun companies which then existed in each British division. But by then the time for training was running out . . . just when it was most needed. For it was the machine guns that would have to provide the defensive backbone along the weakest part of the British front line.

With only twelve infantry and three cavalry divisions (equivalent to about one infantry division), Gough's Fifth Army, still recuperating from its gruelling experience in the Third Battle of Ypres, had to hold forty-two miles of line. Never, during the First World War, had a British Army been spread so thinly. By comparison, the Third Army (on the left flank of the Fifth) had fourteen infantry divisions to cover twenty-eight miles of line and had more artillery as well. Unable, therefore, to hold a continuous line, and with limited artillery support, General Gough placed maximum reliance on his machine guns and on the determination of the infantry to make the best use of their Lewis guns, which now totalled thirty-four per battalion. There was one unfortunate drawback to this faith in machine guns as far as the Fifth Army was concerned. The system depended on 'shell proof' emplacements (such as the pill boxes at Passchendaele) with interlocking fields

*View expressed to author by Major-General Sir John Dunlop, military historian and machine gunner 1914-17.

†A fascinating and prophetic assessment can be found in the Eleventh Edition of *The Encyclopaedia Britannica* published in 1911.

of fire over a deep area. Any attackers who penetrated the thinly held outpost line could be delayed here until a properly organized counter-attack was delivered by fresh troops sheltering in deep dugouts or concrete bunkers behind the battle zone. These were basic conditions to make the defence workable; they were sadly lacking on the Fifth Army front.

CHAPTER FOUR

GUNS, SECRECY, TRAINING

The zone devastated by the Germans when they retreated to the Hindenburg Line in the spring of the previous year had not yet recovered. It was an eerie experience for the columns of British troops marching through that open country dotted with sullen, leafless woods. As their hob-nailed boots echoed from the skeletons of once thriving homesteads, their thoughts may have strayed to the bustling back areas of the Flanders front, where English was as common as French, where the Red Shield canteens of the Salvation Army were a familiar sight, and where the red light establishments had sergeants outside controlling the queues. But here in this silent, rolling wilderness even railways were rare.

If there was consolation, it was that the sector had been quiet for months. After all, if communications were poor, there was no chance of bringing up the millions of shells needed for another Passchendaele-type attack. Alas, the troops were not going to enjoy the quiet atmosphere for long.

Whatever faults may have been found with General Gough in previous battles, no one can say that he did not do everything in his restricted power to prepare for the avalanche about to crash upon his army. His appreciation of the situation as outlined in a number of communications to GHQ, beginning as early as 1 February, made it clear that he had no doubts about the impending attack. Like a man trapped in a nightmare Gough saw disaster looming but was unable to make anyone in authority heed his warnings. When it was all over, he alone of all the people in high places could have said, 'I told you so.' It says much for the generous nature of the man that, although victimized, he did not speak out in his own defence until twelve years had elapsed – and then with tactful reservations.

Haig himself was obsessively certain that the main weight of the attack would come in the north. Not uncharacteristically, Haig seemed to assume that because he had attacked the German army in its strongest positions on the Somme and at Ypres, the enemy would obligingly dissipate themselves against the bulwark of Arras. So certain was he, that he had originally allotted the flabbergasted General Gough a meagre eight divisions for his extended front. Haig grudgingly gave Gough more divisions only when it was pointed out that if Haig *was* wrong, eight divisions would not even delay the enemy, never mind stop him.

One man who did take Gough's warnings seriously and made far-reaching practical preparations was the newly appointed Commander-in-Chief, Royal Flying Corps, Major-General John Maitland Salmond, then only thirty-six years old. At the beginning of February he increased the number of aircraft available on the Fifth Army front by eight fighter squadrons and two reconnaissance squadrons. Even more important Salmond increased the mobility of his aircraft. Reserve airfields were built behind the lines and the reserve vehicles for the RFC brigades were increased by fifty per cent. Special lorries were added for headquarters. The flexibility provided by the extra airfields and the mechanization of the supporting ground staff was to prove invaluable when the time came.[42]

Slowly Gough's repeated warnings bore fruit. On 2 March the Commander-in-Chief held an Army commanders' conference at Doullens at which the GHQ intelligence appreciation included the statement: 'There are strong indications that the enemy intends to attack on the Third and Fifth Army fronts with the object of cutting off the Cambrai salient and drawing in our reserves.' The salient referred to, better known to the troops as the Flesquières Salient, lay at the junction of the two commands but was principally the concern of the Third Army.

That night Haig wrote in his diary, 'I told the Army commanders that I was very pleased with all that I had seen on the fronts of the three armies which I had recently visited. Plans were sound and thorough, and much work has already been done. I was only afraid that the enemy would find our front so very strong that he will hesitate to commit his army to the attack with the almost certainty of losing very heavily.'[6]

A week later the GHQ Weekly Summary of Intelligence asserted that it was improbable that the coming offensive would extend farther south than Epéhy – about five miles from the junction of the Third and Fifth Armies. On 17 March, only four days before the blow actually fell, the same summary stated that there was no reason to change its previous views, adding, 'It is possible . . . that the enemy feels he has not yet sufficient preponderance, either in infantry or artillery, to justify an immediate offensive.' Almost as an afterthought the summary described the increasing concentration of dumps and aerodromes on the Arras–St Quentin front ('indications that the Germans are completing their preparations for attack') but, disregarding the logic of the evidence, the Intelligence Summary concluded, 'The final warning will almost certainly be a short one. Up to the present it has not been given, and, although we must be prepared for an attack at short notice, there is no need to expect an offensive from day to day.'

To Gough, whose predictions seem clairvoyant today, this 'Intelligence report' must have made strange reading. Even some of his own divisional commanders were not convinced that they were the target of the coming storm and they pleaded for time to rest and train their reorganized formations. Incessant work was wearing out the men, they complained. Gough, certain in his heart that he was right, told them to carry on digging. It was their only hope of salvation – and a slender one at that.

And in truth, on the GHQ maps at least, the situation did not look as black as Gough painted it. Behind the neatly shaded area indicating the front line and the battle zone, a bright green line had been carefully drawn by the draughtsmen at headquarters extending the full length of the forty-two mile front. This was the much vaunted Green

Line. Here, according to the plan, would be deep trenches and stout machine gun emplacements, dug-outs that were proof against the shells of even the formidable German 5.9 howitzer, and well-protected headquarters where a CO could maintain his communications in security. It would be a rock on which any German troops who broke through the battle zone would flounder.

It did not exist.

Only the front line was in a state of battle preparedness when the British took over from the French. There were no constructions behind the front lines save belts of wire. The battle zone would have to be prepared by the men on the spot and by whatever labour Gough could extract from headquarters. But not only was GHQ unsympathetic, they ordered Gough to construct an additional defence line for twenty-five miles around the key town of Péronne and another twenty-five miles of works behind that – a total of about 300 miles of trenches. Gough redoubled his efforts to obtain the necessary navvies needed for these gigantic earthworks.

> Some idea of the neglected condition of this front, [he wrote] can be gathered when it is realized that the administrative requirements to ensure proper movement and supply in battle were, sixteen narrow gauge lines, at least four new sidings, the maintenance and strengthening of forty roads, and the building of at least two new bridges . . . Four trains per day, carrying stone and metal for the roads, and four trains per day of engineering material were wanted to fulfil our requirements.

By persistent badgering, Gough managed to build up a remarkable labour force of about 60,000 which gradually filled the area behind the lines with an amazing babel of tongues. There were leather-belted, middle-aged English navvies ('Invicta' steam rollers and all), wiry Chinese coolies, Italians, Indians, and even some 7,000 German prisoners loading and unloading stores. But it was only by the middle of March that the bulk of these labourers were collected and even then they were engaged for the most part on communications, dumps, burying cables, or making airfields. The heavy burden of digging new defence works still remained with the fighting troops.

For the divisional commanders of the over-stretched Fifth Army and, to some extent, for those of the Third Army, it was an insoluble dilemma. If their men had to dig, they couldn't train. Added to this (and quite apart from the difficulties raised by the new structure of divisions) was the need to drum into the men in the field the subtleties of planned retirement. The German army had executed the manœuvre successfully in its retreat to the Hindenburg Line; and certainly the British Army of 1914 would have understood what to do – they were professionals. But the professionals were dead and the British troops of 1918 lacked, in varying degrees, the guile, initiative, and military craft of their predecessors.

Some of the training which did take place was wholly inadequate. On 20 March, the day before the Germans attacked, the 151st Brigade rehearsed counter-attacks across fields in the Marcelcave area. The order read, 'The barrage will be represented by forty men of the 8th DLI with tins beaten by sticks, and drums. The enemy will be represented by a company of 8th DLI with caps reversed.'

And so the unit band solemnly marched over hedges and ditches thumping and drumming in their role as an artillery barrage to where men with their flat caps reversed lay crouched in ditches waiting to fire blank ammunition at their comrades. Many times in the days to come these same men would cower again in ditches while Death's own drummers stalked the same fields.

On the day the 151st Brigade held its training exercise the enemy divisions were already marching to their final assault positions. Their training was finished but unlike the men holding the front of the Fifth Army it had not included a surfeit of digging. From the beginning of January, in practice grounds all over Germany and in areas miles behind the lines, the crackle of musketry and machine gun fire persisted day after day as the assault troops were conditioned to forget the rules of the trenches and adapt themselves to a war of movement. Practice attacks were carried out on dummy trenches with live bombs and ammunition. Casualties among the troops in training did not dampen their ardour, even when a company commander was accidentally shot off his horse. The artillery practised the barrage with live shells, and the infantry were taught to follow closely behind it. Again there were casualties, but the skill and confidence gained was considerably more than that instilled by following a line of men 'with tins beaten by sticks'.

General Ludendorff was taking no chances. He visited the attack formations to see for himself how they were progressing in the transition from the rigid tactics of the trenches to the fluid tactics of open warfare. Whenever he saw problems arising, and there were many of them, he assigned one of the younger German General Staff officers to deal with the situation.[45] Gradually a vast mass of storm troops, in the prime of life, well-armed, well-trained, and enthusiastic was gathered.

In the meantime, the German trenches were manned by divisions of lesser calibre, reduced to the status of garrison troops and equipped accordingly. In forming two such dissimilar bodies Ludendorff was creating a problem that reacted sharply against him later in the year. But at the time he had eyes only for the magnificent spearhead of his striking force, and in particular for the tremendous concentration of artillery that had been assembled. From the searing flame and flailing white hot metal of its barrage he planned to forge the key with which to shatter the deadlock of years.

* * *

They came by night the big guns, ugly and mis-shapen under their tarpaulins on the low flatcars of the long supply trains. In dimly lit sidings, teams of horses emerged from the darkness and hauled them to waiting pits where sweating gunners heaved and pushed them under the camouflage drapes. By morning those at work or on watch in the forward areas would discover that a new battery had arrived. To the infantry this must have been a heartening sight. The gaping, black mouths of 210mm howitzers glared evilly over the walls of shattered cottages (whose foundations made firm firing platforms). Canvas screens hid from prying airmen the ominous tracks leading to the still woods which concealed the long-barrelled 150s. A Bavarian urinating in a sunken road was startled to discover that a battery of vicious 130mm whizz bangs had been installed there since the previous day. The 77mm field guns with their iron shod wheels were hidden in hedges and ruins and thickets. Farther forward, in weapon pits and in the trenches themselves, the shrouded mortars stood silent as the bomb dumps grew beside them.

For the gunners the main topic of conversation was not the mass of guns around them – most of them had seen big concentrations before – but the new orders. Previously when a battery entered a different part of the line it registered, firing a shell or two to check its range and to make various technical adjustments. This had been forbidden. Despite the opposition of senior artillery experts, Ludendorff had given instructions that ranging would be carried out only by the latest scientific methods. And so battery officers pored over aerial photographs, studied the frequent meteorological reports, and painstakingly ranged their weapons with sound locators and flash-spotting equipment. Not that the idea was original. It had been tried very successfully by the British at Cambrai; but not on such a scale. By 21 March 6,500 German guns and howitzers were in position.

Ludendorff was advised by an artillery expert who had retired before the war, but who had served with conspicuous success since his recall. Lieutenant-Colonel G. Bruchmüller and his artillery had paved the way for the successful German offensive in north-west Russia which led to the capture of Riga at the beginning of September 1917. At Riga, the Germans relied on complete surprise, opening fire only six hours before the assault. The infantry and cavalry who made the attack were not brought to their assembly positions until a week beforehand and no new gun emplacements were dug. The bewildered Russians, completely unprepared, were swept away. The breakthrough impressed not only the German higher command but the British and French, too. A paper on the tactics used at Riga – and at Caporetto – was prepared and circulated by French headquarters.

General Gough did not miss the significance of the appearance on the front of another bird of ill-omen, Lieutenant-General Oscar von Hutier. This 60-year-old Prussian, former commander of the German 1st Guard Division, was none other than the victor of Riga, the man who had given Bruchmüller his head. More than six weeks before the start of the threatened offensive Gough had drawn the attention of GHQ to the fact that Hutier had taken command of the German Eighteenth Army newly arrived opposite his front. Shrewdly he pointed out that a number of additional crossings had been built over the St Quentin-Cambrai Canal in the German lines, thus enabling the enemy to concentrate troops and guns in the forward areas quickly and at will.

For the benefit of officers on the southern half of his front who might be lulled into a false security because it was protected by the River Oise, Gough recalled that the battle of Riga had opened with the enemy forcing the line of the Dvina.[28]

What no one on the British side could anticipate was the magnitude of the attack. Ludendorff engaged a massive coordinated attack by three armies against all of the British Fifth Army front and just over half of the front held by Byng's Third Army. The main attack was to be carried out by the German Seventeenth and Second Armies while Hutier's Eighteenth Army was to strike simultaneously and just as heavily at the right of the British Fifth Army with the understanding that its mission might be either to swing to the right, assisting in a vast wheel northwards, or to overwhelm any attempt of the French to assist the Fifth Army. For Ludendorff the ideal solution of the attack was for the Second Army under General von der Marwitz to break through the centre of the British line and strike north with Otto von Below's

Seventeenth Army, while the Eighteenth Army held a huge defensive flank to the south along the Somme. Had von der Marwitz and von Below followed the suggestions about artillery preparation made by the inspired Colonel Bruchmüller this might well have come to pass. Fortunately for the British, although Bruchmüller was empowered to give advice to the other army commanders they were not obliged to take it. In the event they listened with only half an ear, von Below perhaps influenced by the fact that when he had tried to take Riga in 1915 he had only a partial success. Thus when the battle opened it was on the Fifth Army front only that the evil genius of the elderly colonel was fully felt.

Carefully and patiently the old gentleman had worked out his plans for the artillery of Hutier's Eighteenth Army. The long-distance and flanking batteries were formed into one group. Guns for counter-battery work formed another. The remaining and greater part of the ordnance at his disposal was reserved for the most important target of all, the British infantry.

Although it was a compliment they would have willingly foregone, Bruchmüller's master plan was a tribute to the reputation the long-suffering 'PBI' had earned in more than three years of war. For their stubbornness and valour they were awarded a belt of fire which extended for up to four miles behind the British front line. Some idea of the intensity of this moving wall of flame, smoke, noise, and hurtling metal can be gauged from the fact that even the oldest 1896 pattern of the German 5.9 howitzers were allotted 300 rounds per battery for the first day alone. The 1913 pattern, the most modern of the 5.9s, had 600 shells per battery for the same period and most of these would be expended within five hours.

The barrage was to open at 0440 with a rain of gas and high explosive shells on the rear to smash communications. Then at 0530 all batteries would switch to the infantry positions for ten minutes followed by three more ten-minute bursts during which ranging checks would be completed. At 0710 the major barrage was to be loosed on the British strongpoints and trenches for exactly two hours and twenty-five minutes. Special groups of guns would also sweep the areas between the British defence zones during this period just in case anything had been overlooked. At 0930 the barrage would reach its climax.[9]

Howitzers and medium mortars would blast the British front line, while the super-heavy howitzers and heavy mortars flattened a belt just behind it, and the field guns the area behind that. This final holocaust would last five minutes. Then, wrote Colonel Bruchmüller in his suggested plan of operations, 'the infantry will assault without "hurrahs".'

CHAPTER FIVE

KAISER ON THE SCENE

At the beginning of March a new type of bore began to appear in the clubs, drawing rooms, and kitchens of England – the man who knew just what would happen when the storm burst. Everyone, from the Prime Minister to the humblest citizen had his private theory. The so-called military experts and the war correspondents could talk and write of little else.

By Sunday 17 March 1918, however, even newspapers seemed to be in possession of information enabling them to draw conclusions that, in the event, were to prove almost as accurate as GHQ's 'Huns to attack British on West Front – Blow at Channel Ports' forecast one 'expert'.

Newspapers also reflected the manpower shortage that weekend. They carried advertisements urgently calling for 'home service only' recruits for the Royal Garrison Artillery and the Army Service Corps. Men had to be under fifty years of age and not less than five feet in height.

The vexing question of manpower was one of the subjects raised over lunch at Haig's headquarters at Montreuil only a couple of days later. The guests included the Duke of Westminster, a brace of generals, and Mr Winston Churchill, the energetic and resourceful Minister of Munitions. Rather to Haig's dismay, the irrepressible Winston announced that in order to supply the deficiency in men he had ordered, with the blessing of the War Cabinet, a fleet of 4,000 tanks. Testily Haig confided to his diary – not without justification – that no one seemed to have considered where the crews for these machines were to come from. But he was to have a much more interesting and more relevant conversation before the day was done.

It was late and Sir Douglas had finished dinner. His

mind was concentrated on the somewhat comforting subjects raised by two of his guests, questions of supplies and materials. Suddenly there was a familiar tap at the door and in walked Haig's chief of staff, Lieutenant-General Sir Herbert Lawrence, carrying a sheaf of reports. Haig could tell immediately from the expression on Lawrence's face that he had something of importance to impart. He had indeed.

The reports described what on other occasions would have been commonplace events on the Western Front. Two Alsation deserters had stumbled, dirty and dishevelled, into the British lines south of St Quentin. A bewildered German artillery NCO had been seized and dragged away by raiders near the village of Bony. At Villiers-Guislain, infantry had been captured by an enterprising patrol. Near Ly-Fontaine a German plane had crashed and the pilot had been taken prisoner. Insignificant in themselves, taken together they yielded the last parts of the jig-saw being pieced together by intelligence officers. The German attack was imminent.

One can feel a certain compassion for Haig as he studied the reports and maps that evening. For more than two years he had borne the crushing responsibilities of Commander-in-Chief and before that had held posts which subjected him to constant strain. Moreover, he was embroiled again with the hated politicians and just the previous week had been involved in prolonged and sometimes heated discussions with the British and French premiers in London. Nor had his private life been without its anxieties. During the London conference he had been troubled about the health of his wife, who was pregnant. Fortunately all went well and on 15 March she gave birth to a boy, much to Haig's delight. With his mind full of family events, political problems, and military affairs, he had little time after his return to France on 17 March to settle down before the revealing reports of 19 March were in his hands.

In his own diary that night, the British Commander-in-Chief stated that the reports showed 'the enemy's intention to attack about March 20th or 21st'. To his wife, out of consideration for her feelings as much as for the sake of security, he sent a letter on 20 March concealing the concern he must have felt.

> The enemy is rather threatening for the moment. I therefore think it will be better for me to delay coming over to see you for a week. That is to say I'll arrange to come on Friday 29th. The cook is making some soup for you, and I am arranging to send it by King's Messenger. I am very disappointed at having to put off seeing you for a week, but under the circumstances it is right that I should do so. Everyone is in good spirits and only anxious that the enemy should attack. And if he did attack on Saturday and I was in England it might lead to 'talk'. Not that my actual presence in France at the moment of attack is necessary because all reserves and other questions, such as moving up troops to support, have already been settled – but on general principles, I ought to be with the Army when the battle is active.

But Sir Hubert Gough, for one, was unhappy with the movement of reserves. There had been a most difficult telephone conversation between himself and the chief-of-staff after dinner one evening that week. Gough, by then certain that the blow was about to fall on his own extended front, had requested that the two solitary divisions earmarked by GHQ as reserves for his Army should be moved nearer the front line. One of them, the 50th, was twenty-five miles from the front. The other, the 20th, was fifteen miles behind the lines.

Sir Herbert Lawrence, ten years Gough's senior (at forty-seven Sir Hubert was the youngest General in the British Army) was not pleased with this request. To move the divisions would be to 'commit' them he argued. It was premature. Sir Hubert could not see the full picture and it was to be lamented in fact that he had moved the reserves already under his own command nearer the front before he knew where the enemy's main attack would fall. The chief-of-staff concluded with a little lecture on strategy which left Sir Hubert angry.

On 19 March Gough wrote to his wife, 'I expect a bombardment will begin tomorrow night, last six or eight hours, and then will come the German infantry on March 21st . . . everyone is calm and very confident. All is ready.' Even as he wrote, the German assault troops were moving up to shelters just behind the front or to their actual jumping off positions. Could he have lifted the curtain of darkness over the lines on the night of 20 March, Sir Hubert might have had second thoughts about the confidence he expressed.

The grey columns of storm troops, shepherded by bleakly efficient staff officers, had tramped the last miles of their journey through steady rain, the first which had fallen for eight weeks. Up to 19 March, the weather had been mild and sunny and, although the shellhole area behind the front was slippery, the fields were firm enough to allow the passage of troops and guns with comparative ease. Had the spring been a wet one, the collection of such a huge force might have proved an almost insuperable task. Even under the favourable weather conditions which existed, the mounting of the assault during the hours of darkness, in accordance with the strict timetable laid down, was a magnificent achievement. No excuses were allowed for formations which failed to keep to schedules laid down in the movement orders. Battalions or batteries which arrived too late at a rendezvous to take their correct place in a divisional column were condemned to spend long hours in ditches by the roadside or in the fields until such time as a gap occurred.

Near the front, a particular scene was repeated again and again. Guides, wrapped in capes, would appear from the darkness to lead units to positions allocated and signposted well in advance. The columns of heavily burdened infantry halted. Clusters of shadows conferred together, carefully shaded lights flickered palely over maps, subdued shouts relayed fresh orders, and the tramp of boots began again, dying quickly as the infantry squelched off onto the muddy tracks leading to their destination – or perhaps their destiny.

For the most part, the marching men were full of

confidence after their weeks of training. All around them in the darkness they could feel the might of the German Empire. They were conscious of being the cream of its manhood. Just as the New Armies had drawn great inspiration from the gathering of the finest elements of the British Empire before the battle of the Somme, when 'anybody who was anybody seemed to be there', so the Kaiser's soldiers felt a glow of grim pride at the company they were in.

The imperturbable Hanoverians of the 111th Division went into the line alongside the burly Schleswig-Holsteiners of the 17th Division, some of whom spoke better Danish than German. As the Brunswickers of the 20th Division left their billets for the jumping-off trenches, their place was taken by the 39th Division from the conquered province of Alsace. Not fifty years had passed since the fathers of some of the men of the 39th had fought on the other side and now they were among the troops handpicked for the great offensive. Where the Third Army joined the Fifth Army, the German assault was to be made by tough Brandenburgers of the 107th Division alongside carefree Wurtembergers of the 27th Division. But the origins of the German regiments made little difference to the soldiers in weather-worn khaki who manned the British outposts. One German looked just like another through the sights of a Lee-Enfield rifle.

To the attackers, victory was imperative. The war weary didn't hesitate to say that if they couldn't smash the Entente this time then nothing would and they may as well start talking peace.

To the attacking commanders victory was vital for this was the *Kaiserschlacht* – the Emperor's own battle. Moreover, to the experienced eye, there were certain signs of slackening discipline. When things were bad at home it was reflected in the men at the front. A sergeant in a Dresden regiment under orders for the great offensive was surprised to discover that some of the older men in his platoon had no soles in their spare boots. They had cut them out and sent them home so that their children's shoes could be repaired.[53] The commander of a fusilier company turned a blind eye to one of his men reeling drunkenly in the ranks, bawling a song, as they marched off. Harsh words could do only harm at such a time, he decided, and it was left to the rain and the cold air to bring the men round.[40]

British chance fire occasionally found targets among the tightly compressed assault formations. A 9.2 howitzer shell plunged on a company of storm troops resting in a mine crater. By the pink light of burning boxes of machine gun ammunition, eighty mutilated, groaning men were carried to the waiting ambulances. Twenty charred corpses remained in the shell crater. As the survivors of this group mustered for the attack their officers read a special signal sent to the troops: 'H.M. the Kaiser and Hindenburg are on the scene of operations.' Some of the more practical and experienced soldiers said that they would rather have had an extra issue of cheese. The officers tactfully ignored this remark and recorded instead that the message was 'received with enthusiasm'.

Ludendorff, patriot though he was, might have felt the presence of the Kaiser – the 'All Highest' – was not the most desirable omen he could have before the battle. The Kaiser, after all, had presented himself and his staff at the scene of operations just before the first great attack on Ypres; he wanted to be available to ride through the city at the head of his victorious troops. The All Highest was still waiting for Ypres to be captured. But in his turn the Kaiser may have thought that his First Quartermaster General could have selected a more auspicious headquarters for himself than the Hotel Britannique. Fortunately, Ludendorff and Hindenburg had a forward headquarters at Avesnes with a less portentous name and the Kaiser moved in alongside them in his special train.

And so, those who could laid themselves down to sleep on the night of 20 March 1918. The Kaiser and his courtiers in their blacked-out train. Ludendorff and Hindenburg in beds commandeered from the Hotel Britannique. Sir Douglas Haig in his chateau at Montreuil-sur-mer. The commander of the German storm troop company shattered in the mine crater snatched a couple of hours huddled in a burrow in the side of a trench. As for the British infantry they slept for the most part with their boots on.* The warning order 'Prepare for attack' had arrived.

Soon after midnight a white mist began to seep from the damp ground, first turning trenches into milky streams and shell holes into creamy pools, then spreading as a dense, opaque sea across the broken villages and stunted woods, blinding the anxious British sentries, cloaking the waiting German hordes.

*A BRITISH INFANTRYMAN'S EQUIPMENT, 1918. Fighting order consisted of steel helmet, box respirator, web equipment, and ammunition pouches, small pack, water bottle, mess tin, waterproof cape, light entrenching tool, rifle and bayonet. He would probably be carrying 250 rounds of ammunition, weighing some eight pounds plus two Mills grenades each weighing one pound eight ounces. Instead of a greatcoat, he would probably wear a leather jerkin or goatskin jerkin in cold weather. Officers normally wore the jackets and trousers issued to other ranks for action at this period of the war with their badges of rank on their shoulder straps only. Some also carried rifles instead of revolvers.

CHAPTER SIX

'A CURVE OF FLAME . . .'

At half past four in the morning, just about the time the infant son of Sir Douglas Haig was beginning to whimper for his morning feed in his snug nursery in far-off London, a score of soldiers of the 16th Manchester Regiment were sitting disconsolately around the rim of a large shellhole in no-man's-land. The younger ones looked anxiously at the veterans. The veterans either remained impassive or gave an encouraging wink. But it was no use pretending. They were lost. The world ended just a few yards from where they sat waiting for their officer and his sergeant to finish a discussion that seemed to go on an age. The fog had not been too thick when the patrol set out to explore the enemy wire opposite St Quentin, but gradually it had thickened and obscured nearby landmarks as well as the stars. Dawn was an hour or so away.

Eventually the shellhole conference ended. It was decided that they would stay where they were and see if the fog eased or whether they would be able to get some idea of their position at daybreak. Cold and damp, the men settled down, wiping condensation from their weapons and peering vainly into the gloom while they waited. At precisely 0440 an overwhelming, unendurable, tidal wave of noise shattered the stillness of the early morning and roared over and past them.

Panting, shaking, they hurled themselves to earth, and lay stunned as shells whistled, groaned and screamed over their heads in the unbroken thunderous bedlam of the German barrage on the British lines. For ten minutes the terrified Manchester men clung to the pulsating earth. Then the sergeant hammered on the shoulder of his officer and bellowed in his ear, 'At least we know which way to go now, sir.'

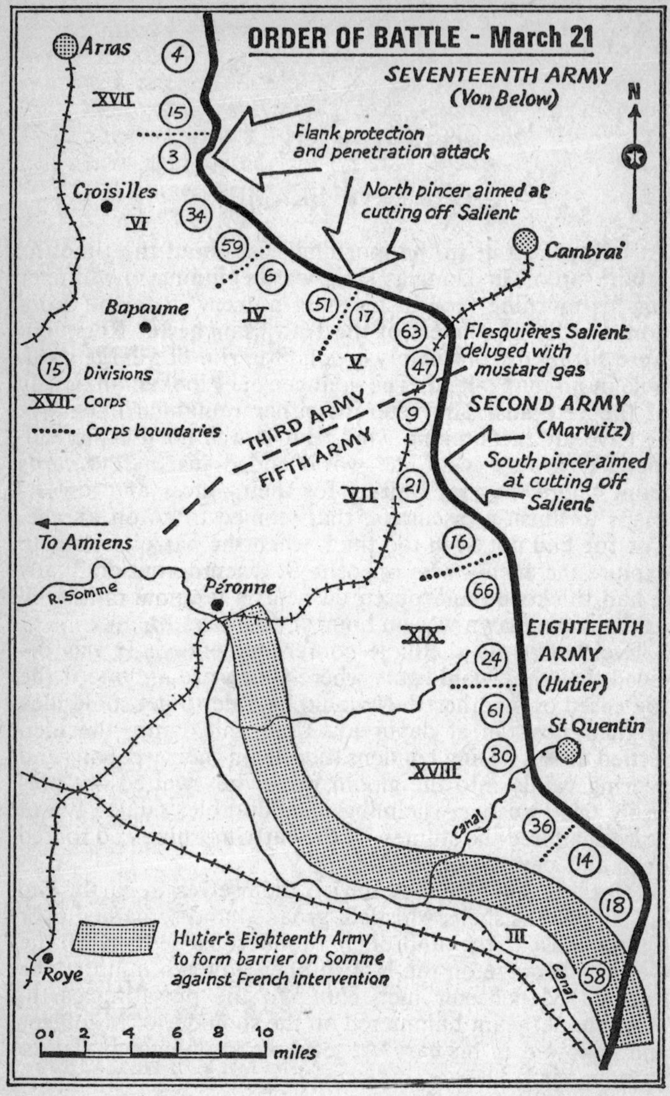
ORDER OF BATTLE - March 21
SEVENTEENTH ARMY
(Von Below)
N
Arras
XVII
Flank protection
and penetration attack
North pincer aimed at
cutting off Salient
Croisilles
VI
Cambrai
Bapaume
IV
V
Flesquières Salient
deluged with
mustard gas
15 Divisions
XVII Corps
Corps boundaries
SECOND ARMY
(Marwitz)
THIRD ARMY
FIFTH ARMY
South pincer aimed
at cutting off
Salient
VII
To Amiens
R. Somme
Péronne
XIX
EIGHTEENTH
ARMY
(Hutier)
St Quentin
XVIII
Canal
III
Canal
Hutier's Eighteenth Army
to form barrier on Somme
against French intervention
Roye
0 1 2 4 6 8 10
miles
4
15
3
34
59
6
51
17
63
47
9
21
16
66
24
61
30
36
14
18
58

At that very moment, the battalion's commanding officer, Lieutenant-Colonel Wilfred Elstob, was listening to the shells bursting around his headquarters, a strong-point known as Manchester Hill, and worrying about his lost patrol. The rest of his men sat in their rocking dug-outs waiting for the moment when the barrage would lift and they could scramble up the steps, dragging boxes of ammunition and bombs with them. They had already been told what was expected of them. 'There is only one degree of resistance,' Elstob had said, 'and that is to the last round and the last man.'

Fifteen miles behind the lines, the barrage that had stunned the Manchesters' patrol roused the commander of the Fifth Army from his sleep just after 0500. Although it sounded muffled from his headquarters room in Nesle it at once gave him 'the impression of some crushing, smashing power'. Pulling a greatcoat over his pyjamas, Sir Hubert crossed the corridor to his office and reached for the phone. When Gough put it down again, he had a keen, thoughtful look. Automatically he pulled back the heavy blackout curtain. The garden was wrapped in mist. Trees were dim shapes at forty yards. As the window rattled to the distant gunfire Sir Hubert returned to his bedroom, threw himself down, and tried to think. The first reports of the bombardment had confirmed his worst fears and forecasts. The barrage stretched along the whole of his forty-two-mile front and along ten miles of the front held by the neighbouring Third Army. After an attempt at a nap, Sir Hubert breakfasted, read the latest reports, and then made his battle plans. There was nothing he could do to help the troops already engaged, but he could do something which would have a far-reaching effect on events. Without consulting GHQ he ordered the 20th and 50th Divisions to move up to reinforce the front. Although he did not yet suspect it, there was some doubt as to whether there would be a front left by the time they arrived.

To the German observers it seemed quite possible that the tremendous weight of shells might well have achieved what the artillerymen always dreamed of and what attacking infantry always prayed for – the complete annihilation of the enemy's first lines.

Another observer was Winston Churchill attending a chemical warfare conference at St Omer. He had decided to spend the night with his old friend Brigadier-General Tudor, temporarily commanding the 9th Division. When the barrage descended Churchill dressed and went out to see for himself what was happening. Tudor met him and announced that he had ordered the British batteries to reply. He would be able to hear them at any moment.

> 'But the crash of the German shells bursting on our trench lines 8,000 yards away was so overpowering that the accession to the tumult of nearly two hundred guns from much nearer to us could not even be distinguished,' Churchill wrote. 'From the Divisional Headquarters on the high ground of Nurlu, one could see the front line for many miles. It swept round us in a wide curve of leaping red flame. . . . There were still two hours to daylight, and the enormous explosion of the shells on our trenches seemed almost to touch each other, with hardly an interval in space of time. Among the bursting shells there rose at intervals, but almost continuously, the much larger flames of exploding magazines.'[12]

To a tall young captain leading up a company of the 4th Seaforth Highlanders, the colours of the barrage were fascinating. The vivid oranges, blues, reds, and greens created their own terrible beauty. The Seaforths, in reserve to the 51st Division, had been roused from their beds and sent hurrying up to man a deep, well-sited trench at Beaumetz, which would serve as a breakwater for the forward troops to fall back on. As they trudged forward, their shadows flickered in the rainbow glare and muted snatches of pipe music drifted on the wings of the barrage which continued in impressive and deadly earnest.[71] Many of the waiting enemy assault troops were so delighted with this display of their Army's might that they left their trenches and dug-outs and stood on the parapets looking towards the British lines.[40]

Where the fog was thick there was little to see, but in areas of improving visibility, particularly in the north of the Third Army area, a pale, rosy curtain of fog and flame seemed to tower over the British trenches, glowing deeper where super-heavy shells burst, and twitching and dancing under the violence of the explosions.

About 0900 the first German patrols started to explore no-man's-land and soon afterwards the storm troops, lugging their light machine guns and followed by sections dragging mortars and flame-throwing equipment, began to pass through gaps in their own wire in preparation for zero hour. They had been trained to stay close to their own barrage regardless of the danger from flying splinters. This was the chance to put teaching to the test. Suddenly the noise of the barrage redoubled itself and clods of earth and fragments flew over their heads in the frenzy of Bruchmüller's last five minutes when 'all howitzers will fire as near as possible to the front line of the first position without endangering our own infantry'. The huge black projectiles of the heavy mortars could be seen whirling overhead to dump their two hundredweights of high explosive on the target. A German officer tried to light a cigar. Three times the blast of mortar bombs falling short blew out the match. As he threw the cigar away the oppressive, crushing noise faded. Zero hour had arrived.

In a matter of seconds the first storm troops, wearing leather knee-patches and puttees in place of the traditional jackboots, stumbled over the broken earth towards the British positions. As they did so, long lines of support troops filed over their own front line and spread out in no-man's-land. A Jäger lieutenant happily smoked a long green huntsman's pipe as he marched at the head of his men. His rifle was slung over his shoulder. What was there to worry about after such a barrage?

What indeed. The British outpost line had ceased to exist. A few strands of wire and heaps of bloody sandbags marked its position. Here and there khaki-clad legs and arms protruded from the shattered trenches. One or two survivors paralysed and numbed by concussion gazed through uncomprehending eyes as the grey waves swept over and past them. There were trenches where all the defenders lay gassed. The mixture of high explosive and Blue Cross shells had caught them unawares.

Hurrying where visibility was improving, advancing carefully but steadily where the fog lay thick, the German infantry pressed on. The officers made a mental note of the pale red orb of the sun that gradually rose above the low-lying layers of mist. It would help them to keep direction. At some time, only a few minutes after the lifting of the German barrage from the outpost line, a British private, spitting dirt from a near-miss, saw dim figures approaching through the fog. Acting on the principle 'in an extremity fire first and ask questions after', he squeezed the trigger.

Any of the handful of British who survived that morning and didn't apply the same maxim paid dearly. The first that some of them knew about the arrival of the enemy was the flash and bang of bursting grenades. According to plan, of course, this should never have happened. Once the German barrage started, the outposts were supposed to fall back to redoubts and fortified positions. No one had reckoned on fog, however, certainly not fog as dense as this. Thus, not only were the men in the outpost positions handicapped, but those in the redoubts as well. To sweep the mist-blanketed area blindly with machine gun fire might do more harm than good.

The attackers, having silenced the last defiant shot from the outposts, reached the redoubts about thirty minutes after zero hour. News of the extent of the attack was brought to some garrisons by dishevelled survivors of the initial encounters. Sometimes the Germans themselves delivered the message.

The experience of the 2/4th Oxfordshire and Buckinghamshires at Enghien Redoubt, was typical. All night the garrison, the equivalent of a company, had huddled in dugouts behind drawn gas curtains, waiting for the assault. At about 0600 the commander of the redoubt, who knew the locality well, decided to make a last minute inspection of his defences and plunged into the mist escorted by a rifleman. After fifty paces he stopped, completely lost.

For fifteen minutes he stumbled through the milky maelstrom before he found his bearings and regained his headquarters. Thereafter he stayed put. When shells ceased to crash in a quarry which was part of the defences, he ordered his men to their positions on the fire steps and machine gun posts. As the men groped their way through the gas-laden fog some of them fell, hit by stray bullets. Straining their eyes into the mist, they at last discerned a line of dim figures filing out of a sunken road – Germans all right, and walking straight into the sights of the dedefenders of Enghien.

Lost in the fog like a lot of people that morning, the Germans came steadily on, their outline growing clearer with every step. Fingers exerted 'first pressure' on triggers, the ugly muzzles of Lewis guns twitched slightly with last-minute adjustments. Then the sharp crack of rifles and the urgent, angry splutter of automatic fire echoed and re-echoed throughout the sandbagged fire-bays. The attacking force was hurled to the ground by the hail of bullets. A few survivors crawled back to cover. Nobody in Enghien doubted that they would soon be back – with friends. Wherever the fog was really thick, similar scenes were re-enacted that morning. Groups of Germans infiltrated between redoubts and tried to rush them from the flanks or rear while supporting waves made frontal attacks. But well-wired in, and sited for all-round defence, these networks of trenches and dugouts, proved formidable.

Three miles south of Enghien Lieutenant-Colonel Elstob had ceased to worry about his lost patrol and concentrated on the more immediate problem of the Germans swarming round Manchester Hill. As the telephone wire linking his post with 90th Brigade HQ was dug in deeply and had not been cut, he was able to keep them informed of events in the periods when the enemy withdrew to lick their wounds. These periods were infrequent. From 1100 onwards the Germans tried everything to break into the trenches. The Manchesters responded in kind. About midday the Germans bombed their way into a strongpoint and Elstob personally led the attack that bombed them out again. Another post ran short of ammunition and, as there was no one to spare, Elstob himself humped the heavy small arms ammunition boxes to the hard-pressed riflemen. Using his revolver, he led a counter-attack which hurled the Germans back from another threatened point. Snatching a rifle from the lifeless hands of a private, Elstob joined in rapid fire as an ominous line of panting, shouting men in field grey lumbered bravely in yet again, only to join the dead and wounded strewn over the disputed area. With one of his men trying to bind a splinter wound in his head, Elstob reported at about 1400 that Manchester Hill was still holding out.

It was a painful moment for the acting brigade commander, Lieutenant-Colonel H. S. Poyntz. Standing in the gloom of a dug-out, the officers and clerks on his staff remaining still so that he might understand every word, Poyntz could hear and feel the crashing and thumping of the bitter fighting only a few miles away. And over the crackling wire came the voice of a man in the centre of that furnace – a man who despite his wounds remained cheerful. Elstob's only regret was that the enemy had now managed to break into the redoubt and there was not much hope of throwing them out with the men left, nearly all of whom were wounded or exhausted. At that very moment vicious hand-to-hand fighting was going on. He'd better get back to his men. Poyntz wished him luck. He would rather have been able to promise Elstob reinforcements or order him to try to break out, but that was impossible. Poyntz left the dug-out and stood staring in the direction of Manchester Hill. The roar of battle seemed to grow deeper.[58]

An hour later, a signaller managed to contact Elstob again. In a hurried conversation Elstob said nearly all the garrison were casualties and the end was near. His last word to Poyntz was a simple 'Goodbye'. His last word to the German storm troops was a shot from a rifle. Late in the afternoon the Germans dragged up field guns and blasted their way into the redoubt from close range. Elstob, already bleeding from three wounds, was killed on the fire-step of a battered trench. He was awarded the Victoria Cross.[60]

Ironically the fog which enabled the Germans to close the ring around Elstob had helped his lost patrol reach the British lines. Elstob might be dead but there were still men of the 16th Manchesters in action.[58]

About the same time as the field guns were blasting Manchester Hill at point-blank range, the Oxfordshire and Buckinghamshires in Enghien were smashing the phone in the headquarters dug-out and frantically burning their papers. The place was unrecognizable. Bombarded at close range by mortars, and swept by machine guns, the defenders had stubbornly refused to be wiped out. Ugly bundles sagging on a long belt of wire to the rear of the post showed where an attacking line had been caught by a Vickers gun sited in enfilade. Again German field guns were called forward to deliver the *coup de grâce* at close range. On this occasion the garrison got the order to withdraw before the final deluge. With fixed bayonets, and grasping bags of grenades, they plunged into the haze of smoke and dust that hung over the cratered ground, and over the wreckage of their stronghold and the bodies of their friends. A lieutenant and a handful of men eventually reached the main defence line in the Battle Zone but the rest were killed or captured.

There was no lack of courage that day. Men who had survived the bellowing shrapnel storm in the fog and the waves of exultant storm troops that swamped the outer defences, crawled, ran, or staggered back to the British Battle Zone trenches and volunteered again to man the new defences. The survivors of two forward companies of the 8th Queen's provided an invaluable reinforcement for a strongly defended locality around the village of Le Verguier where they were distributed among nine small posts. With their blood-shot eyes, hoarse voices, and torn webbing they could have been a demoralizing influence. Instead, their accounts of the German onrush seem to have inspired the Le Verguier garrison. All attempts by the Germans to penetrate the triangular position were defeated, the cleverly sited detachments of the 24th Machine Gun Battalion playing a major part in the fight. Only as night began to fall did the enemy seep around the flanks of the village.

Located on a relatively high point overlooking the battlefield, Le Verguier gave its defenders a grandstand view of the attack. To the south they could see German columns halted on the main road to Vadencourt while the enemy tried to subdue a company of the 3rd Rifle Brigade in 'Cooker's Quarry'. An order to withdraw failed to reach the riflemen but they were not overrun until 2000 hours. To the north the Le Verguier garrison noted a sudden billowing of dense oily black smoke. Undeneath it the 2/6th Manchesters were falling back choking and retching under a flame-thrower assault. Recovering, the Manchesters rallied on a little wood with the pretty name of Carpeza Copse.

In a tortured strip of land three to five miles wide, that ran from Croisilles in the north, to La Fère, fifty miles south, thousands of British soldiers sacrificed themselves that day in a bid to blunt the momentum of the German attack. Some held out longer than others. The vitally important Essigny Redoubt, on the St Quentin road, was overwhelmed by midday and its garrison from the 12th Irish Rifles destroyed. At Grugies, a sister battalion, the 15th Irish Rifles, held out until 1800 under a subaltern, Edmund de Wind. At thirty-five, de Wind was rather old to be only a second-lieutenant, but he had joined the Canadian Army as a private at the outbreak of the war and had not been commissioned until 1917 when, as a native of County Down, he had joined his fellow Ulstermen. For four hours, the 15th repelled attack after attack on the railway embankment they were holding. Although hit twice, de Wind carried on; his valour and leadership that day were summed up by that arid phrase of officialdom. 'V.C. (Posthumous)'.[60]

Many other Irishmen had more than their fair share of the fighting. The 16th Division, in particular, sustained terrible casualties defending a salient on the forward zone too small to defend comfortably but too large for the German guns to overlook. Shells burst on it from all sides in the initial barrage, wiping out two companies of the 7th Royal Irish and shattering the defences of the 7th/8th Royal Inniskilling Fusiliers. A counter-attack supported by two tanks was crushed by well-directed artillery fire and machine gun fire from low-flying aeroplanes. As the two brigades of the 16th holding the forward lines were gradually cut to pieces, the Germans pressed forward. For a time a gap opened between the left of the 16th and the right of the 21st Division but it was plugged by reserves in the evening.

If fog cost the British infantry heavy casualties, it proved equally treacherous for the artillery crews. Frequently they found German infantry upon them before they had time to open fire. Many were forced to abandon the guns and defend themselves from nearby trenches. Not far from Hinaucourt, the men of 'C' battery, of the 83rd Brigade, RFA, turned themselves into a veritable redoubt after being driven from their guns. Holding off the Germans in front with a hail of fire from rifles and Lewis guns, they also turned two machine guns on supporting columns trying to by-pass the position. Opposite St Quentin a young artillery officer called Russell anticipated the German dual-role '88' by twenty years, when he turned his lorry-mounted thirteen-pounder high angle anti-aircraft gun on advancing columns. The redirection of the recoil to a horizontal position instead of vertical was spectacular . . . but the shells still found their targets.[71]

The situation of the British batteries on 21 March was desperate. They had been smothered with gas during the opening bombardment and forced to wear masks even when serving the guns. Their fog-bound observers could not spot enemy positions. Worst of all, for the first vital hours of the assault on the Fifth Army front, they could not see SOS flares sent up from the hard-pressed redoubts.

Once the Germans began to infiltrate past the forward zone it was difficult for artillery officers to decide whether to limber up and pull out or to stay in the hope that the fog would clear and reveal targets. By the time some commanders made up their minds the enemy had often made the decisions for them. The 2nd Green Howards, for example, had moved through the German barrage to defences at Roupy in the main battle zone and about midday they saw the enemy massing in a valley about 800 yards away. 'They presented a very fine target for artillery fire,' an eye witness recorded, 'but owing to most of the guns [our guns] being on the move we could get no weight of shell fire.'[68]

The Germans came in time after time against the Green Howards, sometimes preceded by strafing Fokkers which fired flares to warn the attackers of hidden strongpoints. A post on the left of the battalion was captured; 'C' company led by a subaltern counter-attacked. The Germans shot them down with concentrated machine gun fire. The rate of firing from the main trench in front of Roupy gradually dwindled and the Germans rushed it and found its defenders sprawled dead, dying, or wounded over their smoking weapons. Hoarse and perspiring, the *feldwebels* and *unter-offiziers* rallied their weary men for another assault. They had orders to take Roupy or die in the attempt. Hastily improvising steps and ladders from the debris they clambered over the rear of the trench. Within seconds coal-scuttle helmets were clanging and rolling on the duckboards and the bodies of the victors in grey joined the khaki-clad corpses of the vanquished. The strongpoints behind the main trench were still manned by determined men.

Just after one o'clock in the morning, grenades banged and flared briefly. In a confused clatter of boots on rubble, shouting, and shooting, a battalion of the King's Regiment launched a counter-attack in which they recovered a little lost ground but, confused by the unfamiliar terrain, gradually drifted into the posts still held by the Green Howards.

In the north, the Third Army had endured an equally bloody day. There the fog cleared much sooner than in the Fifth Army area and, furthermore, the Germans found themselves faced by twice the density of troops than those who fought under Gough. Despite its strength, however, the Third Army took a savage battering from the barrage (which in some cases was doubly effective because of the greater concentration of troops in the forward zone). Just as the crushing of two forward Irish brigades had caused a crisis in the south, the havoc which befell the 59th Division caused chaos in the north. The 59th's two forward brigades were destroyed by midday and a counter-attack by the third brigade was delivered with more courage than skill. The

2/5th Lincolns plunged blindly and doggedly through well-aimed, carefully controlled rifle and machine gun fire and were forced to take cover in a trench which was eventually assaulted from both sides and captured. The 2/4th Leicesters ran head on into a superior mass of advancing storm troops and fell back fighting desperately. By early afternoon the only infantry battalion of the 59th Division still intact was the 4th Lincolns held in reserve. Its artillery too had been overrun and at the end of the day only fifteen guns could be mustered. As a significant force the 59th Division no longer existed.[14]

Disastrous though the day may have been for this division, it had left its mark upon the attacker. A remarkable account of the battle on this front is contained in Ernst Junger's *Storm of Steel* in which he makes it clear that machine gun nests in particular caused heavy casualties. Whereas from some positions the British 'emerged with arms uplifted and knocking knees', and handed over their cigarettes and water bottles before hurrying off to the rear, at other places 'the fellows put up a superb show'.

After one defiant post had finally been overrun Junger found a Lewis gun almost buried beneath a heap of empty drums. 'It was still nearly red-hot and smoking.' The gunner, a man of athletic stature, lay dead beside it, shot through the head. The fact that Junger's regiment met strong opposition later in the day speaks well of the cooks, clerks, and gas specialists of the 59th who, along with the divisional pioneers, were hurriedly thrown into the gap which had been blasted open.

In the meantime, the danger to the formations on each side of the 59th increased as the Germans tried to strike them from the flank and rear. A violent battle developed around and near the village of Croisilles where the headquarters of the 102nd Brigade refused to surrender a strong position, although completely surrounded. This resistance, with the possession of trenches being settled by bomb and bayonet, continued until early evening. (The 102nd Brigade belonged to the 34th Division and if it still contained any of the original volunteers they might well have reflected that they seemed to have made quite a habit

"TOMMIES" ASKED FOR.

News Wanted by Relatives.

Comrades of the following are asked to give what information they can concerning them to relatives and friends. Date, indicating when news was last received, refers to last year unless otherwise stated.

BEESLEY, Rfm. R., 737, Rifle Brigade.—H. Newbold, 8, Elmington-ter., Camberwell, S.E.

BIDGOOD, Lance-corpl., 25676, R Warwicks.—May 4.—Mrs. Bidgood, 53, Edgecombe Park-rd., Plymouth.

BROWN, Drvr. S., 9017, R.G.A.—Mrs. L. Weller, 1, Ostmandene, Dorking, Surrey.

DUKE, Pte. F., 68709, R. Fus.—Nov. 30.—Mrs. Duke, 17, Minster-rd., Bromley, Kent.

EATON, Pte. E., 37532, R. Fus.—July 31.—Mrs. Eaton, South-st., Mayfield Sussex.

GOODING, Pte. A., 233609, R. Fus.—Aug. 16.—Mrs. A. Gooding, 106, Ilderton-rd., S. Bermondsey, S.E.

HIGGS, Sergt. J., 31832, Rifle Brigade.—Oct. 8.—Mrs. J. Higgs, 135, Becklow-rd., Shepherd's Bush, W.

HINES, Pte. W., 32184, Som. L.I.—April 28.—Miss J. Rowland, 32, Springfield, Wellington, Somerset.

HOGGETT, Rfm. W., 41698, Irish Rifles.—Aug. 16.—Mrs. W. Hoggett, Little Cressingham Arms, near Watton, Norfolk.

MACLAUGHLIN, 2nd-lieut. A., R.F.C.—Oct. 29.—Mrs. MacLaughlin, Drummins Manse, Armagh, Ireland.

MATTHEWS, Corpl. B. H., 40291, Lincolns.—Aug. 8.—Mrs. H. Garner, Fen End, Waterbeach, Cambs.

RAWLINGS, Pte. C., 515429, London Scottish.—Nov. 24.—Mrs. Rawlings, 26, Abbotsford-ave., West Green, Tottenham, N.

SANDERSON, Pte. F., 24857, S. Staffs.—Oct. 12.—Mrs. Baker, 109, Maplewell-rd., Woodhouse Eaves, near Loughborough.

SCOTT, Pte. A., 096525, A.S.C.—July 9.—Miss H. Uvary, 153, Huddleston-rd., Tufnell Park, N.7.

SMART, Pte. G., 291108, Devon Regt.—Nov. 25.—Mrs. Smart, The Drive, Long Newnton, near Tetbury.

TAYLOR, Pte. W., 241383, North'd Fus.—Oct. 26.—Mrs. W. Jacobs, 12, Dudley-rd., Queen's Park, N.W.

TUCKER, Pte. C., 26698, Devon Regt.—April 23.—Mrs. C. Tucker, 2, Castle Cottages, South Town, Dartmouth.

WALLIS, Pte. E., 23694, R. Warwicks.—Oct. 31.—Mrs. E. Wallis, Jock's Lodge, Four Marks, Hants.

WHITE, 31827 Lance-corpl. H. R., Lewis Gun Det., D.C.L.I.—Nov. 6.—Mrs. White, 105, North Allington, Bridport.

WOODLEY, Pte H., R.W. Surreys.—Sept. 25, 1915.—Mrs. Stopps, 3, Malthouse Cottages, The Vineyard, Abingdon, Berks.

A correspondence coupon, cut from page 9, must accompany each inquiry, which should be marked 'Tommy,' and addressed "The People," Milford Lane, Strand, W.C. 2. An interval of at least six weeks must elapse before an inquiry can be repeated.

1. MISSING. By the beginning of 1918 nearly every home in the country had been affected to some extent by the war. Every week the Sunday edition of *The People* carried a pathetic list of soldiers who had vanished without trace. In the list produced here, under the title 'Tommies asked for', some of the men had disappeared during the desperate fighting at Passchendaele, some at Arras in the spring of 1917 and one referred to a private in the Royal West Surreys, missing since the battle of Loos in 1915.

of getting involved in 'firsts', for the division went into action on the first day of the Battle of the Somme and on the first day of the Battle of Arras – suffering heavy casualties on both occasions.)

While the 34th fought with sturdy contrariness to avoid envelopment, the 6th Division faced a similar predicament with ferocious professionalism somewhat to the south. The 2nd Durhams actually went so far as to capture four machine guns and turn them on their former owners. By mid-afternoon rifle ammunition began to run short, despite reserve dumps of 70,000 rounds formed behind each battalion and the 200 rounds carried by each rifleman. Killing and being killed, the Durhams were gradually whittled away. When the last round had been fired that day, they were reduced to one officer and ninety-four men. The 1st West Yorkshires who had fought alongside them could muster only two officers and 110 men. The whole of the 18th Brigade totalled only nine officers and 410 other ranks and the other brigades in the division were little better off, as were the 152nd and 153rd brigades of the 51st Division.

The 4th Seaforths were now settled into good positions at Beaumetz, a well-constructed and well-wired, but broken trench line from where later they could see columns of Germans pressing down the Cambrai-Bapaume road, unfortunately out of range. There were plenty of other Germans to shoot at, however, and the 154th Brigade, which had suffered least in the opening attack, exacted considerable vengeance for their comrades. The Highlanders were considerably heartened in the afternoon by the appearance of reinforcements accompanied by twelve tanks, but a counter-attack by the Gloucesters through the Beaumetz defenders towards the captured village of Doignies did not begin until early evening when it was too dark for the tanks to operate.

The menace of the thrusts on the left wing of the Third Army made even more precarious the position of the three divisions committed to defending the Flesquières Salient. The Salient, a firm buttress of the Third Army immediately on Gough's left, was the dubious fruit of the Cambrai offensive. Well fortified and strongly garrisoned, it would not fall easily to direct attack. In his comprehensive work *1918, The Last Act*, Barrie Pitt described the Flesquières Salient as an 'iron spike' driven into the ground on which adjacent parts of the front could rely to absorb any recoil that might be necessary. Unfortunately an iron spike is useless unless rooted in concrete and on this occasion there was no good reason for clinging to the Salient. It was held for reasons of pride, not logic. It was the most glamorous trophy Haig had to show for the dreadful autumn-winter campaign of 1917 and it was not to be expected that it would be given up lightly despite the excellent reasons which could be put forward. It was not actually attacked frontally but instead was drenched with mustard gas. Hundreds of hoarse, blistered, blinded, and vomiting British soldiers were the result of the bombardment.

As the convoys of ambulances and lorries rumbled rearwards over the broken roads, and the braver spirits tried to cheer up their comrades in the gloomy interiors, General Byng, their commander was counting the cost of the day's fighting. Finally he picked up the telephone and, after a long conversation with GHQ, was given Sir Douglas Haig's permission to pull back a mile or so, the divisions which had clung so faithfully to the reeking, ochre-stained trenches round Flesquières. Still they remained dangerously exposed.

General Gough was also on the line to GHQ that night but once again General Sir Herbert Lawrence, the chief-of-staff, left him frustrated and angry. Gough, having identified forty enemy divisions on his front, had no doubts about the outcome of the battle if drastic actions were not taken soon.

All eleven British divisions in the Fifth Army first line that morning had been in action and had suffered in varying degrees. Gough's only immediate reserve division, the 39th, was already helping to plug the hole left by the annihilation of the two brigades of the 16th Division. The 20th Division, which he had ordered forward the moment the attack was launched, was using one brigade to fill a gap between the 14th and 36th Divisions. Three dismounted cavalry divisions, each the size of an infantry brigade, were being drawn into the battle piecemeal along with sundry entrenching battalions, gas companies, field companies of the Royal Engineers, and odd detachments of machine gunners. The only help Gough could rely on the following day was from the 50th Division, now making the long trek from its billets twenty-four miles behind the lines. This was the very unit that Gough had earlier asked should be moved close behind his front, a move vetoed by Lawrence.

To have the 50th nearer the front would undoubtedly have been a great assistance to Gough, but one infantry division would not replace the overwhelming losses suffered that day. Gough required supports as quickly as possible; French troops or British troops, it did not matter as long as they were able to fight.

The cogency of Gough's arguments did not impress Lawrence. Lawrence was sure that 'the Germans would not come again the next day'; after the heavy casualties they had suffered, they would be 'busy clearing the battlefield, collecting their wounded, reorganizing and resting their tired troops.'[28]

Gough, whose sole aim was to make GHQ comprehend the vast weight of the offensive, got the impression that Lawrence was merely jollying him along. 'I was quite ready to deal with facts, however menacing, and to handle the situation, however precarious it might be,' Gough wrote, 'but it was important that GHQ should realize the position, stripped of all illusions. . . . I began to think that I had not succeeded in making GHQ understand.' All the same, he did receive permission to withdraw his right wing some five miles to the line of the Crozat-St Quentin Canal. Haig also asked the French to support Gough's right.

'Having regard to the great strength of the attack . . . and the determined manner in which the attack was everywhere pressed, I consider that the result of the day is highly creditable to the British troops,' the Commander-in-Chief wrote in his diary on the night of 21 March, adding: 'I therefore sent a message of congratulations to the Third and Fifth Armies for communication to all ranks.'

It was not a message which would be read by Elstob, or

de Wind, or the obliterated companies of the 7th Royal Irish. It would not be read that chill, foggy night by the survivors of a company of the 7th Buffs repairing breaches in the blackened, pitted walls of the old French fort of Vendeuil. Instead they checked their ammunition reserves and waited for the morrow.

Perhaps the surviving rats (for gas and shell kill rats as well as men) poking their way through the debris, alone saw and heard what really went on that night in the tortured strip of earth fifty miles long and three or four miles wide. They could watch from the shadows as the German stretcher bearers loaded dimly lit ambulances on the sunken road near Enghien, where British casualties lay on one side and their enemies on the other. They could listen with their sharp ears to the last frantic efforts of men buried alive in deep dug-outs or hear the sobs of forgotten wounded. They could run lightly over the freezing feet of Lieutenant Junger slumbering uneasily among his Fusiliers in a shellhole in the area of the ill-fated 59th Division, or they could scuttle past the kilted figure of the tall Seaforth officer watchful on the firestep at Beaumetz among his Highlanders and their comrades in the Gloucesters. But, in truth, the rats did not care. They weren't on anyone's side. They made war only on the dead. The rats too waited for tomorrow.

CHAPTER SEVEN

EXIT THE AWKWARD SQUAD

Readers of the *Vossische Zeitung* on Friday 22 March, were informed at their breakfast tables that, 'With the old élan and spirit of 1914, our battalions stormed over the ground and broke the enemy's resistance all along the line. It is unanimously declared that the defenders fought bravely, but the British leadership was not equal to the colossal blow.' The exuberant correspondent went on, 'West of St Quentin . . . a thick mist which only the noonday sun dispersed, considerably disturbed our operations. Curtains of mist gathered so thickly that the men of our field artillery, which was advancing immediately behind the infantry, could hardly see their horses. Nevertheless, there was no pause.'

Unfortunately for the British defenders, there was also no break in the mist on the morning of the 22nd, when, cold and stiff, they manned their posts. Some of those who had already endured the shambles on the Somme, at Arras, and at Passchendaele, had reached the end of the road. These veterans were without illusion and were so physically and mentally weary of dodging Death they no longer feared him. They no longer cared what happened, but with the dawn nearly all of them stood to arms. War had become a habit.

At 0400 the soldiers of the German 185th Regiment rose from their damp blankets and cloaks in the fields and set off through the mist towards Le Verguier. In a matter of minutes they were approaching the barbed wire entanglements which surrounded the defiant little fortress, barriers still piled high with corpses of their comrades killed the previous day. Obediently the Germans followed their officers and NCOs towards gaps in the defenders' wire, hurling grenades to clear the way. In reply, the rifles and Vickers guns of the 24th Machine Gun Battalion stabbed through the fog and traversed steadily on their prearranged arcs. Under the weight of the fire the attackers became disorganized and ran frantically about searching for a weak spot. Groups gathered, shouting together hoarsely, only to scatter when bullets from the unseen British smashed into human targets.

At 0930, the baffled 185th disengaged briefly and a storm of shellfire swept the area as every gun in the 4th German Guard Division and the 208th Division concentrated on the defences. Then the burly figures of the 5th Foot Guard Regiment swept in from one side while the remnants of the 185th tried again from the other. In all, detachments from five battalions stormed forward. This time the defences were overwhelmed with rifle, bayonet and bomb but, unbelievably, Lieutenant-Colonel H. J. C. Piers managed to lead a fair number of men through the mist and milling Germans back to the British trenches losing only one other man on the way. At about 1000 the soldiers of the 185th Regiment tramped over the ruins of Le Verguier – twenty-four hours after the village should have fallen according to Ludendorff's carefully prepared schedule.

Ludendorff's timetable suffered even greater disruption at Travecy Keep. From this vantage point, the 2/2nd Londons plagued the Germans all that day, shooting up transport on the St Quentin road, on one occasion scattering a group of German staff officers who were rash enough to hold a conference within range. The guns of the Keep fell silent at dusk when ammunition ran out. The garrison had expended 18,000 rounds of rifle and Lewis gun ammunition, 200 mortar bombs, 400 grenades. Forty-four men, of which a high proportion were wounded, fell into German hands.[50]

Wherever units were settled into sound defensive systems the Germans were dealt with severely on the 22nd. Young Walter Boylan, a private in the 9th East Surreys, found so many good targets among the Germans trying to overwhelm the 24th Division that he almost forgot that the attack had robbed him of a well-earned spell of leave. Boylan had actually been given his warrant and pay when all leave was abruptly cancelled. Marched up urgently to a support position, his battalion had experienced no difficulty in holding fast and he had enjoyed a good night's sleep despite the cold. When the Germans came on again at daybreak they appeared to the lad from Wolverhampton to be as 'thick as blades of grass'. Three times groups of them reached the wire in front of the East Surreys only to be shot down and driven back. Then shells began to burst on the position – British shells. The artillery was unaware that the battalion was holding out and the position became untenable. The order to retire was given and the Surreys left their crumbling trenches and ran back under heavy German machine gun fire and British high explosive.[71]

To the right of the Surreys, another support unit was having an equally exciting time. After positioning themselves along a sunken road protected by a thin belt of wire, 'B' Company of the 5th Duke of Cornwall's Light Infantry, waited patiently for daybreak. When it came, the Cornwalls were puzzled by the antics of a thick curtain of mist which would rise about three feet and then suddenly drop again. Lieutenant R. G. Ross, who had spent most of the night compulsively checking his revolver, recorded the shock which ran through the pioneer company when

> During one of the three foot lifts . . . a first glimpse of the German hordes was obtained . . . one officer tried to shout 'Fifteen rounds rapid', but found that his throat had suddenly gone dry and only a faint croak emerged. Again he tried and this time the order rang out; it was carried along the line by each platoon officer. It seemed minutes before the men started shooting, but to get things going one officer plugged away with his revolver, and actually fired all his rounds before our men realized what was happening. It was a glorious ten minutes we had. We were positive nothing could break our lines: the men were cool and collected, bombs were thrown and [rifle] grenades fired. The casualties were terrible to the Germans, because they were in close formation. Then down came the mist again and our view was obstructed. We waited patiently, gripping rifles and revolvers as we had never gripped them before. At last the mist cleared and we

found to our surprise some of the most daring of the enemy on our wire just about twenty yards in front of us.

This time there was no need for fire orders . . . the casualties to the enemy were again horrible, one cannot describe the slaughter. We were all now positive that the survivors would have to withdraw when all of a sudden we were enfiladed by machine gun fire from our left.

The company determined to hang on but it proved impossible 'because the troops on the left had given way and we were in danger of being surrounded'.[69]

It was the same old story. However solid a defence the infantry might offer in an unbroken line, the moment the Germans turned a flank there was not enough depth for protection, nor were there reserves to counter-attack. The Cornwalls had no option but to withdraw a few hundred yards and try to find friendly troops with whom they could link up. This time they were fortunate.

When we reached a small, hurriedly dug trench we discovered it to be manned by a brigade of another division [continues Lieutenant Ross]. As soon as we were under cover they played the devil with the Hun, and when we had secured ourselves, we joined in. We discovered that French native troops had given way on our left, thereby necessitating the retirement. Needless to say we were furious because we were positive that all the German army could not have broken the line held by us. We now thought our turn had come to hold and attack them in turn, but many dreadful days were in front of us before that took place.

The Cornwalls were the pioneer battalion of the badly mauled 61st Division. The use of a single company to strengthen a threatened part of the front shows how few reserves were available.

As has been said, Gough's main hope was the 50th Division which had been warned of the imminence of the German attack late on the 20th and had sent out a telegram alerting its units the same evening. The following morning, about 0430, hundreds of hobnailed boots clattered over the cobbled streets of the villages where its three infantry brigades were in billets. As the distant roar of the barrage rose to its crescendo the battalions mustered and received orders placing them on four hours' notice. Most of the troops had spent the past few days engaged in strenuous training exercises and the grumblers moaned that not only was peace denied the wicked but slumber too. The few hours sleep they snatched on the night of the 20th were to be the last many would enjoy for a long time. For some the last ever.

All morning and afternoon the packing and stacking went on, as dispatch riders sped back and forth from the harassed battalion headquarters. Then, around 1500 the final order came. Soon the solid, khaki columns of fours were on the march, disturbing the water-fowl on the banks of the peaceful little river Luce with their noise. As they tramped the four miles to the entraining station at Guillaucourt, the men of the Lewis gun sections of the 8th Durhams cursed steadily. The guns and panniers, normally carried on limbers as near as possible to the scene of action, now had to be carried by the gunners. By 1800, however, the division's infantry, Lewises and panniers, were crammed into ancient French trucks; steam engines groaning and whistling in protest at their load, rattled towards the battle. To the left of the railway line the steady clip clop of horses and the rumble of cartwheels echoed on the long, straight Villers Bretonneux-St Quentin road as the 50th Division transport plodded to the pre-arranged rendezvous. On the rear of the wagons, the divisional sign, the head of a fierce red unicorn on a white background, gradually faded in the soft dusk.

The fifteen-mile train journey took the 50th Division about two and a half hours. At Brie, on the banks of the Somme, the trucks ground to a halt and, stiff and aching from the uncomfortable ride, the battalions formed up in the cold evening air almost immediately to be ordered forward again. As the night deepened and the fog thickened the three brigades marched on diverging roads through the silent and strange countryside. The sounds of the fighting which had persisted through the day, and which they had heard clearly during occasional halts, faded to silence. Only odd flashes and muffled bangs in the distance hinted at what lay ahead.

Gough had placed the 50th Division at the disposal of his weakest corps, the XIXth (only two divisions, the 24th and 66th) and the corps commander, Lieutenant-General Sir Herbert Watts, ordered it to form a screen over a wide front so that the hard-pressed forward troops could fall back through it. According to theory the 50th should have occupied the vaunted Green Line that looked so fine on all the HQ maps. Instead, their astounded officers were shown a strange-looking excavation about one foot deep and six feet wide, meandering across the countryside. This spit-locked trench, with notice boards indicating where dug-outs and machine gun posts should be sited plus a few stretches of barbed wire, was all that existed of what should have been an impenetrable bastion. Thus, after long periods of marching (six hours in some cases), the first order to the weary troops was to 'dig in' – a somewhat optimistic command since none of the heavy tools, picks, spades, or shovels had arrived. This equipment with the spare Lewis guns and ammunition, reposed in the limbers of the transport column which had halted overnight (horses at least must rest) at a point behind the line. So it was that, at 1030 hours on the 22nd, the Durhams and many other battalions were still scratching futilely about with their puny entrenching tools. It was just as well that they were not aware that the division's machine guns were also 'back there' with the transport.

The line to be held by the 50th stretched for a frightening distance; it reached nearly eight miles from the small Cologne River in the north, to the equally small and marshy Omignon River in the south. The 151st Brigade (5th, 6th and 8th Durhams) held the left, the 150th Brigade (4th and 5th Green Howards and 4th East Yorkshires) held the centre, and the 149th Brigade (4th, 5th and 6th Northumberland Fusiliers) the right. Throughout the long night they had pecked and scraped, trying to improve the pathetic Green Line. As they dug, various administrative and supply units filtered through them heading for the rear. At dawn infantry stragglers trudged in out of the mist. By 0900 Brigadier Riddell of the 149th had collected nearly 800 strays and placed them in support positions.

As the fog cleared the troops paused briefly to look at the scene before them. Against a backcloth of bursting shells, fires, and blazing dumps, small parties of British troops could be seen picking their tortuous way back between the woods and across the countryside. Some retired in thin lines, one wave covering the other. Others came in clumps. Those farthest from the enemy plodded along the roads with automatic, leaden steps. There was the thud and crash of gunfire mixed with the sporadic crackle of small arms. Occasionally the gaily coloured biplanes of both sides swept overhead dipping and turning to strafe troops on the roads or in the trenches. Now and again one of the planes would fail to pull out of a dive but the splintering crash was unnoticed in the general uproar. The dishevelled appearance of the retiring troops was hardly encouraging. Many of them had slight wounds, indifferently bandaged. They were filthy and invariably thirsty. All of them were unutterably weary. Exhaustion seems to have affected the German troops as well. According to the British Official Historian, 'The behaviour of the Germans on different parts of the front varied. On some parts they permitted troops to walk back across the open undisturbed, being too tired to follow: on others they endeavoured to sweep forward in large numbers. In the rear-guard actions which ensued heavy casualties were inflicted on the enemy. . . .' The price paid for these delaying actions was often severe. After one vicious skirmish ended the Germans captured fifteen unwounded men, the remainder of a covering group formed from two companies of Lancashire Fusiliers and forty dismounted cavalrymen.

By about mid-afternoon most of the 66th and 24th Division troops had passed through the waiting screen and the approaching masses of enemy began to deploy for an assault on the 50th. By that time the waiting troops, still minus their transport, had scrounged what ammunition they could from dumps in the area. The 8th Durhams had only 170 rounds per man when at 1600, much to their relief, the spare Lewis guns and ammunition arrived. They were barely in time. Spread over the undulating plain the masses of advancing enemy infantry were an easy target. The 6th Durhams, who proudly wore the black buttons of a rifle regiment, noted with satisfaction that they were able to make themselves felt at long range.

As evening drew on the battle grew in ferocity. Despite an excellent field of fire which enabled the 50th Division to mow down wave after wave of attackers, the Germans, with great gallantry, pressed home hand to hand attacks against the centre of the line. At Nobescourt Farm, a ruin distinguishable by a few shallow trenches, the enemy even threatened to break through, but a counter-attack led by the commanding officer and the adjutant of the 4th Green Howards restored the situation and forced the Germans to take cover. The CO, Lieutenant-Colonel B. H. Charlton, and the adjutant, Captain J. S. Bainbridge, were both killed. The commanding officer of the 5th Durhams, actually holding the farm, discovered that his headquarters, like it or not, was in the firing line and he ordered his clerks, signallers, and orderlies to join in with their rifles until the danger was over.

The 8th Durhams, assailed by bursts of machine gun fire from the flank as well as massed fire from the front, suddenly found themselves attacked from the rear. 'Our own artillery now commenced to calibrate, but the shooting was very short and several 4.5s fell behind our line and in the wire,' records the battalion diary. 'The eighteen-pounders (shrapnel) also burst short and casualties followed, particularly in 'C' company.' The battalion was forced to withdraw some troops from forward positions until an artillery observation officer appeared and was duly 'informed of the situation'. The informing must have been a memorable event for the unfortunate gunner officer.

The intensity of the fighting encountered by the 149th Brigade can be gauged by the fact that Brigadier Riddell, who controlled his three battalions of Northumberland Fusiliers on horseback, had five bullet holes through his saddle equipment and a sixth through his coat. This last bullet was deflected from doing serious damage to the brigadier by the metal case in which he carried his safety razor. The Fusiliers fought their action in the classic style, with two battalions holding the line while the third counter-attacked through them with the bayonet when called upon. They gave up little ground. Considering their long and exhausting march, their unfamiliarity with the terrain and the lack of proper defences, the men of the 50th performed magnificently that day.

Even more remarkable, perhaps, was the strong opposition put up by the divisions which had borne the brunt of the previous day's attack. On the 50th's left wing the survivors of the Irish regiments fought stubbornly until they were gradually forced back by sheer weight of numbers. Of two companies of the 7th Leicestershires fighting a rearguard and covering action near Peizière only one officer and fourteen other ranks fell unwounded into enemy hands; Epéhy, held by the 6th and 8th Leicesters with two companies of Royal Engineers, was taken only after what the Germans themselves described as 'heavy bloody sacrifice'. At Revelon Farm a company of the 11th Royal Scots was wiped out by field guns, swarms of bombing, strafing aircraft, trench mortars, and three German regiments. Only a mile to the south of them, 'C' Company of the 2nd South African Regiment also fought to the finish when cut off although the rest of the South Africans withdrew skilfully, fighting all the way.

On the southern wing of the Fifth Army it was a similar tale. Fighting at Roupy began with the dawn and grew in violence as the day lengthened. The 2nd Green Howards and the men of the King's Regiment refused to budge from their strongpoints and the enemy finally had to reduce these one by one. A survivor of the battle recalled in a matter of fact way: 'At 2.30 p.m. Colonel Edwards was wounded; at 3 o'clock the battalion on the right was withdrawn. By 4 p.m. the right and left platoon keeps had been captured . . . while at this hour the Germans opened a strong attack from both flanks, using trenches already captured to mass their troops, making use of cover offered by the ruined village, and bringing machine guns to bear on us from the left rear.'

The position became untenable shortly after 1700 and the same eyewitness continues: 'We withdrew to a system of trenches . . . but as these were only three feet deep they afforded no protection; so after a short time we withdrew to the Flesquières defences, where we found troops of the 20th Division. In this position we were heavily shelled as the German gunners had these defences taped.' After re-organizing in a less vulnerable spot, the battalion finally got orders to disengage and march into reserve to a village about five miles behind the line.

The quartermaster of the Green Howards records with some pride: 'We got the rations up quite easily this day and had them cooked in the travelling kitchens for the battalion.' There was more than enough. Many men would not draw their rations ever again.[68]

On the right wing of the Fifth Army, Vendeuil Fort held out for the best part of 22 March. During the previous day's fighting its commander, Capt. Fine, had signalled constantly by flag the same message: 'Counter-attack essential.' He had been told that in the event of a major assault it was vital that his post be held and that special arrangements had been made for the divisional reserve to come to his aid. Major-General R. P. Lee, of the 18th Division, had to make the unpleasant decision that it was more important to use his reserves to keep in touch with his flanks. He regarded the forward area as enemy-occupied. And so it was, apart from Captain Fine – and the Awkward Squad.

Fine's garrison in Vendeuil Fort consisted of a platoon of the support company of the 7th Buffs, a section of Royal Engineers, two mortar sections, and two motley platoons (formed by order of divisional headquarters) which in peaceful times were employed as unskilled labourers by the Royal Engineers. These consisted of men – let us be kind – who were not born soldiers. Some were old. Some were bad marchers. Some were not too bright, or not too strong, or regularly in trouble. But whatever trouble they may have caused their own officers in the past, it was nothing compared with the chaos they caused the German columns trying to push down the roads nearby. The enemy gave it up finally and concentrated on putting the old fort out of action. Perhaps it was the thick walls, perhaps it was their thick skulls, but the Awkward Squad and their comrades did not surrender, what was left of them, until nearly 1700.[48]

In the Third Army area the fighting had been just as severe. Despite their success against the 59th Division on the 21st, the Germans found themselves repulsed by determined troops when they renewed their attack. The 2nd German Guard Reserve Division, brought up fresh from the rear in order to put new vigour into the attack, found itself locked in combat with survivors of the much-tried 177th Brigade. After initial successes their attack bogged down against apparently irrepressible rifle and Lewis gun fire. When night fell German guardsmen were still trying to take the village of Mory.

Where the Germans were still trying to close their pincers around the 34th Division, a bewildering dog fight took place in which the artillery of both sides splattered the area indiscriminately. The 15th Royal Scots had to retire nearly a mile to avoid their own barrage, while the 6th Bavarian Division, attacking St Léger Wood, had to contend not only with the resolute defence of the 1st East Lancashires, 13th Green Howards, and 9th Northumberland Fusiliers, but the lethal contributions of their own gunners as well.

The Germans attacking the 51st Division persisted in mass charges during the day and suffered accordingly. The mixture of Highlanders, Gloucestershires and Worcestershires in the long Beaumetz trench fired box after box of ammunition as the enemy slowly worked round the flanks of the position. According to the 4th Seaforths, the battalion killed more Germans that day than they had accounted for during the whole of the war up to that time. And the riflemen were not the only people to harass the dogged attackers. A ferocious German bombardment intended for the 153rd Brigade fell short on storm troops dug in before the Highlanders and many of them, stunned and terror-stricken, risked the bullets of the Scots and staggered forward with their arms upraised. In all, 200 prisoners were taken. Other German troops, appalled by the devastation wrought by their own super-heavy howitzers, streamed towards the battery positions swearing to take revenge on their own side.* They were restrained, says one German account, 'only with difficulty'.[26]

The German air arm was much criticized too, for the storm troops suffered heavily from the activity of British planes. In later wars, of course, commanders would try to ensure that the opposing air forces were neutralized on the ground before an offensive. (The 1939 campaign in Poland, and the air strikes in the Lowlands and Scandinavia in 1940, show that the Germans learned their lessons well.) But in 1918, close air support was a glaring (and peculiar) omission from Ludendorff's usually comprehensive battle plans. It was a mercy for the hard-pressed British ground troops that Ludendorff did not possess an aeronautical Bruchmüller to advise him.

*The barrage also hit the 6th Black Watch severely.

CHAPTER EIGHT

ORDERS FROM CORPS

Although the infantry were not always conscious of it, the assistance they received from the Royal Flying Corps during the 1918 offensive was probably one of the most valuable and effective contributions made by the air arm during the whole war. The endeavour and sacrifice of the airmen in March 1918 has rarely been equalled.

At the beginning of the Great War, the Royal Flying Corps was in its infancy. When it expanded it automatically recruited its pilots from the army's junior officers. Thus many of the men in the squadrons supporting the Fifth and Third Armies knew first hand the full horror of the battle going on below. They had been through it themselves. They were aware also of the isolation and despair that afflicts troops who have to endure enemy air attacks without seeing their own planes in action. The RFC's commander, Salmond, had seen to it that the RFC was in a position to strike no matter how far the Germans might advance and his pilots made sure that when they did strike it was with all their strength.

Generally speaking the aircraft of 1918 were poorly suited for strafing columns of well-armed infantry. Their slowness gave light machine gunners and riflemen a chance of hitting them. They were fragilely constructed, vulnerable, and covered with a highly inflammable fabric. Although the Germans were beginning to produce an all-metal biplane, the Junkers J–1 (known as the Flying Tank) most airmen went into the fight sitting cheek by jowl with an unarmoured petrol tank, and behind two machine guns mounted on engines of uneven performance. Parachutes were practically unknown. (Some peculiarly military thinking had concluded that if pilots wore them, they might be tempted to use them unnecessarily.) The British pilots had other troubles from above, some containing a certain grim humour. As the airmen of 5 (Naval) Squadron were working desperately to clear their D.H.4s from the threatened airfield at Mons-en-Chausée, with hangars already in flames and the landing strip under fire from the advancing enemy, Squadron Commander S. J. Noble received a message. According to Noble, the message referred 'to plans for providing vegetables, in view of the shortage, and instructed me to prepare frames at once for planting of seedlings'. Commander Noble was still dwelling on the implausible communication when a shell struck his headquarters, fortunately without damage to himself. Needless to say, the only things planted by his airman that afternoon were 200 twenty-five-pound high explosive bombs.[49]

The heavy fog interfered with air operations on the first day of the offensive but squadrons took off as soon as visibility cleared.

The headquarters of the 2nd Bavarian Regiment was bombed in a sunken road near Urvillers, its signals officer was killed and the brigade major seriously wounded. Sixty horses were killed by a single airman who caught a German artillery regiment on the march near Honnecourt – a serious loss in view of the enemy shortage of sound draft animals. Both the German 66th and 116th Regiments complained of British spotting planes directing heavy artillery fire on them, while two battalions of the 10th Bavarians forming up on high ground near Ecoust St Mein endured 'a rotten time' according to their historian. 'About a dozen English low-flying battle aeroplanes whizzed up, and from an incredibly low height, bombed our advancing troops. This caused great confusion and to make matters worse, our own artillery frequently fired short, so that further advance became impossible.'

On the morning of the 22nd fog once again hampered air operations but when it cleared, about midday, engines roared on the emergency fields (seventeen squadrons had been forced to move back) and the fast, square-nosed S.E.5 fighters of 24 and 84 squadrons which had been armed and fuelled for hours, rolled over the smooth turf, and took to the air. They were joined by the ugly 'Big Ack W's' (Arm-strong-Whitworth F.K.8s) of 35 Squadron, and by 53 Squadron's cumbersome 'Harry Taits' (R.E.8s) plodding along with their huge exhaust pipes sticking up like stovepipes from the engines. Normally the slow F.K.8s and the R.E.8s were used only for artillery observation and reconnaissance missions but on this occasion they went in at low level with bombs and machine guns.

As the day drew on, more and more squadrons joined in the battle; D.H.4s bombed bridges, railway junctions, and dumps, while Sopwith Camels, Bristols, and other fighters took on the Fokkers, Albatrosses, and Pfalzes. At night the dark-hued F.E.2b 'pushers' of 101 and 102 Squadrons whirred high over the German back areas bombing every stray light – and sometimes finding their own airfields under attack from German night bombers when they returned.

Salmond's closely co-ordinated handling of aircraft as virtually another infantry weapon became more impressive as the battle continued and the weather improved. It certainly influenced German officers who suffered under his relentless harrying, for in the years before 1939 the Luftwaffe made a speciality of close-support planes.

The RFC also became indispensable for observation as the battle progressed. Nearly all other communications had gone and with them the means of controlling the fighting troops; a breakdown which had not been anticipated properly in either the Third or Fifth Army areas. And there had been warnings. In the mud of Ypres in 1917, for example, Scottish troops of the 51st Division were reduced to hoisting their kilts and showing the whites of their thighs in order to indicate to spotting planes just how far they had advanced. But in March 1918 the problem, after the first day or so, was getting in touch with anyone at all. Once the battle and forward zone communications had been smashed there was nothing left.

One may ask why the British were able to maintain communications and cohesion so much better during the retreat in 1914 when scientific aids were even more primitive. The answer is that the army of 1914 was composed of professionals fully equipped for a war of movement. There was also a proportionate abundance of cavalry in the early days, and a good use was made of it. But by 1918 the 'arme blanche' had been greatly reduced in size and indeed the greater part of the three cavalry divisions in the Fifth Army area were thrown into action dismounted. Had more of them been used to maintain contact on horseback, many commanders would have been spared agonizing hours of ignorance.

The hasty and frequent moving of artillery units caused a great deal of frustration to the RFC. 'Many wireless calls from the air for fire on German advancing troops went unanswered because of the rapidity with which the British batteries had to move and to the fact that they could not, or did not, erect their wireless aerials,' says the official account of the war in the air. In fairness, however, the radio equipment of 1918 was clumsy and the aerials were difficult to erect quickly. Artillery tended to ignore them once a war of movement had broken out.

Just as communications gradually became haphazard, difficult, or non-existent, so supplies too became a problem. 'The note of these days is not the breakdown of the infantry resistance but of the elaborate organization behind the lines, for which the fighting strength of the front line troops had been ruthlessly sacrificed and on which the infantry had been taught to rely,' says one contemporary historian. 'In the first place there were no rations. . . . More important, there were no working parties and no carrying parties. The trench mortar batteries simply faded out of the picture, buried their guns and joined up as infantry. There was no place for them in the warfare of the moment.'[39] These were the conditions on the Third Army front where, in fact, the situation was less perilous than it was to become. There Sir Julian Byng had been attacked on a front of ten miles and had five divisions in reserve plus the comforting proximity of the Arras bastion. As he withdrew his divisions, the line actually got shorter – at first.

Gough had to worry about a vast front forty-two miles long, every section of which was under attack. His meagre reserves had already been drawn into the battle and a solitary division was on its way from the British army. His only other salvation lay with the French divisions arriving

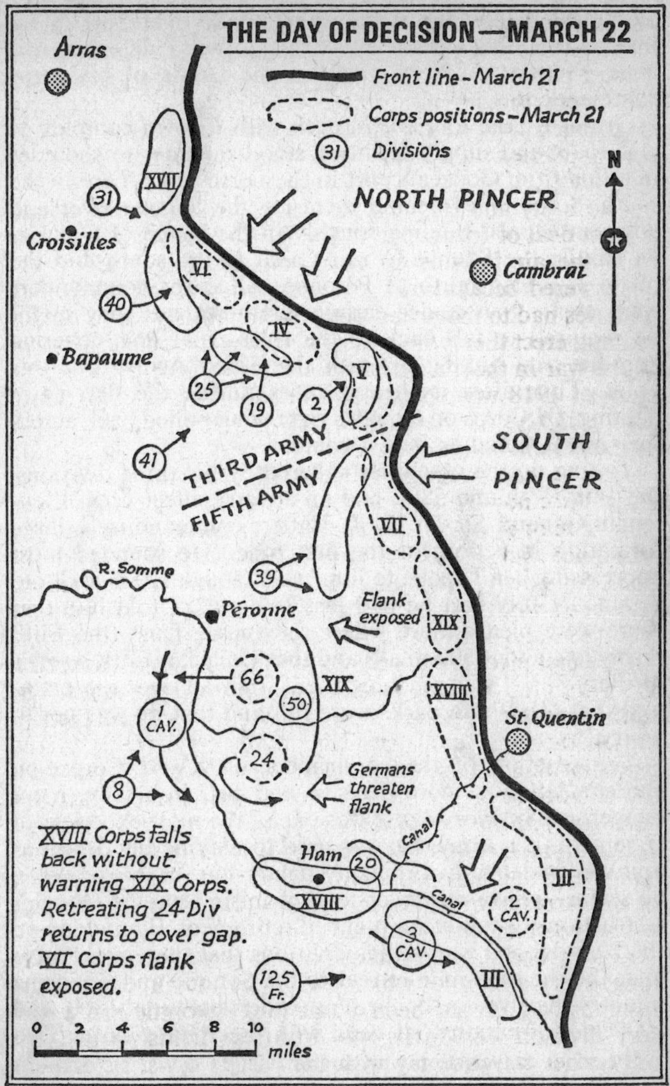
THE DAY OF DECISION—MARCH 22
Front line-March 21
Corps positions-March 21
31
Divisions
NORTH PINCER
SOUTH PINCER
N
Arras
Croisilles
Bapaume
Cambrai
Péronne
St. Quentin
Ham
R. Somme
Canal
Canal
XVII
VI
IV
V
VII
XIX
XVIII
III
XIX
XVIII
III
31
40
25
19
2
41
39
66
50
1 CAV.
24
8
20
2 CAV.
3 CAV.
125 Fr.
THIRD ARMY
FIFTH ARMY
Flank exposed
Germans threaten flank
XVIII Corps falls back without warning XIX Corps. Retreating 24 Div returns to cover gap. VII Corps flank exposed.
0 2 4 6 8 10
miles

piecemeal behind his right wing to take over part of his front. Once the hard shell of his forward defences had gone, Gough was very much in the hands of his corps commanders.

Originally the four corps, each with its own complex of rail, road, and supply facilities, stood shoulder to shoulder in a line from Gouzeaucourt in the north to La Fère in the south. Some miles behind them lay the Somme river and adjacent canals, running roughly in the shape of a sickle, its handle the Somme-Crozat Canal in the south and the blade sweeping north to Péronne. All corps commanders were aware that under certain circumstances they might be required to fall back to the river-canal line, covering Péronne and linking up with the Third Army near this point. Thus after its heavy losses during the first day's fighting, III Corps on Gough's right wing pulled back across the Crozat Canal as best it could.

Totting up the casualties suffered by his three divisions, the 14th, 18th and 58th, had an adverse effect upon Lieutenant-General Sir R. H. K. Butler, commanding a large formation in action for the first time. 'He sounded most depressed when I spoke to him,' said Gough later, 'and told me mournfully that he had lost 100 guns. I told him that there were plenty more where they came from (the Fifth Army lost about 500 in all) and that Uniacke [Fifth Army's artillery chief] was pinching them from all over the place, and that GHQ gun parks were full and that he was not to worry.'*

The reaction of the commander of XVIII Corps, on Butler's left was more decisive and yet, ironically, more dangerous. Sir Ivor Maxse was one of the most experienced generals in the army. He was used to making big decisions and was undeniably a doughty fighter but on this occasion he seems to have misunderstood or misinterpreted Gough's instructions to conduct a planned retirement. By midday on the 22nd he had warned his divisions that they might have to make the nine-mile retreat to the Somme and when the infantry received a confirming order between 1800 and 1900 his formations fell back with precipitate haste. Two

*Personal conversation with author.

of his divisions, the 30th and the 36th, having fought furiously all day, now found energy enough to outpace their pursuers. The 61st Division had a more difficult time, a whole company of the 6th Shropshires being cut off and captured by two German battalions, but by late evening most of XVIII Corps had arrived on the Somme, some units having covered fifteen miles, digging, fighting, and going without food.

Too late Gough heard of their feat. Immediately he ordered Maxse to maintain touch with XIX Corps on his left, but by then the retirement was in full swing and it was impossible to contact Maxse's headquarters. This left Sir Herbert Watts, the sixty-year-old son of a Cambridgeshire parson, in an unenviable position. He now had a full-scale battle going on to his front, where the 50th Division were covering the retreat of the 24th and 66th Divisions, and a vulnerable right flank where Maxse should have been. Reluctantly Watts had to order the bone-weary 24th Division to retrace their steps to fill the danger spot, while the exhausted 66th, looking forward to a night's rest behind the 50th Division screen, had to force their limbs to carry them a further four miles to the rear to take up positions to cover the Somme crossings and bridges. To make the task of the 24th Division a little easier, the 50th were ordered to pull back a couple of miles to line up with them. At this point a German bomber scored a direct hit on Watts' headquarters. In the confusion, and with the failure of communications, Watts could not inform the corps commander on his left of his movements until early morning.

It became the turn of Sir Walter Congreve, commanding VII Corps to try to sort out the situation, which was fast getting out of control. He had difficulty too in convincing other units of the scope of the attack. The flank formation of the Third Army, the 47th Division had not been seriously hit in the Flesquières Salient and could see little reason for deserting their superior positions without a fight. According to the Official History an absurd situation existed in which 'every effort was made to impress upon the 47th Division the magnitude of the German offensive and to explain the policy of retirement. But the 47th Division insisted it was the business of the 9th to form a defensive flank to keep up connection if the latter retired.'

In the end Gough motored to Albert to talk to his fellow army commander Byng, but the best he could extract was a promise that a brigade would be embarked to fill any gap that might occur between the 9th and 47th Divisions. There was to be little sleep for either Gough or his troops that night. The general had to move with his headquarters back to Villers Bretonneux and maintain contact with his harassed corps commanders. His men had to march. And dig.

The order to pull back was both irritating and puzzling to the men of the 50th Division. Nobescourt Farm was still in the possession of the 5th Durhams and although the Northumberlands had withdrawn slightly behind Caulaincourt they regarded themselves as being in a strong position. Now all the hard work expended on the infamous Green Line was to be wasted. The order to withdraw reached the 8th Durhams at 0100, just when some the men were hoping to snatch a little rest. Numb with lack of sleep and the exertions of the fighting the battalion struggled to its feet grumbling because packs, which had been dumped elsewhere, could not be collected. There were more groans because boxes of bombs and rifle ammunition 'which the transport was unable to move owing to the short notice given' had to be abandoned. Says the War Diary of the battalion: 'A bright moonlight made the withdrawal difficult to conceal but by 4.30 a.m. all companies had been withdrawn successfully and a start was made linking up the companies in the new line which required consolidating . . . as no trenches existed.'

One can only assume that there must have been a fair leavening of miners in the Durhams, for by 0600 the trenches linking the companies had been dug, a task made even more onerous by the thick mist which arose again about dawn. It must have exasperated even those stalwarts to be told just before 0700 that their work had been in vain – new orders had arrived for a further retreat.

There was in fact little else Gough could do, once the full extent of the XVIII Corps retirement was learned. To have the 50th and 24th Divisions five miles east of the river and five miles in front of Maxse's Corps on their right would be to court disaster. The 8th Division, which he had hoped would fill the gap and link up his line, had just begun to arrive and would have to be committed brigade by brigade to hold the Somme bridges until the troops on the other side had crossed. In the meantime the troops on the rest of the front would have to carry on fighting as there was little doubt that fresh German divisions would soon be hurled in again.

CHAPTER NINE

A GOOD DAY FOR TENNIS

Originally it had been intended that the 8th Division would maintain a support line about five miles on the 'enemy side' of the river but the breakdown of communications and the consequent disorganization had made this impossible. A billeting party of the 2nd Northants which arrived at a village they were expecting to occupy on the night of 22 March, found Germans already there and they had to fight their way out and billet elsewhere.

This report did not make pleasant reading for Major-General 'Billy' Heneker.* In fact, there had been very little to impress him earlier that day when he made a personal reconnaissance of the area into which his division was moving. As his car drew nearer the battle, it slowed to a crawl in face of the diverse transport coming down the roads away from the enemy. Guns, ambulances, motor lorries, mobile pigeon lofts, water carts, cookers, limbers, all moving westward. And men too, walking wounded with bloody bandages and tattered clothing, scurrying messengers and runners, worried staff officers and exhausted stragglers.[8]

The picture by night was equally disconcerting. Having been ordered to establish his troops along the west bank of the Somme, Heneker had driven to the detraining centre of Chaulnes, a busy rail junction. It was a fantastic sight. Sparks were rising in showers from the shunting engines which had just brought in the last of the 24th Brigade. A bonfire blazing outside a huge American Red Cross hospital marquee danced strange shadows across the face of Brigadier-General St George Grogan as he listened to his commander's instructions. A dull droning overhead suddenly became louder and the shrill whistling of a bomb

*Heneker was regarded as one of the best types of young generals and he left a remarkable diary.

drove veterans to the ground. When the blast had died away the marquee was a shambles. Seventeen nurses, orderlies, and patients lay dead. Grogan's men had to leave it to others to clear up the mess; their duty was to the living not the dead. As they marched away into the night they looked back occasionally. The blaze grew smaller but not less bright as the distance increased.

As far as the Germans were concerned the battle had become a race to cut off the units still on the east side of the Somme, and, if possible, to seize the bridges intact. To the assembling troops of the 8th Division it appeared to them at dawn on 23 March that there might be little to stop the enemy attaining their objective.

Captain Essame, adjutant of the 2nd Northants, was shocked by the condition of many of the retiring troops. 'I got the impression that the Army had definitely been broken,' he states. 'We didn't even bother to try to rally the stream of fugitives coming across the bridges. An awful lot of them had had enough. They were making for somewhere way back.

'For the first time I saw British soldiers coming back without their rifles. They weren't men of labour battalions or non-combatant troops. They were men from infantry regiments. I'd seen men retiring on the Somme and at Passchendaele, but they had always brought their rifles with them. This was the first time I'd seen men come back without them.'[71]

Miles to the north, in the Third Army area, another young officer was experiencing similar qualms about the fighting quality of the troops. Lieutenant Richard Gale (now General Sir Richard Gale) was serving with the machine gun battalion of the 42nd Division rushed by bus into the storm centre which had already sucked in the reserve 40th and 19th Divisions. They 'debussed' many miles behind the line and were ordered forward on a march which lasted twelve hours. The young Machine Gun Corps officer noted:

> 'We heard no fighting, nor had we seen any formed bodies of troops; but what we had seen appalled us. Dumps of kits and valises lay on the side of the road,

disorganized transport and guns were moving to the rear, all intermingled with pathetic groups of refugees. Canteens had been abandoned and their stores of spirit rifled. This was a retreat with all the horrors of panic. There was, as far as we knew, nothing behind us and the Channel ports, save this wretched rabble that seemed to have lost all cohesion and will to fight.' With the voice of experience, Gale adds: As is so often the way, the closer we get to the battle the less the panic.'[19]

Certainly nowhere was panic less in evidence than in the Beaumetz defence line where the Seaforths and survivors of the Gloucesters were holding out for the third day against numerous frontal assaults and close range fire from field guns. The enemy dead lay thick in front of the position. Even the most stubborn Prussian now realized that it was wasting men to tackle the 'pigheaded Scotsmen' head on. Storm troops began to work their way down the trench from the flanks and in many places the Germans were in the rear of the defenders.

Already the tall Seaforth captain had stopped his men using their Lewis guns because they were wasting ammunition. It was a question of rifles only. Every round was made to count. One bullet, one German. Nonetheless, as the afternoon wore on it became clear that ammunition would not last. Cartridgeless Seaforths began making their precarious way back. As they slipped over the parados the officer covered them trying to pick off the enemy who looked the most dangerous to them. Then, while he was engaged in a quick conference with an officer of the Gloucesters, the Germans made another frontal rush. A Gloucester private was hit and slid from the parapet, blood gushing from his throat. Seizing a rifle the Seaforth officer leaped onto the firestep and opened fire at close range but was brought down with a flying rugby tackle.

'You're a bloody hero, but also a bloody fool,' shouted the shrewd Gloucester officer sitting firmly on his kilted comrade. And round the traverse of the trench appeared a German officer with a stick bomb in his hand. There was an awkward pause. Then both Britons stood up. Salutes were exchanged. The German made solicitous inquiries about their wounds, then sent his prisoners to the rear. Uhlans, with grey service covers over their helmets, escorted the last defenders of the area on the first steps of the long road to Germany. The tall captain, who could not remember sleeping since he had entered the trench three days previously, noted with some surprise that he did not feel tired![71]

With no knowledge of such bitter actions being fought miles ahead of them, the advancing British reserves were shaken by the signs of disorganization and panic everywhere as they entered the rear areas. Officers of the 2nd Grenadiers, coming into the line behind the Third Army, recorded, 'Many people seem to have taken leave of their senses and not only have innumerable camps full of every kind of stores been incontinently abandoned, but in this village [Boiry-St-Rictude] alone a large Expeditionary Force canteen has been set on fire with all its contents and a water reservoir supplying the surrounding districts has been blown up, although neither is in the slightest danger of capture.'[31]

In truth, of course, many of the apparent signs of disorder were due to the haste with which the supporting infantry had gone forward, not back. The 1st Buffs, for example, had dumped their much-prized band kit in Favreuil before hurrying forward to take their place in the 6th Division's battle line. (The bandsmen were needed as stretcher bearers.) When the battalion was withdrawn, some of the surviving bandsmen set off to collect the instruments but were turned back by the military police. Only the highly illegal action of two drummers enabled the big drum and three side drums to be retrieved.[48] A small incident in itself, but it illustrates the way in which troops who entered the area subsequently got the impression of kit having been abandoned in flight. Similarly some of the piles of packs dumped by the roadside were undoubtedly left there at the instructions of officers urging forward reinforcements.

Once again the weather took a hand on the 23rd. After a cold night, fog blanketed a large part of the battlefield and played its tricks on both sides. Tommy Gilpatrick, a diminutive private in the Durhams, had managed to lose himself completely. Desperately anxious to catch up with his platoon, which he knew had fallen back, he found himself trudging along parallel to an apparently endless, if not very thick, belt of barbed wire. In the end he decided to squeeze his way under a likely spot.

He squirmed half-way through when he stuck. The pride and joy of his life, a warm (and now, somewhat pungent) goat-skin jerkin was stuck firmly fast on the wire. For ten minutes Tommy pulled at it, slowly growing aware of a roar of laughter and shouting as he struggled. He looked up. The fog had lifted and he lay exposed to the view of a German battalion marching in column down the road. Tommy and his goatskin finished the war in a prison camp.[71]

Near Ham, where the Germans had actually crossed the Somme Canal in the mist, a desperate brigadier came across two disgruntled companies of Cornwalls who had been put to work digging again after their long march the previous day. Immediately they were ordered to drop their picks and shovels and to prepare for an attack on the village of Verlaines, west of Ham. It was 1000 and an officer recorded in his diary:

> Off we go in artillery formation. The mist has cleared and it is quite hot – a good day for tennis. Suddenly I hear a band and on the road is the band of the 7th Cornwalls, trying to cheer us up. We go on for quite two miles. We then see the village, extend, fix bayonets and trudge slowly on, very hot, tired and hungry. Several men faint. As we enter the village we run about a bit . . . most of the Boche in the village bolt. As we pass through . . . I see a half a loaf of stale bread and a bottle of lukewarm wine on the ground which I pick up as I rush on. We are now nearing the crest of a ridge so we go on in short rushes. When we halt I pass the bread along the men and eat some myself as it seems one's only chance of ever getting food inside you. Next rush urged on by Tyacke [Captain C. N. Tyacke] and we are on the crest with the houses of St Sulpice adjoining Ham.
>
> We are now getting it in the neck from machine gun

and rifle fire especially from snipers in the houses. Tyacke is shot through the heart.[69]

The Cornwalls had actually gone beyond their objective. The officer's diary continues, 'The men are knocked out as they lie and the stretcher bearers, who were splendid, all killed. We get our Lewis guns on to about twelve Boches who run from the houses and scupper them. I get a rifle and kill one to my intense satisfaction.' The Cornwalls eventually withdrew to a safer position but they were not yet finished. A German aeroplane swooped down, strafed them, and was shot down by the concentrated fire of every weapon the pioneers could bring to bear, crashing into nearby woods. ('Loud cheers from everyone.')

Not far away, the demise of another German airman was recorded in less dramatic terms. A battalion of the 7th Durhams was resting from its labours on the Villers Carbonnel road 'when several E.A., flying low, fired machine guns at traffic on the road. We retaliated with rifle and machine gun fire and one machine was brought down.'

At this moment, as the shocked 8th Division was watching exhausted stragglers trailing across the Somme bridges, a full-scale rearguard action was being fought on the other side of the river. There, the troops of the 50th, 24th, and 1st Cavalry divisions were making their way slowly back across the flat grassy plain called the Santerre in order to reach the marshy scrubland that borders the Somme and cross to the other side. Although the early morning mist had assisted them in getting a good start on their five-mile march, the enemy had also pushed vigorously and enterprisingly ahead. The Germans had a glorious opportunity before them. Apart from the numerical weakness of the forces opposing them, there was the tricky nature of the crossings for the retreating British.

For at this point the river divides into numerous streams and canals (running parallel in places) each of which has to be crossed by a separate bridge. If the Germans could bring these bottlenecks under machine gun fire there was a good chance that they might overwhelm troops waiting to make their way over. If, better still, they could direct their

TABLE I III Corps, *Lieutenant-General Sir R. H. K. Butler* Front: 19 miles. Artillery 356 guns (incl. 106 heavies.)

14TH DIVISION	18TH DIVISION	58TH DIVISION	2ND CAVALRY DIVISION (in reserve)*
41 Brigade	53 Brigade	173 Brigade	3 Cav. Brigade
8 KRRC	10 Essex	2/2 London	4 Hussars
7 Rifle Brigade	8 R. Berks	3 London	5 Lancers
8 Rifle Brigade	9 R. West K.	2/4 London	16 Lancers
42 Brigade	54 Brigade	174 Brigade	4 Cav. Brigade
5 Ox and Bucks	11 R. Fusiliers	6 London	6 Dragoon Gds.
9 KRRC	7 Bedfords	7 London	3 Hussars
9 Rifle Brigade	6 Northants	8 London	Oxfordshire H.
43 Brigade	55 Brigade	175 Brigade	5 Cav. Brigade
6 Somersets	7 Queen's	9 London	The Greys
9 Scottish Rifles	7 Buffs	2/10 London	12 Lancers
7 KRRC	8 E. Surreys	12 London	20 Hussars
Pioneers	Pioneers	Pioneers	
11 King's Own	8 R. Sussex	4 Suffolk	

*Two brigades behind right of corps, third at Jussy.

The German forces opposing the IIIrd Corps were part of the VIIIth Corps (1st Bavarian, 7th Reserve, 9th, 10th and 36th divisions); the IVth Reserve Corps (33rd, 34th, 37th and 103rd divisions) and Group Gayl (13th L., 47th Reserve and 223rd divisions).

artillery on the crossings, the divisions to the east of the Somme might be eliminated or captured.

Destruction of the bridges seemed to be almost haphazard and British troops were sometimes marooned on the wrong bank. The 9th East Surreys, having been re-formed after their adventures of the previous day, now found themselves holding the approaches to a bridge near the village of Falvy. One company was formed up in arrowhead formation (point towards the enemy) on the right side of the road to the bridge, the other in similar formation on the left. Officers controlled the firing lines formed by the arms of the arrowpoints from a position in the centre.

Lying behind his rifle in the left company, Private Boylan reflected on his evil luck. In lulls in the firing he looked enviously at troops crossing over to safety. Then he studied the men of his own unit and noted that the young, raw troops were showing no sign of breaking, although he was quite sure that they were just as frightened as he. This was surprising for on the way up Boylan had seen one man break down and take shelter in a dugout . . . a long-service man with the Military Medal. Now the only sign of panic came from yet another veteran who jumped up and looked about to run. An officer bellowing a threat to shoot the man on the spot, brought him to his senses. Finally Boylan's company took their turn in crossing the bridge, whereupon it was promptly destroyed and the Surrey's other company was trapped on the far bank and had to swim for it. (The fact that the swimmers were immediately reclothed, given rifles, and sent into the line is a remarkable tribute to discipline if nothing else.)

Detachments of the 1st Cavalry Division, now mounted, faced a particularly hazardous crossing at Pargny because of damage to bridges. Some men tried to swim their horses across the river but they became bogged down in the marshy banks and had to be hauled out. Others tried to lead their mounts over the wreckage but came under machine gun fire and soon terror-stricken wounded animals were racing riderless over the countryside. The cavalrymen finally crossed on foot and settled down with their rifles to provide cover for any further arrivals on the opposite bank.

Five tanks arrived in fighting order on the bank of the river at Brie. To their commander's disgust they were too wide to cross without destroying the upper lattice work of the bridge. The sponsons housing their guns would have to be moved first, but there was no time. The crews removed Lewis guns and ammunition, set their machines ablaze, and tramped across to join the infantry. The bridges also presented problems for the infantry of the 50th Division. Its 150th Brigade reached the river almost intact and crossed safely, despite having been pressed by the enemy all the way. The 149th Brigade, although some platoons of the 6th Northumberlands were overrun in savage hand-to-hand fighting as the withdrawal commenced, crossed the plain to the river, according to one eye-witness, in a manner that resembled a 'set piece at Aldershot, one company retiring in perfect order covered by the fire of another, while an officer . . . controlled the field with his whistle.'[58] Eighty men of the 5th Northumberlands who covered the crossing from a village on a slight rise were cut off by the Germans. That night forty of them managed to break away and sneak over the wrecked bridge which the cavalry had used. The 151st Brigade after receiving orders to withdraw in the early morning, got away under cover of the fog. The War Diary of the 8th Durhams records: 'By this time the troops were becoming very exhausted as they had been marching and preparing defensive positions continuously since detraining at Brie on March 21st.' They were back almost where they had started from; a round trip of sixteen miles as a crow flies – and a lot farther as a soldier covers ground.

By 1230 heavy fighting had developed again, the Germans attacking under concentrated machine gun fire and low flying planes. Then, at 1300 the order for a 'methodical retirement' to a bridge at Eterpigny was received. 'By this time the enemy was within 300 yards of our position and enfilading our hastily consolidated shell holes from both flanks. Our artillery was giving no support being in the process of retirement. . . .' Happily for the 8th Durhams the final stages of their retirement were successful and in the early afternoon they crossed the river.

Now the strain began to tell. Although the battalion had done all that was required of it the release of tension, once the bridge had been crossed, led to a temporary slackening of discipline. But by 1530 some indefatigable officers discovered that the bank of the river was not protected and rallied their sleeping, foraging, troops. 'Accordingly the battalion took over a line of posts on the bank of the Somme, digging in and consolidating.'

The 8th Durhams did not move again until 0400 when 'our own artillery were shelling our own front line severely.' They pulled back 1,000 yards, before they were eventually ordered into reserve. They marched rearwards under the full observation of enemy balloons which directed large shells from long range guns onto the crowded roads, and the Durhams' officers led them cross country to avoid further casualties.

Earlier, the 6th Durhams, heading for a 300-yard long footbridge across the swampy river banks, ran into trouble in the village of Le Mesnil-Bruntel. Germans had penetrated the woods to the rear and opened fire as three companies (the fourth had already crossed) marched through the village street. Men dropped in their tracks; there were cries of pain and anger. They were trapped. Before them was the slender footbridge and the marshy unknown river bank; behind them a determined enemy. Some men ran for it, hoping their comrades across the river would provide covering fire. A few bolted into the swamps and hid there. Others milled around in confusion. With a supreme effort Captains Cardew and Aubin made their orders heard and finally a private threw himself down and fired back at the enemy. Another, about to make a dash for it, turned and joined him. A Lewis gun team went into action from a ditch. The panic and possible massacre were over. Gradually the 6th Durhams deployed and fought a rearguard action towards the bridges. In the end, the three companies crossed safely although two officers and twenty men lay dead on the rubble-strewn cobbles of Le Mesnil and in the marshes by the roadside. There might have been easily ten times that number.

Farther to the north, where the Somme twists and turns

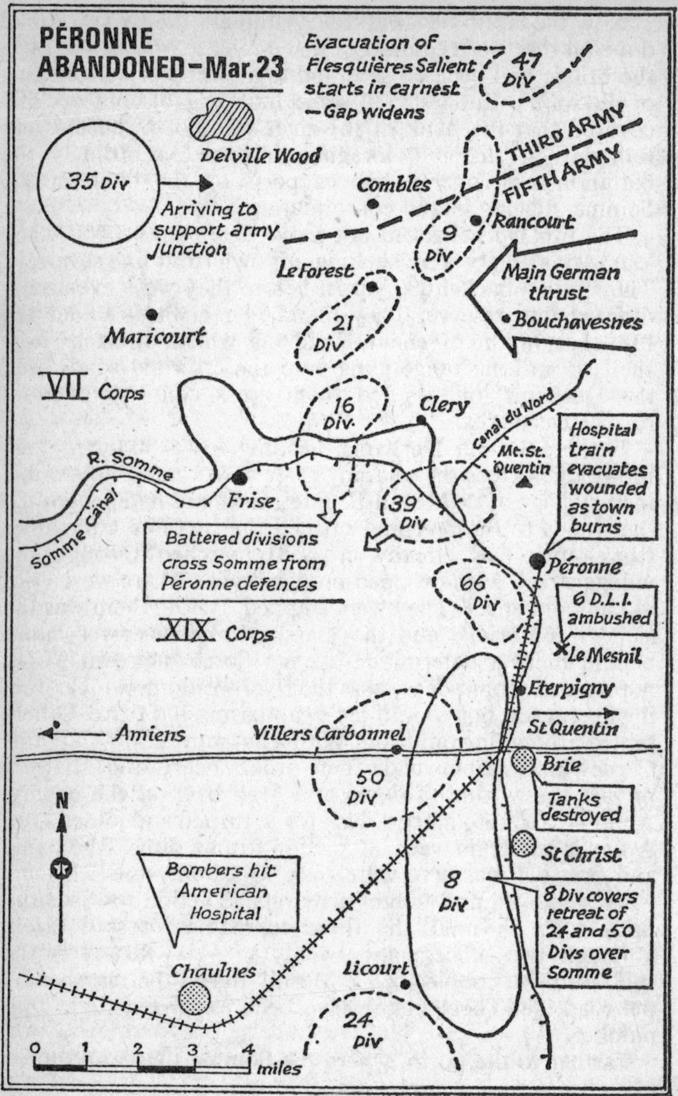
PÉRONNE
ABANDONED – Mar. 23
Evacuation of
Flesquières Salient
starts in earnest
– Gap widens
47
Div
THIRD ARMY
FIFTH ARMY
35 Div
Delville Wood
Arriving to
support army
junction
Combles
Rancourt
9
Div
Le Forest
Main German
thrust
Bouchavesnes
21
Div
Maricourt
VII Corps
16
Div.
Clery
Canal du Nord
Mt. St.
Quentin
Hospital
train
evacuates
wounded
as town
burns
R. Somme
Frise
Somme Canal
39
Div
Battered divisions
cross Somme from
Péronne defences
Péronne
66
Div
6 D.L.I.
ambushed
XIX Corps
Le Mesnil
Eterpigny
St Quentin
Amiens
Villers Carbonnel
Brie
50
Div
Tanks
destroyed
N
St Christ
Bombers hit
American
Hospital
8
Div
8 Div covers
retreat of
24 and 50
Divs over
Somme
Chaulnes
Licourt
24
Div
0
1
2
3
4
miles

west, were scenes of greater confusion. The Germans threatened to sweep behind the divisions covering the important railhead and communications centre of Péronne. As early as February Gough had been told that in the event of a German offensive pressing him back to the Somme he must cover the town at all costs. An order to construct a vast network of trenches and strongpoints stretching for fifty miles around Péronne had been given to Gough and had he been able to create this mighty fortification no one would have been happier. But with the labour at his disposal the idea was ludicrous. As a result three much reduced divisions (the 16th, 21st, and 39th), found themselves trying to cover the town from extemporized positions and it became obvious that unless they were withdrawn across the Somme they would be overwhelmed. Congreve, commander of VII Corps, reluctantly gave the order to abandon Péronne after allowing the civilian population and the rear installations as much time as possible to evacuate the town. Gough could only concur. In the casualty clearing stations a race against time began to clear the scores of wounded from the hospital tents and into a train which had miraculously arrived. It became a grisly business of deciding who was worth trying to save and who was obviously going to die and might as well be left behind. A padre conducted a non-stop burial service while the still warm bodies of men who died while awaiting evacuation were hastily lowered into a row of gaping graves.[30] Military policemen stood at every corner directing the retreating troops who poured into the cobbled streets. The devastation of the fields and surrounding area made it impossible for traffic to leave the roads and anxious eyes scanned the sky, now darkened by the smoke from burning dumps and installations. 'The evacuation of Péronne . . . offered exceptional targets. Every road out of the town became blocked,' said a VII Corps report afterwards. 'Some infantry were able to make their way across the fields, but the masses on the roads were such that had the enemy's aircraft been active, enormous damage could have been done.'

Out of this mess, the universally despised Redcaps brought about some semblance of order. The traffic, including the strings of ambulances, began to move again, and still the German aircraft did not appear. While this was going on, the three divisions covering Péronne clashed fiercely with the Germans and slowly retired on the Somme crossings, covered by gunners who kept their 18-pounders in action in many cases until the infantry had passed through them. As a belated reward for their efforts the Germans caught the 282nd Regiment of the Royal Field Artillery as it was limbering up and in a welter of shell bursts, neighing horses, and exploding limbers knocked out eleven guns.

With the unavoidable retreat of the troops covering Péronne, the price of clinging too long to the Flesquières Salient was now paid in full, and a bitter price it proved to be. Péronne lay in the right rear of the bulge which still contained four divisions of the Third Army, although one of them was much under strength. Their line of retreat (now inevitable) lay due west. But because Péronne lies at a point where the Somme turns at a right angle from north-south to east-west, the natural line of retreat for the Fifth Army divisions lay in a more southerly direction across the river. Only the worn 9th Division was left to maintain contact in the ever-widening gap between the two armies. The 35th Division was *en route* from Flanders but could not arrive in time. The so-called 'iron spike' had been drawn as easily as if it had been planted in porridge and the original occupants of the Flesquières Salient, who had been loath to leave their strong positions and had therefore been retiring slowly, now had to withdraw at full speed to escape the threat of envelopment. Among them were the 47th Division which had refused to heed the insistent warnings of the 9th Division at the opening of the battle. Lieutenant-Colonel E. L'Estrange Malone of the Royal Fusiliers with the 63rd Division in the Flesquières Salient had felt able to hold out forever if need be. On the second day of the offensive he had been irritated by the order to abandon the front line and to retire to the intermediate position. On 23 March he was further annoyed when the 47th Division had to retreat once again, especially as he gained the impression as he fell back that 'everybody' except the infantry seemed to have fled.

After the battle, while recovering from wounds, Malone wrote, 'March 23rd, 1918, will always remind me of a bad nightmare. Daybreak found us in our inadequate trench [the spitlocked Green Line] without any cover, with but little water and no means of communication with anyone. It was a glorious morning and we lay and basked in the sun among the anemones waiting for the Germans and waiting for orders. At last we saw the rearguard of our brigade falling back towards our lines. Our artillery promptly opened on them, mistaking them for Germans.'

Then came further orders to retire: 'Through the wood in single file we wound our way, and out into the wooden track at Neuville. Progress is slow; the day is as hot as midsummer; the men are over-loaded. Lewis guns and magazines all have to be carried by hand as there are no limbers. Where our transport has gone no one knows.'

The Fusiliers refreshed themselves at Neuville with the contents of an abandoned canteen. Then on they marched again. 'We pass a beautiful new German aeroplane, which has been forced to land at the end of the wood. No one has attempted to destroy it; it is thoughtfully left for the enemy to recover. From every village a huge column of smoke is ascending to heaven. These are the dumps being destroyed, the piles of stores that could not be carried away – at least a portion of them, for the whole countryside is littered with material.'

As the battalion continued to retire, carrying its wounded and collecting stragglers from other units it seemed to Malone that he was running a 'mixed commando'. Whenever they stopped at a village it was only a matter of time before heavy artillery shells ranged in on them and Malone himself narrowly missed being hit by the baseplate of a ten-inch projectile. In the afternoon the Fusiliers had to fall back across open ground, 'Walking slowly over the grassy plain while black shrapnel burst overhead and high explosives made craters in the ground.' The were now in range of enemy machine guns and the battalion became scattered only to be rallied later by an officer with a hunting horn.[50]

The Third Army was in a serious predicament on the

night of 23 March. Its left and centre were locked in battle and the situation in front of Bapaume was desperately fluid. The Third Army's right wing was in disorder, with bands of stragglers wandering in a darkness lit by the eerie glare of burning dumps.

Any hesitation by the Germans to push on now became a lost opportunity to exploit the gap between the right of the Third Army and left of the Fifth.

Considering that Haig had foreseen the possibility of the retirement of the Fifth Army to what was optimistically termed the Péronne bridgehead and the line of the Somme, one wonders why he did not give special consideration to the corresponding role of the divisions in the Flesquières Salient; in particular to the need to cement the joint between the two armies. Had this been done, Gough might have been able to concentrate on the enemy to his front, and on clearing up the penetration across the Crozat Canal. With a threat to both flanks this was impossible. Unluckily for Gough, news of the serious disorganization of divisions retreating from the Flesquières Salient travelled slowly, chiefly because it was an area occupied solely by the military. The nurses and civilians who abandoned Péronne, however, carried back lurid tales to Amiens and Abbeville, where many of the wounded were treated, and from there in no time at all rumours of the disintegration of the Fifth Army spread across the Channel.

As the red-eyed, rubbery-legged, parched men of the Third and Fifth Armies fought for their lives that Saturday afternoon, thousands of Britons at home were doing their bit too . . . cheering on their football teams. There were some good matches that day. Bury beat a Liverpool that had never heard the name Bill Shankley, and Burnley defeated a Stoke that had to wait years for the arrival of a boy called Stan Matthews. Whether the civilians appreciated the full gravity of the situation across the channel from the sparse reports available is unlikely. War correspondents did not have the speed of communication which now make their reportage almost a simultaneous account of events. Even the men at the heart of things had little idea of the seriousness of their plight.

Sir Douglas Haig, for example, had formed some harsh opinions of the way his men were conducting themselves. Despite his message of praise for all ranks on 21 March, he confided to his diary on the 22nd: 'Our 16th (Irish) Division which . . . lost Ronssoy village, is said not to be so full of fight as the others. In fact, certain Irish units did very badly and gave way immediately the enemy showed.' A stern judgement to pass on the companies of the 7th Royal Irish who were obliterated by the barrage; the men of the 7th/8th Royal Inniskilling Fusiliers who were assailed from three sides but fought until evening for the smoking ruins of Ronssoy; or the 2nd Royal Irish, the garrison of Lempire, who held out until the whole battalion was overrun.

The fighting quality of Irish soldiers was the subject of further remarks by Mr W. Shaw-Sparrow in *The Fifth Army in March 1918*. 'They were badly shaken by the day's ordeal. A good many of them, I fear, did not fight as well as they might have fought. . . .'

Be it noted that Mr Sparrow's book was published in 1921. Ireland had just gained her independence after a series of bloody and unhappy events and the atmosphere of the times may have influenced the remarks he made, just as events in Ireland in 1916 may have had an effect on Haig's assessment of Irish soldiery. For months, with the backing of many senior army officers, he had been urging the government to introduce conscription in Ireland. The officers were opposed by Lloyd George who suspected that conscription could be forced on the Irish only at gunpoint. The Army was still trying to change his mind the following autumn, but in vain.

Haig's jaundiced view of the prowess of his troops was not confined to the Irish. On the evening of the 23rd, after a visit to Gough's headquarters, the Field-Marshal again picked up his pen and opened his diary. The thud of artillery could be heard distantly as night fell over the sprawling battlefield. At Le Verguier, darkness covered the dead of the 24th Machine Gun Battalion, silent and rigid beside their empty weapons. At Roupy, the shadows hid the battered tangle of trenches where the corpses of the

Green Howards and the King's Regiment lay indivisible in a heap. The white armbands of the slaughtered stretcher bearers of the Cornwalls glimmered palely in the dusk between the lines at Ham, and tiny fish nibbled tentatively at the limbs of the Durhams slowly stiffening in the marsh at Mesnil. 'I cannot make out why the Fifth Army has gone so far back without some kind of stand,' wrote Haig.[6]

CHAPTER TEN

OUR ALLIES

The lorries of a German machine gun company bumped slowly down the road from St Quentin, mixing with columns of reserves moving forward. Labour gangs were tardily repairing the damaged surfaces of the highway and there were frequent halts. Sergeant Ludwig Renn, a veteran of three years' service, noted that as his unit drew nearer the boom of the guns three German captive observation balloons 'swayed now towards and now away from each other, and never came any nearer. That meant they were advancing too.' He also observed dead Scots lying near a small stream in 'their short kilts' with 'their boots and stockings . . . removed'. Several of his men were now wearing 'good English laced boots'.

When the column stopped and the unit bivouacked, Renn noted the speed with which his hungry comrades threw themselves on a dead horse and hacked off chunks to supplement their rations. As the smell of roasting flesh spread over the camp, the sergeant pondered over a map of the French front. 'Were we trying to penetrate to Amiens and cut the French off from the English?' he wondered. 'Would that mean the end of the war? For it must be ended.'[53]

Miles behind the lines, the War Lords of both sides pondered over their own maps. Seldom has there been such a bustling of brasshats as occurred on Sunday, 24 March 1918.

The normally urbane Haig bristled with apprehension. He had reason to. The previous day he had met his French opposite number, General Phillipe Pétain, and concluded what appeared to be a satisfactory arrangement based on the plans drawn up at the beginning of the year. These plans allocated areas of concentration in which the French would come to British aid in the event of a major attack, and vice versa. It was an arrangement the two men had made themselves after they successfully thwarted the plan of the loathed politicians to set up a central reserve under General Ferdinand Foch. On Saturday, Pétain appeared prepared to keep his part of the bargain. He said he would do everything he could to cement the junction of the Third and Fifth Armies and had given instructions for a whole army under General Fayolle to take over part of the front on Gough's right. Pétain also promised that another reserve army would be formed farther back. But then Pétain reminded Haig that his own front in Champagne was threatened.

Perhaps detecting a note of uncertainty or betrayal in Pétain's tone, Sir Douglas afterwards decided to make arrangements of his own and conferred with Plumer, commanding the Second Army in the useless Passchendaele salient, and Horne, commanding the First Army in the Flanders plain. The two generals were able to promise Haig six divisions, three of them Australian divisions with twelve battalions each.

This was meant to be good news for Pétain. But whatever Pétain may have promised on the Saturday, he had undoubtedly changed his mind by the Sunday. By then, of course, Pétain was in possession of alarming reports from his liaison officers proclaiming the disintegration of the Fifth Army. The British were showing less than 'bulldog' tenacity in defence. The Fifth Army's organization and communications were so disrupted that it was 'incapable of serious resistance'. It had virtually ceased to exist, Pétain's liaison officers claimed. French units which had entered the battle so far had suffered severely (mainly because they had gone into action without artillery and in some cases with only eighty rounds of ammunition per man).

During the day Pétain had received calls for support from the French corps (Pellé's) coming into action on the British right wing and he had to divert one of his precious reserve divisions to its aid. Pétain was shaken at dinner that evening, when M. Clemenceau, the 76-year-old prime minister,

TABLE II XIX Corps, *Lieutenant-General Sir Herbert Watts*

Front: Seven miles. Artillery 366 guns (inc. 130 heavies)

24TH DIVISION	66TH DIVISION	1ST CAVALRY DIVISION*
17 Brigade	197 Brigade	1 Cavalry Brigade
8 R. West Surrey	6 Lancs Fusiliers	2 Dragoon Guards
1 R. Fusiliers	2/7 Lancs Fusiliers	5 Dragoon Guards
3 Rifle Brigade	2/8 Lancs Fusiliers	11 Hussars
72 Brigade	198 Brigade	2 Cavalry Brigade
9 E. Surrey	4 East Lancs	4 Dragoon Guards
8 R. West Kent	2/5 East Lancs	9 Lancers
1 North Staffs	9 Manchesters	18 Hussars
73 Brigade	199 Brigade	9 Cavalry Brigade
9 R. Sussex	2/5 Manchesters	8 Hussars
7 Northants	2/6 Manchesters	19 Hussars
13 Middlesex	2/7 Manchesters	15 Hussars
Pioneers	Pioneers	*In reserve near Peronne where it could support VII Corps too.
12 Sherwood F.	5 Border	

The enemy forces opposing the XIXth Corps were the XIVth Corps (1st, 4th Guard, 25th and 228th) and L1 Corps (19th, 208th and Guards Ersatz divisions).

revealed that he was prepared to withdraw the government from Paris if necessary, showing once again how rumour increases proportionately to its distance from the front line. The old warrior even spoke dramatically of 'leaving last by aeroplane to rejoin the armies'. This added to reports of the German threat in Champagne (where an enemy captive balloon had been found with papers indicating that an offensive was imminent, though this may have been a ruse), had a further depressing effect on the already solemn Pétain.

As he drove through the night to Haig's advanced headquarters at Dury his gloom deepened. By the time he was shown in at 2300 his pale blue eyes clearly revealed his sombre thoughts. Seeing with some alarm the expression on the face of the French Commander-in-Chief, Haig did not wait for him to pour out his forebodings but launched into what he expected would be received as cheerful news. By thinning out his northern front Haig now had a force of six divisions with which he would be certain to secure the line of the Third Army.

Then according to one French account, Haig added: 'Thanks to this reinforcement he was hoping to stop the enemy's progress on that front, at least temporarily. As for the operations south of the Somme [i.e. on the greater part of the Fifth Army front] the British commander-in-chief, though following them to be sure with the most lively interest, nevertheless holds them since the previous day as a matter more especially concerning the French. . . .'[3]

But Haig underestimated French comprehension of his own guile. Here he was asking the French commander to take over a battle which from all reports was already lost. Pétain had heard few details from British GHQ on the first two days of the great offensive but descriptions of the conditions prevailing in the rear areas of the Fifth Army, mainly from his own sources, were depressing, almost unnerving. How could he believe Haig's assurances about the resolution of the British Third Army?

Pétain was not the usual caricature of a French general. It was perhaps his very knowledge of the capabilities of the ordinary soldier, his awareness of the mortality of the infantry, his experience of the true lengths of human endurance, that made him simultaneously the best and worst general in France. He was in fact unique among the War Lords of the Western Front.

Haig, Joffre, Foch, Nivelle, Hindenburg, Falkenhayn, and many others acted as though their men *were* equal to any two of the enemy. They set superhuman tasks, issued impossible orders, and ignored the legions of the dead. If disregarding cost is the hallmark of good generalship, they were brilliant. But Pétain lacked this grisly virtue. He had seen what happened to the French army at Verdun. From the steps of his headquarters in the Mairie at Souilly in 1916 he had watched the youth of France march past full of life, heading for the inferno, and seen those who survived come back, in a matter of days, staggering and staring as old men.[37]

Because of his compassion for the sufferings of men in the front line, Pétain was the man the French turned to when a number of divisions refused to obey orders after the disastrous Nivelle offensive in 1917. Pétain succeeded in ending the mutiny mainly because he was able to convince the troops that never again would the impossible be asked of them. He had to sanction executions (although of more than 350 sentenced to death only fifty-eight were actually shot).[67] He had to exhort, cajole, and flatter and all the while admit the truth unto himself: the self-evident truth that there was a limit to what flesh and blood could stand. Lloyd George seemed to have discerned this when he observed that Pétain was a good and able soldier but 'his métier after the 1917 mutinies was that of a head nurse in a home for cases of shell-shock'.[44]

It was logical that he should suspect that the British Army, which had suffered so heavily on the Somme in 1916, at Ypres and Cambrai in 1917, and now, in 1918, on the Somme again, might have reached its limit of endurance. Unlike the French it had not reached breaking point previously, but why should 'Les khakis' be immune? And if they *were* broken, Pétain must decide where his duty lay.

As commander-in-chief of the French field army there were three main alternatives for Pétain to consider:

(i) immediate steps to repair any breach in the Allied line;

(ii) the protection of Paris and the left wing of his own army if the British and French separated;

(iii) the preservation of the strength, including its reserves, of the French army.

Was his duty, in short, to his Allies, to his country, or to the future (for a strong French army would have to be preserved if France was to have influence in any peace proposals)? In the event, Pétain concentrated on the first two propositions but his frankness was undoubtedly the greatest contribution he made to the conference. For although Haig subsequently described Pétain as being 'very upset, almost unbalanced and most anxious',[6] the tall, broad-shouldered old soldier, was patently sincere however gloomy he may have been, and it seemed to him now that as he stretched out his hand to close the breach, so Haig was withdrawing his.

Pétain, therefore, had ordered Fayolle to regard his main task as the covering of the French left wing, although he should, if possible, maintain contact with the British. In other words, Pétain put the security of the French Army first. Unity with the Allies came second.

He had not yet told Haig his decision. It was midnight. The room was dominated by maps and uniforms and the anxious faces of British and French staff officers. Haig had many arguments he could have used to back up his case that the French should take over responsibility for the unknown chaos that was said to reign south of the Somme. The French had a considerable number of divisions in reserve; it was part of their agreement; the English were expecting further heavy attacks (and they came) on other sectors of their own front line. But the time for subtlety and closely reasoned argument was past.

Bluntly Haig asked if General Pétain meant to abandon the British right flank. For a moment the burly, sad-faced figure was silent. Then a movement. He nodded his head. Yes that was what he meant. Silence. There was nothing to say. Pétain eventually broke it himself: 'It is the only thing possible, if the enemy compels the Allies to fall back still farther.'[3]

Dogmatic and obtuse Haig may have been on occasions, but this was not one of them. Adept at thwarting politicians when it suited him, he was far too intelligent not to know when to let them in on the act, especially when it looked as though things were collapsing around his ears. As his car raced through the night to his main headquarters at Montreuil, he mentally framed the messages which would spark London into action to consider this 'serious change in French strategy'.

Arriving at 0300, he immediately began work on cables to Sir Henry Wilson, Chief of the Imperial General Staff, and Lord Milner the Secretary of State for War. The cipher clerks worked until the early hours. His diary for that date – although it is not clear whether he made the entry the following day in view of his late return to GHQ – states, 'In my opinion, our Army's existence in France depends on keeping the British and French armies united.'

Note the expression 'our Army's existence'. He does not say 'the Allied armies'. He appears to have been as exclusively concerned with the British army as his 'almost unbalanced and most anxious' counterpart had been with the French, an impression strengthened by the entry in his diary for the previous day when he talked of the British probably being 'rounded up and driven into the sea' if touch between the two armies was lost, and by a secret letter he sent to Foch the day after his momentous meeting with Pétain. In this letter Haig stated that unless large French Forces were employed to fill the threatened gap between the armies, the British army 'must fight its way slowly back covering the Channel ports'.[44] The shades of Dunkirk were cast long before the sun-kissed summer of 1940.

The days that followed the confrontation of Sunday 24 March, became a nightmare for those involved. After nearly four years of the Great War, the men who were running it had finally created seemingly irrevocable confusion and distrust.

There were some fascinating cameos. Lord Milner, arriving at Doullens for a conference, was seized by Clemenceau who, according to Lloyd George, 'startled him by the announcement that Haig had just declared that he would be obliged to uncover Amiens and fall back on the Channel ports'. The 'secret' letter to Foch had come home to roost, and although Haig may have meant merely to indicate that his primary consideration was to protect his most sensitive sector, a hasty reassurance had to be given by Haig that he had been 'misunderstood'.

At the same conference Clemenceau plucked at the sleeve of Raymond Poincaré, the President of France, and muttered, 'Pétain is annoying because of his pessimism. Just think of it, he said to me what I would tell no one but yourself. It was this: "The Germans will beat the British in open country; after this they will beat us too!" ' Indignantly the old man they called The Tiger added, 'Ought a general to talk, or even think, like that?'[4]

General Foch who had been in a military limbo for more than six months, now found himself in a strange position. Earlier that year Haig and Pétain had done all in their power to prevent the setting up of a general reserve under his command. Haig in particular had been obdurate and finally Foch had been found a harmless planning job on the War Council at Versailles. Now he was popular with everyone and after three days of talks Foch found himself with the task of coordinating the action of the Allied armies on the Western Front. Haig, the arch-enemy of the general reserve scheme, was now ready not only to back Foch to the hilt in order to maintain the junction of the two armies, but, in his diary, actually took credit for forcing the issue through.

After the war, nearly everyone claimed that the appointment of Foch was their own brainwave but the colourful, dapper little artilleryman himself was undeceived – 'You give me a lost battle and tell me to win it,' he told Clemenceau.

Well might Haig seem 'not only willing but quite pleased' to take Foch's advice. Well might Pétain lose some of the 'appearance of a commander who was in a funk'. Now that Foch had taken over responsibilities they, at least, could not be blamed for losing the war. How Foch would perform the miracle asked of him was his business.

Without a proper staff, lacking the necessary means of communication, with his powers still restricted (for he had no troops actually under his command) Foch was thrown back on his two natural resources; courage and vanity. No one was as brave as General Foch when it came to ordering troops to hold to the last man. No one was more certain of his ability to win battles; in truth, he regarded even the bloody fiascos he had initiated earlier in the war as victories. Lacking the subtlety of Haig and the realism of Pétain he was nonetheless, in some respects, the ideal man for the job. At least he was sure to fight all along the line; he could be counted on to keep the war going.

Fortunately, considering his inherent qualities, General Foch received the able assistance of an unsuspected ally. The day before Haig and Pétain met for their fateful talks, General Ludendorff made a decision that, had they known it, would have cheered them immeasurably.

Up to 23 March, all had gone well for the Germans. They had achieved surprise. They had hit the British front at its weakest point with tremendous force. They had correctly judged that the French would hesitate at the crucial time. Seven weeks before the offensive was launched General von Sauberzweig, chief-of-staff of the German Eighteenth Army, in submitting his written plan for attacking the Fifth Army, had stated confidently, 'It need not be anticipated that the French will run themselves off their legs and hurry at once to help their Entente comrades. They will first wait and see if their own front is not attacked also, and decide to support their ally only when the situation has been quite cleared up. That will not be immediately as demonstrations to deceive the French will be made. . . .'[14]

Von Sauberzweig knew what he was writing about. The first senior French officer to reach Gough in person was General Georges Humbert, titular commander of the French Third Army designated to take over the right of the Fifth Army front. A skilled, conscientious soldier he was welcomed warmly by Gough, who thought that it would be only a short time before French divisions would be arriving in support. Gough could hardly believe his ears when the straight-forward Humbert shrugged his shoulders and exclaimed that apart from himself, his army consisted only of the flag on his motor car. 'This was not exactly the support that the moment seemed to require,' was Gough's laconic comment.[28]

For the first time Gough learned that the divisions of Humbert's Army, which he thought had been concentrated for training and rest in his own rear, had been dispersed along the French line. French units, scattered as they were, had little choice but to come into the battle piecemeal and their tardy arrival on the battlefield did not go unnoticed by the German General Staff. The Germans were certain that the Allied leadership was beginning to waver; that the Alliance itself was in danger of disintegrating through bickering, indecision, and a divergence of national interests. And from the Franco-British conferences held on 23 and 24 March we know that the German assessment was not wildly overstated. It left Ludendorff with a tantalizing problem. Should he stick to his original plan and concentrate on the defeat of the British army in the open field, while merely holding off the French? Or should he assault the centre of the Allied line along its whole front and win the war with one blow?

Ambitious though his plan may seem now, it did not seem so improbable in the eyes of many German generals. Crown Prince Rupprecht thought the British might have received a mortal blow. Hutier in the southern sector had made enormous gains without coming up against serious French intervention. German aviators reported that dumps were burning all over the rear areas and that the roads were blocked with troops and transport moving back. Could this be the beginning of the end? On the morning of 23 March, Ludendorff abruptly announced a change in plan. The scale of the attack would be widened to include the whole front.

The very afternoon that Pétain was studying pessimistic reports of the Fifth Army's condition, and Haig was preparing his statement about the reserves he had scraped up from the Ypres front, German staff cars began to disgorge immaculate figures at Avesnes – Ludendorff's forward H.Q.

Inside, Ludendorff – the unmistakable Prussian officer with his cropped head, heavy jowls, pink face, and monocle – studies the scene. On the table are maps. Below the table cluster highly-polished boots topped by smart grey-green trousers with the broad red stripe of a staff officer. Above the table Iron Crosses glitter arrogantly on the left breast pockets of well-pressed tunics. Here and there around the table the dainty blue enamelled *Pour le Mérite* glints at a collar. Ludendorff himself wears the *Pour le Mérite*, giving perhaps a rare insight into his character for Ludendorff was more than a military bureaucrat, he too was a risk-taker and an opportunist. Today he has decided to improvise. After all, his armies have just made the greatest advance accomplished on thc Western Front up to that date. Anything is now possible.

His orders were clear. 'The object is now to separate the British and French by a rapid advance on both sides of the Somme.'

North of the Somme, attacks would be sustained at different places against the British not only 'to drive them into the sea' but 'in order to bring the whole British front into ruins'. There would be a linking assault in the centre of Ludendorff's attacking line and south of the Somme the French would be attacked and beaten. It was a formidable concept. It was tenable only if the British had truly been beaten, and only if the French (as the Germans were sure they would) put their national interests before unity.

'Such a dispersal of the Armies in three directions,' General von Kuhl, Crown Prince Rupprecht's chief of staff wrote later, 'was thinkable only when . . . the enemy had been beaten on the whole front.' This, in his opinion, had not been achieved when Ludendorff made his decision.[41]

As we know, if it had been left to the generals, the unity of the French and British armies would have been shattered at this stage. But the final decision was left to the despised politicians who still enjoyed an independent freedom of action unthinkable in Germany. It was a factor that Ludendorff did not take into account. Certainly he paid tribute to the determination of the Western statesmen after the war.[45]

THE GENERALS CHANGE THEIR MINDS

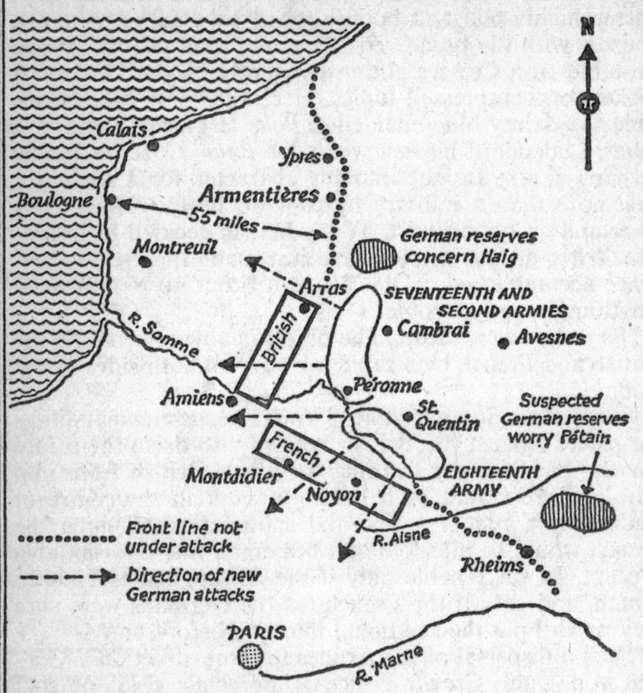

Originally, HAIG and PÉTAIN had promised to come to each other's aid if attacked. In the event, PÉTAIN, believing wrongly that the Fifth Army had broken, concentrated his reserves to protect Paris, towards which they retreated. HAIG's barrier pivoted on Arras and swung back to cover the Channel ports. LUDENDORFF, in the meanwhile, decided to drop his shield along the Somme and attack in three directions at once, thus diluting his strength.

In March 1918, however, Ludendorff, who acknowledged only the Kaiser as Supreme War Lord and Hindenburg as his titular commander-in-chief, regarded himself as the sole instrument of victory. To him civilian leaders and diplomats were weaklings. Strength lay only in his faithful legions and Krupp canon. Germany would march forward on an ever broadening front until the British were trapped against the Channel coast and the French were driven back past Paris and begged for peace.

But there is an inertia about major military operations and while the Germans were expanding the scope of their attack, and while the British and French were frantically trying to sort out their command problems, the battle developed of its own accord presenting the junior officers on the spot with a continuous flow of difficult decisions.

The French coming up on the right of the Fifth Army discovered that if the British had retired with what seemed undue dispatch in certain areas it was for two very good reasons. One was the sheer weight of the German attack; the other was to avoid the ever present menace of being cut off because there were insufficient troops to form a continuous line. It took the French only a short time to learn the rules of the new game. When it came to retreating they proved able to march back even more quickly than the British – if only because they were fresher and their boots were in better shape.

This is not to say that the French troops showed signs of the malaise which had afflicted many of their divisions after the spring mutinies of 1917. Not at all. Moreover, they were in excellent physical condition. An Australian observer remarked: 'The French troops . . . looked splendid, bronzed men, almost all of a good age – twenty-five to thirty-five.' As Major-General Sir Edward Spears points out in *Liaison 1914* the rank and file of the French army consisted mainly of peasants . . . 'What is more they were big men. It came as rather a shock . . . to observe, as the industrial population of England became absorbed in the British Army, that the French Army of '16 and '18 was composed of bigger, burlier and stronger men than the British, probably a stone heavier on the average, and an inch or so taller.' Splendid virtues, but bigger men make bigger targets – a fact not overlooked by the Germans.

A regiment of the French 125th Division arriving on 23 March, went straight into an attack on the town of Tergnier, lost its commanding officer, and after gamely carrying on under Lieutenant-Colonel Christopher Bushell (who won a V.C. by joining in with two companies of the 7th Queens), fell back. 'They seemed a fine, resolute lot,' wrote an eye-witness, 'and they said that they had gone up with only 35 rounds of ammunition a man and had expended the lot.'

Of another counter-attack essayed by the French in the area the same writer records, 'There was no artillery preparation. The attempt was beyond praise as regards the gallantry of the soldiers who made it, but the brave Frenchmen were met with a perfect storm of machine gun bullets and they could not go on. After lying down for a few minutes they got up and retired, and the retirement took the whole of the English first line with it.'[48]

During Sunday 24 March, as the clergy of England intoned pious prayers craving the Deity's partiality (the newspapers had now printed the brutal truth about 'the 15-mile retreat'), French infantry and cavalry units continued their futile attacks on the Germans as and when they came up. Then they fell back to the weary British line. Originally it had been intended that the French divisions would build up a new front and that the battered British divisions would go into reserve behind them. In practice the British found themselves shoulder to shoulder in the same line as the French, or even counter-attacking to take pressure off French units. The bemused troops of the 18th Division actually found themselves covering the retirement of the newly arrived French 9th Division. Even the battered 14th Division had to deploy on occasions to cover the retreating French.[13 28]

It was a situation repeated regularly during the German offensive. Relieving units would find themselves faced by a larger opposing force than they could handle and the tired troops they were supposed to replace would be called back to thicken a line which the enemy continued to grind down to near bursting point.

Thus it was with the 8th Division covering the main Somme crossings. On Saturday evening, once the 50th and 24th Divisions were over, the bridges were blown and the advancing enemy checked. But during the cold night the Germans crept forward to the river bank and warmed themselves by felling trees and knocking together makeshift rafts to attempt a crossing at dawn. Protected by the troops who had crossed the Somme-Crozat Canal farther south, the enemy achieved a foothold on the right of the 8th Division. Thus, while holding firm along six miles of the river against all frontal attacks, the division suddenly found its flanks endangered. But instead of concentrating on the crossings on the right already in their possession, the German battalions unimaginatively tried to seize crossings overlooked by the 8th. Groups of Germans which succeeded in reaching the western shore were bayoneted in fierce counter-attacks.

Of course, this fighting took its toll of the British and gradually support troops and others snatching a rest behind the 8th Division, were drawn into the battle. A confused action ensued, in which some defending battalions found themselves pinned down by major frontal assaults, while the units on either side might be completely free from attack and yet helpless to come to their aid without disrupting the sacred continuity of the line. An officer in one of the luckier battalions, which was unattacked for a lengthy period, watched the battle going on all around him and commented later: 'Really we held the line very badly, with all four companies in a row.'[18]

Although the defence may not have been based on the soundest tactical principles, it was sufficiently stubborn to inflict considerable casualties and disorganization on the Germans.

The mainstay of the Fifth Army clinging to the river now became XIX Corps. Maxse's XVIII Corps although originally acting in concert with the French, now concentrated on defending the right flank of its dogged neighbour. Butler, however, allowed III Corps to be sucked irrevocably down the line of retreat most suited to the French and to Pétain, i.e., towards Paris and away from Maxse's right and the axis of the British retirement. So much for the Fifth Army. The situation behind the abandoned Flesquières Salient was even more chaotic. Many HQ, overwhelmed by the hasty withdrawal, had lost control of the situation. Recorded the 63rd Division: 'From a great railway centre like Rocqigny, the whole of the administrative staff had withdrawn, taking everything portable, and leaving not a telephone behind. The result was that the only people who knew from direct observation what the situation was, could neither direct their troops how to meet it, nor enable the troops under their command to do so.' The commander of the Drake battalion of the 63rd was just in time to stop a group of Royal Engineers from carrying out orders which would have sent the trenches holding his whole battalion to Kingdom Come. The Artists' Rifles in the same division were not so lucky. A huge ammunition and RE dump at Ypres was blown sky-high in a spectacular pillar of flame just behind their trenches inflicting numerous casualties. Even the enemy was suitably impressed for a time. When the Germans did show their heads again the light from the blaze enabled the survivors of the blast to pick them off.

This lack of control persisted all Sunday as divisions from the Flesquières Salient fell back.

Over a wide, sprawling area, with pillars of black smoke rising from burning supply dumps and abandoned camps, scattered columns tried to find their way back across the bleak land that had been wrecked by the Germans during their retirement in the spring of the previous year. The empty plain stretched back to the wilderness of the old Somme battlefield where flattened villages were recognizable only by signboards. In places vast crater fields, now partly overgrown, showed where the barrages of 1916 had fallen and tangled wire, like tattered blackthorn hedges, writhed over the silent, decaying strongpoints of forgotten battles. Guns strayed into cul-de-sacs formed by the ancient entanglements, and were abandoned. Veterans recognized their whereabouts by the graves of friends long dead.

The Germans, whose comrades were buried equally thickly in the area, used their local knowledge to mount ambushes. Regiments crossed danger points with barely a casualty; in what appeared to be the safest places, shells and bullets suddenly rained down. Inexorably, slowly, the Third Army's right was forced back. Contact with the Fifth Army was lost and the gap widened. And once again the 9th Division suffered. Since early morning its two weakened Scottish brigades had fallen back fighting. The South African brigade, which formed the remainder of the division, stood fast in an entrenched position on a ridge near the scattered shell holes and splintered trees of Marrières Wood. The commander of the South Africans, Sussex-born Brigadier-General F. S. Dawson, had no doubts as to the seriousness of the situation. The previous day he had watched in admiration the 21st Division retiring on his right, two lines lying down to cover the retreating third with Lewis gun and rifle fire, while the German columns came on 'wave after wave, and column after column'.

He knew also that not all the British troops in the area were as reliable – including some from his own division. Part of the line that day had to be held by a battalion of 'details' – troops that had formerly been left out of action – transport men, signallers, clerks, and men returning from leave. And this scratch formation did yeoman service holding the line. The Germans came up platoon after platoon and were shot down 'like tame rabbits', he recalled after the war. Then came the order to retire. Describing the incident, Dawson added, 'In five minutes the battalion of details was in full retreat and once they got going like that there was no stopping them. The Germans . . . got up and began to fire, but although within forty yards, they were so excited they could hit no one at first. Then they cut the wire and . . . got the machine guns and riflemen on the parapet [of the trench which had been held by the details] and did a great deal of damage. Details', Dawson declared, 'will put up a scrap all right, but will not endure the absolute hell they will go through with their own platoons and companies.'[58]

The same day Dawson came across two officers and forty men of the 21st Division and ordered them to hold a small hill on his left. Their commander told him that they were all that remained of 300 men who had been in action without food since the offensive began. Dawson supplied the

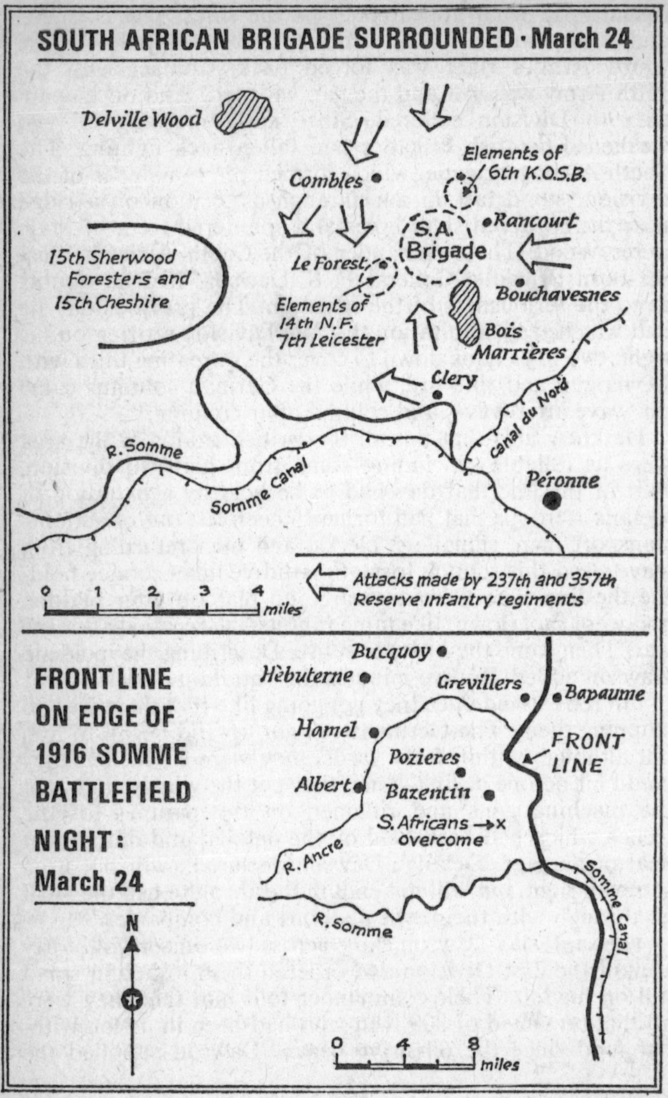

SOUTH AFRICAN BRIGADE SURROUNDED · March 24
Delville Wood
Combles
Elements of 6th K.O.S.B.
S.A. Brigade
Rancourt
15th Sherwood Foresters and 15th Cheshire
Le Forest
Elements of 14th N.F. 7th Leicester
Bouchavesnes
Bois Marrières
Clery
Canal du Nord
R. Somme
Somme Canal
Péronne
Attacks made by 237th and 357th Reserve infantry regiments
0 1 2 3 4 miles
FRONT LINE ON EDGE OF 1916 SOMME BATTLEFIELD
NIGHT: March 24
Bucquoy
Hèbuterne
Grevillers
Bapaume
Hamel
FRONT LINE
Pozieres
Albert
Bazentin
S. Africans overcome
R. Ancre
R. Somme
Somme Canal
N
0 4 8 miles

men with rum and rations and ordered his brigade major to place them in position. Half an hour later when he went to visit them they had vanished.

'I ought to have realized,' he said, 'that they'd had a bad time of it and had reached that stage when troops were no longer reliable. In this stage there is only one way to hold troops – by the influence of an officer or non-com with a stronger personality, who will use his fists, and if this does not work, will use his revolver.'

In such a situation, with units falling back all round him, Dawson himself might have pulled out that night. Instead he decided to stand fast. The misty dawn that broke on Sunday was the last most of his South Africans would ever see.

From 0900, although they had only 200 rounds of ammunition per man, the Springboks gamely shot it out as the ring around them tightened. The Germans clawed their way ever nearer as the day wore on, attacking under the cover of barrages which filled the air with dust and fouled the rifles of the defenders. The enemy set fire to the rank dry grass and crawled close behind the billowing smoke. From two hundred yards, a line of men of the 357th Reserve Infantry regiment suddenly burst from the swirling white clouds, but were precipitately shot down. A courageous field gun crew which tried to manhandle a 77mm into action at 1,000 yards range, were eliminated by a crack Lewis gunner. A second field gun team galloped up at full speed and overturned as the same Lewis brought down horses and riders in a thrashing, frantic huddle.

The fight continued with similar ferocity all that day with the South Africans encouraged by the knowledge that units of the fresh British 35th Division were trying to cut their way through to them. Whenever the noise in their own battle area declined, they could hear the sound of the 15th Cheshires and 15th Sherwood Foresters battling towards them. It was a forlorn hope, for the Germans were so thick around the South Africans (and two small parties of the 14th Northumberland Fusiliers and the 7th Leicesters who stayed with them) that the end became inevitable. They had started the day only 500 strong and as the hours passed, their numbers dwindled. Mortars began to hammer the trenches from close range. Ammunition was running low and the bandoliers and pouches of the dead and wounded were scoured for stray rounds. Hopes rose briefly when the Germans coming in behind the South Africans suddenly scattered – but they were merely fleeing a barrage of their own guns firing over the encircled Springboks. Gradually Brigadier-General Dawson lost control of his command, now scattered over a wide area and hidden by drifting smoke and dust and bursting shells. Some men even surrendered in error when they mistook a signal by a white German artillery flag, but that didn't stop others from fighting. In one trench which had been partly blown in by shells bursting on the parapet, only two men remained alive; Father Hill, a padre who had been tending the wounded, and a private who had been a draper in civilian life but proved to be a formidable warrior at this time of crisis. It was with some surprise that the padre heard the intrepid draper confess, after firing his last bullet, that he had been praying for four hours. The padre himself then revealed that he had been praying himself only the last three – but then as a man of the Cloth he had not perhaps appreciated the danger they were in.

Not far away, Major Ormiston of the 1st South African Infantry Regiment, argued with a private who had crawled across the open to where Ormiston lay wounded.

'I am dying,' Ormiston said. 'I'll be gone in an hour or so. Don't waste your time.'

It was only when the soldier convinced the officer that it would at least do no harm to try that Ormiston discovered that his legs were no longer paralysed.

At about twenty minutes to five, the noose was drawn around the trapped brigade. Three fresh battalions of the German 237th and 357th Reserve Infantry Regiments swept forward straight into the mouths of Vickers guns hung with empty belts and over Lewis guns surrounded by expired drums.[36] Here and there a shot saved for just this moment rang out, but it was all over. There was no more ammunition. The survivors, about one hundred in all, were led away. Those who were fit to march noted with satisfaction that the roads were jammed with men and guns delayed by their stand. A regiment of the German 1st Division marching through the area later noted that the trenches were filled with the dead from both sides who bore obvious bomb and bayonet wounds 'proof that there had been bitter hand to hand fighting'.

Whether the willingness of the South Africans to 'get themselves killed' led them to be wasted unnecessarily is a moot point. Their commander himself had doubts about his decision to adhere so literally to the order, 'hold on at all costs', although this had been given him personally by the acting divisional commander, Brigadier-General Tudor.

Up to the early afternoon there had been an opportunity for him to break out. As most of his ammunition had been fired away by that time it may be wondered why he did not consider that his men would be of more use back in the British lines rather than in German prison camps. Dawson, however, had to make his decision in the heat of battle and, furthermore, he knew that the 35th Division was on its way (its troops penetrated to within two miles of the South Africans).[14] Still the doubt nagged him and he confided to his diary later: 'I cannot see that under the circumstances I had any option but to remain till the end. Far better to go down fighting against heavy odds than that is should be said we failed to carry out our orders. To retire would be against all traditions of the service.'[58] Without detracting for one moment from the bravery of Dawson's men, he might have taken into account the fact that the traditions of the service were being flouted with monotonous regularity by many other officers that day – men who were concerned with keeping their units in being so they could live to fight on.

The other brigades of the 9th Division fought a severe rear-guard action. But whether to fight or to run? That was the question plaguing hundreds of individual officers in those dark days, and particularly on Sunday, 24 March 1918.

The most difficult thing for the junior officers and men to comprehend was the lack of reserves and the total failure of higher command to control the situation. During the earlier years of the war, when the army was committed to incessant attack, the generals had always been able to find fresh divisions to keep up the tempo. Now that they were on the defensive, the apparently inexhaustible supply of cannon-fodder seemed to have dried up. What is more, during the offensive battles of 1916 and 1917, the Germans had always contained potential breakthroughs by falling back onto prepared positions and by throwing in carefully placed counter-attack divisions. It was a shock to the British troops to discover that, not only were their rear defences virtually non-existent, but that often they were expected to carry out any counter-attacks themselves. The strain told.

A brigade of the 17th Division pushing forward to try to cover the gap between the 9th and 47th Divisions came across '. . . a crowd of haggard, exhausted men streaming back along a country road and moving westwards. Some officers with them were doing what was possible to get them into some kind of order. There were about 1,500 in all, many of them wounded. It was a sign that for not a few, the breaking strain was already past . . .'[14] Near Sapignies, a tough sergeant in the 2nd South Lancashires shot and killed two men whose behaviour was generating panic. (It was stated later that he thought they had been Germans in disguise, but no one believed that hoary tale.)[59]

On the evening of the 24th, according to the Official Historian, two brigades of the 47th Division assembled at Bazentin-le-Petit after a gruelling march and many adventures. 'The spirit of the men, for once, was somewhat shaken. They had been under the belief that the retreat was 'according to plan' and that when the devastated area [of the old Somme battlefields] had been crossed they would pass through fresh troops already in position – the names of the divisions coming up for the purpose had actually been mentioned. Now they found themselves still in the front line. Some began to wonder if all was as well as it was represented.'

Fortunately the German air force was unable to take advantage of the situation, mainly due to the furious activity of the Royal Flying Corps, the only people who could see how critical the situation was. One pilot reported, 'Congestion behind our Third Army was extraordinary. Peasants were fleeing westwards on the Arras–Albert front carrying anything that could be saved . . . they blocked the roads with slow moving carts and barrows. Our relief battalion and rear service vehicles were struggling eastward to the aid of troops in the line . . . the result was chaos.'[3]

Captain Hubert G. Wilkins, the Australian official photographer, was standing at another vantage point on the old Somme battlefield, where he watched British transport and artillery columns making their slow way across the moorland roads and down the main Bapaume–Albert road. 'Down the roads came long lines of guns. There was no disorder. Just two or three guns were firing. The British infantry was retiring down the Bapaume road in excellent order – tired but not routed. The officers said they did not know where they were intended to go. They were without orders except to retire to some position farther back.'

Wilkins spoke to some of the retiring troops. A few of them said 'The Boche can have this country as far as I'm concerned.' But 'the majority seemed to be anxious to get to some place where they could get a rest and then turn on him [the enemy].' Pilots of the 71st (Australian) Squadron told Wilkins that the roads were just as crowded with transport and guns behind the German lines, that the German reserves were massing behind Bapaume, and that there were many dead Germans lying in the fields near the town.

Although the main concern of the day was to disengage from the pursuing enemy, there were many bitter clashes. At one point the rearguards of the 41st Division looked in danger of being overwhelmed. At that moment a detachment of six tanks was discovered moving to a rear position according to its orders. Obligingly the tank commander postponed the move and soon his Mark IVs were crawling across the fields near Sapignies, adding the boom of their six-pounders to the general racket. Sensibly the German infantry went to ground. Cynics among the British troops who fell back under cover of the tank guns said that the real reason for the counter-attack was to give the VI Corps officers' club (which indeed was in the area) time to evacuate its supplies of liquor. There were few officers (and men) who couldn't have used a stiff drink as dusk fell.

Gloomy though the day had been, the Third Army did have cause for optimism. Although their own reserves had already been drawn into the fray more help was on the way. The Guards division was now involved in the battle on the left flank, the 42nd Division was completing a twelve-hour trek and going into the line that night, while two British divisions, three Australian, and the New Zealand Division were concentrating in the rear. (The Fifth Army, on the other hand, had to depend on the charity of General Pétain for any reserves and as has already been stated, it was not likely to be bountiful.)

It was almost as though GHQ had decided to disown Gough and his men. Under a reorganization, ordered that evening, the battered VII Corps, north of the Somme, was now placed under the command of the Third Army and the boundary between Gough and Byng became the river itself – a blatant denial of the established principles of modern warfare which have shown that under such circumstances both banks of a river should be under control of one commander. This lapse was to have a telling effect on operations within the next few days. Moreover, Gough was informed that he now came under the direct orders of the French General Fayolle, and the Fifth Army would thus be in Fayolle's group of armies. In effect Gough was no longer in direct contact with British GHQ. At the same time the depleted divisions of Butler's III Corps were put under the orders of the French corps under General Pellé.

What about reinforcements? It seems that Gough was expected to solve that problem by employing the formations relieved by the French. The idea that these, by now, pathetically small detachments could be used as 'reserves' was simply callous. The Liverpools, Cornwalls, and Somersets who made up the 61st Brigade of the 20th Division, for example, were now formed into four companies and placed in support of the French 9th Division. General Gregoire, commanding the French 1st Division, was told that he would have 'the debris' of the British 18th Division under his command.

The intermingling of soldiers of both nations was the delight of propaganda merchants who hastened to display photographs of French and British shoulder to shoulder in the field. Nothing could have been more unsatisfactory. Different temperaments, methods of training, and a lack of understanding purely on the basis of language made co-operation an arduous task. To alter the higher command structure at this stage added to an already difficult problem. Gough himself writes: 'Placing the Fifth Army under Fayolle's group of armies made no material difference. He issued no orders to me and I only saw him once for a few minutes.'

Philip Gibbs summed up the situation on 24 March with a certain amount of caution. 'It seems certain now,' he wrote, 'that our armies are able to control the situation within the limits of ultimate safety, though our losses in men are inevitably severe, and the situation still requires all our abilities in strategy and generalship. Our armies are holding good lines and the black clouds are beginning to lift.'[23]

The men in the 'lines' would not have agreed.

CHAPTER ELEVEN

A VILLAGE CALLED MISERY

In the early hours of 25 March, an urgent message from Sir John Salmond was delivered by dispatch rider to the officer commanding the 9th Wing, Royal Flying Corps. 'I wish you as soon as possible after receipt of this to send out your scout squadrons and those of Nos. 27, 25 and No. 62 Squadron . . . on to the line Grenvillers-Martinpuich–Maricourt. These squadrons will bomb and shoot up everything they can see on the enemy side of this line. Very low flying is essential. All risks to be taken.' The RFC more than obeyed the spirit of their orders. They threw in not only scouts and fighter bombers, but five squadrons of lumbering observations planes as well. Salmond wrote: 'Our machines were so thick in the air over the threatened point that there was every danger of collision in the air.'

On the ground too, the forces necessary to stem German inroads north of the Somme began to thicken and gather in strength as Haig's reserves arrived. The fresh 42nd and 62nd Divisions provided a formidable breakwater in the sector most immediately menaced. The New Zealand Division and the Australians were also on the march. For a time at least General Byng could reasonably hope to contain the German advance. Far to the south on the other wing of the German assault, two fresh French Divisions were arriving and others were on their way. So Fayolle also had reason for optimism. Even the Fifth Army found reserves of a kind. General Gough thinned out his grooms.

Being a groom at Army or Corps headquarters was probably the best billet in France. It was like being an officer (and a high ranking one at that) but without the responsibilities. To a man, the infantry would cheerfully have given anything for such a 'cushy' number. Now, however, every soldier in the Fifth Army was needed in the front line and nine headquarters grooms were attached as mounted orderlies to a make-shift force of 2,000 men formed under the command of Major-General P. G. Grant, Gough's Chief Engineer. Gough had scraped together 500 Americans from the 6th U.S. (Railway) Engineers (many of whom had never fired a shot in anger), Royal Engineer electricians, tunnellers, surveyors, and men from various Army and Corps schools (including the sniping school). With twenty GS wagons carrying supplies and signallers from the Army Signals School this motley collection became a 'mobile reserve'.

Not all British troops in the back areas rushed to help their stricken comrades. A sergeant major placed in charge of a section at the rest camp in Boulogne subsequently reported:

> You never saw such bastards. There'd be a notice put up in the morning that all men for the 3rd and 18th Divisions would parade at twelve, and for the 36th and 56th Divisions at five. When the time came, there wasn't a man of these divisions to be found. Oh no, they all belonged to the 57th and 47th. And next day when the parade was for the 57th and 47th, they all belonged to the 3rd and 18th Divisions. They tore the badges off their jackets and lay doggo.[11]

Inevitably there were dodgers, but the great mass of men rallied behind leaders like Colonel W. B. Little. Colonel Little, of the 5th Border Regiment – pioneers of the savaged 66th Division – was on leave in the Lake District when he heard the news that the offensive had opened. His own battalion had been involved in the fierce action on 21 March holding Templeux le Guerard until the Germans smashed the defences with mortar fire and burst in at dusk capturing sixty men.

After a hasty journey, during which he had the frustrating experience of standing on the quayside at Folkestone waiting for fog to clear before the boat could leave, Little eventually reached the Somme at Corbie and immediately set about collecting troops from the reinforcement camp there,

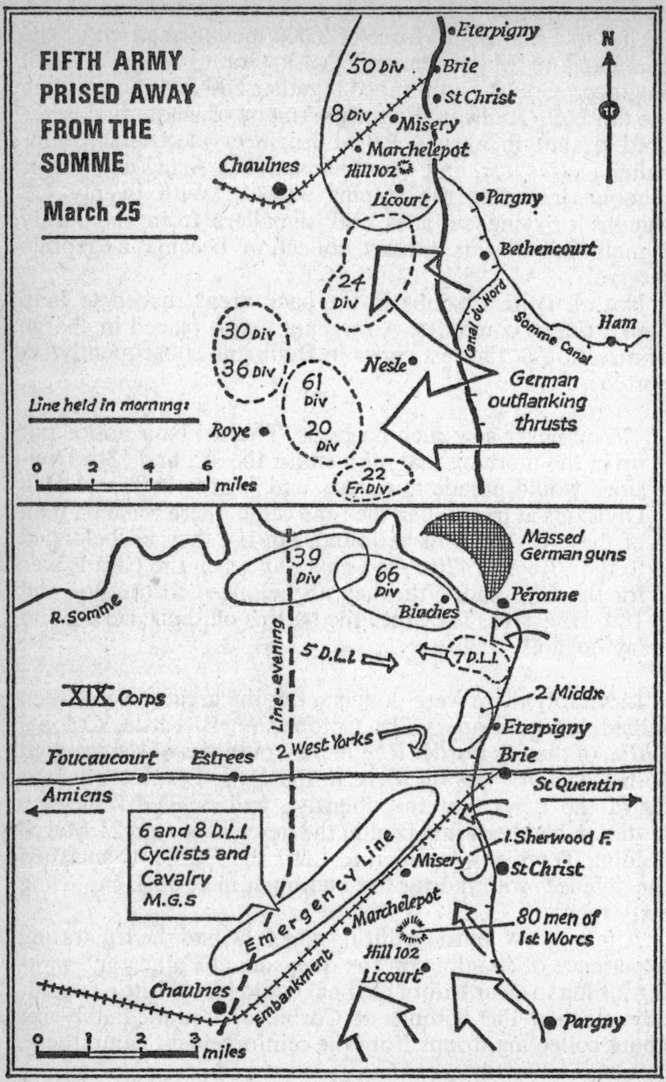
FIFTH ARMY
PRISED AWAY
FROM THE
SOMME
March 25
N
Eterpigny
Brie
St Christ
50 Div
8 Div
Misery
Marchelepot
Chaulnes
Hill 102
Licourt
Pargny
Bethencourt
24 Div
Canal du Nord
Somme Canal
Ham
30 Div
36 Div
Nesle
German
outflanking
thrusts
61 Div
20 Div
Line held in morning:
Roye
22 Fr. Div
0 2 4 6 miles
Massed
German guns
39 Div
66 Div
Péronne
R. Somme
Biaches
Line-evening
5 D.L.I.
7 D.L.I.
2 Middx
XIX Corps
Eterpigny
2 West Yorks
Brie
Foucaucourt
Estrees
St Quentin
Amiens
6 and 8 D.L.I.
Cyclists and
Cavalry
M.G.S
Emergency Line
1. Sherwood F.
Misery
St Christ
Marchelepot
80 men of
1st Worcs
Hill 102
Licourt
Embankment
Chaulnes
Pargny
0 1 2 3 miles

1. MARCH 1918. A wounded German soldier is carried back through the streets of St Quentin in comfort by British prisoners. Two more prisoners, one of them wearing a goatskin jerkin, support a wounded comrade. German reserves trudge past on the pavement bound for the front.

2. A SECTION of a party of 4,000 British prisoners wait for the train that will take them to Germany at a railhead behind the lines. Their faces express a variety of emotions: resentment, resignation, bewilderment and relief. Some of them, like the three in the foreground on the right, appear to be mere boys.

3. SOLDIERS OF THE CROSS. British mothers had to be convinced that their sons' spiritual welfare was being looked after as well as their bodily comforts. This Salvation Army officer with his banjo would do his best to take the men's minds off other pleasures. The church, and the public, were actively working to close licensed brothels.

4. WISH YOU WERE HERE. Eight jolly Germans make merry with even more glasses of beer plus a barrel for reinforcements. Propaganda pictures like this taken behind the lines in France were designed to reassure German mothers.

5. LOOK NO WINGS. A boldly marked fuselage of a German plane which had been forced to land behind the British lines in March 1918, is towed away as a trophy after the wings, machine guns and pieces have been removed. British air operations played a vital part in holding up the German advance.

6. A CUSHY NUMBER. At least that is how the Army Service Corps was looked upon by the infantry. With sacks from the interminable supply of oats for cavalry and gun horses, these supply depot men made themselves a tidy little tent. But in April and May 1918 many of them found themselves in the firing line.

7. ENIGMATIC ALLY. French North African troops of the 45th Division held Rheims when the great blow fell on 27 May, 1918. Their stout defence enabled the British 21st Division to pivot on them and secure the right flank of the breach. The British found themselves intermingled with tough troops like this Spahi seated at a trench loophole. Note the 17-inch bayonet – and the sandbag 'cushion'.

8. 'WHAT ALLIES TO FIGHT WITH,' Haig wrote scathingly in his diary in 1918 after the French had lost Kemmel Hill. Only Pétain realized the terrible sacrifices the sturdy poilus had made during the previous years when, like these men of the 164th Regiment, they were hurled into fruitless attacks again and again. The expression on the faces tells its own story.

9. HEROIC ALLIES. At least that was what the Americans tried to indicate by this somewhat obvious propaganda picture of a headquarters in a front-line shell-hole in France, April 1918. Ignoring the psychology that reality should be suppressed in case it stopped recruitment, corpses are dramatically positioned, although their equipment is undisturbed and even a veteran was unlikely to tolerate a dead man's head on his map. The officer in the centre of the picture is dispatching a carrier pigeon.

10 and 11. THE REAL THING. Real front-line soldiers did not look at all smart, the Americans soon found out. This trio in a battered trench are a far cry from the heroes in U.S. propaganda pictures, while the infantry going 'over the top' are loaded down with spades and all the paraphernalia so vital in battle.

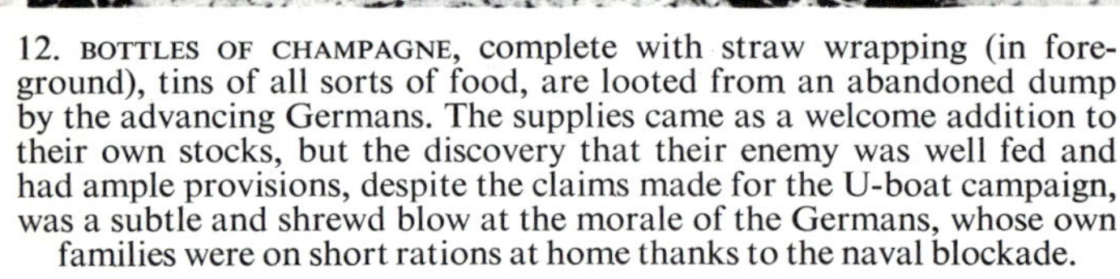

12. BOTTLES OF CHAMPAGNE, complete with straw wrapping (in foreground), tins of all sorts of food, are looted from an abandoned dump by the advancing Germans. The supplies came as a welcome addition to their own stocks, but the discovery that their enemy was well fed and had ample provisions, despite the claims made for the U-boat campaign, was a subtle and shrewd blow at the morale of the Germans, whose own families were on short rations at home thanks to the naval blockade.

13. KEMMEL CAPTURED. German infantry relax in reserve just under the crest. But the rest of the line of hills remains in Allied hands. Kemmel was the summit not only of a blasted hill but of their successes in Flanders.

14. WITH THE SPRING, the buds returned to the orchards and the guns continued to reap a harvest which had been gathered non-stop for four years. The leaves provide cover for these 100-mm cannon (Langrohrgeschutze). The piece nearest the camera has just recoiled after firing. Those in the distance are delivering their shells.

15. COMRADES (Part 1). Ludendorff complained that the 'arrangements for dealing with the wounded had not sufficed at all points', during the great offensive in March. Improvisations for moving men like the badly wounded soldier pictured above, slung in a tarpaulin, were commonplace. The 'stretcher bearers' appear to be his own comrades, with rifles slung, rather than medical corps troops.

16. COMRADES (Part 2). 'I cannot understand why the Fifth Army has gone so far back without making some kind of a stand,' wrote Sir Douglas Haig on 23 March. In fact, many of them had fought to the death . . . men like these filling a mass grave at Peronne where they were buried by their enemies.

17. COMRADES (Part 3). General 'Billy' Heneker, commander of the 8th Division, at his headquarters probably during the occupation of the Rhineland. His intense gaze and finely-drawn look indicate the immense pressure placed upon divisional commanders in 1918.

18. GENERAL HENEKER, right, beams broadly at a function attended by an elderly French general in pince nez and a member of his staff. Collaboration was not always so cosy. Until they had been well and truly beaten on the Aisne, the French scoffed at the warnings of British generals that they were heading for disaster.

commanding equipment and organizing stragglers. Within a few hours he had a unit of 600 men and twenty-six officers prepared to march.[15] Other determined officers, detached from their units on courses, or in transit to and from leave, impressed stray soldiers and led them towards the front. The demand for Lewis guns for these 'irregulars' was insatiable. Heavy machine guns, although more devastating, were less flexible, and there was no time to organize the requisite ammunition trains.

For the Germans, the machine gun supply problem was not as acute. The very fact that they had been halted on the Somme for two days by XIX Corps actually helped their supply lorries to catch up. Ludendorff himself was responsible to some extent for this state of affairs, by having encouraged German industry to concentrate on the production of lorries rather than of tanks.[45] Proof that the supply lorries had done their work well came early Monday morning.

To start with, a planned counter-attack by the depleted 24th Division and elements of the French 22nd Division, essential to restore a gap in the line, did not materialize. It failed simply because the Germans struck first. The British troops, who had been marching to the jumping off area since 0500 abruptly found themselves under heavy machine gun fire from an area which was supposed to be in French hands. (The French, it turned out, had asked for a postponement of the attack from 0800 to 1100.) The Germans had thrust in force against the small groups of the 61st and 20th Divisions in their path. The gap that the counter-attack was supposed to close began, if anything, to widen.

The 8th and 6th Durhams who had spent the night in reserve four miles behind the line reorganizing and resting were hurriedly ordered forward. German observation balloons were now more numerous than ever and their efficiency was demonstrated by a continuous and dusty rain of heavy shells. The Durhams had to force their way past a growing stream of retiring stragglers, guns, and walking wounded. Ahead of them lay the village named Misery and beyond the battling 8th Division gradually being prised away from the line of the Somme by an enveloping movement from the right. Germans had also crossed the river, unnaturally low for the time of year, near Eterpigny to the north. A British unit holding part of the line had been relieved during the night and, by accident, a post covering a crossing place had not been replaced. This permitted a German machine gun crew to sneak across; by dawn they were in position to cover the advance of their comrades.[2] Taken in the flank by this gun and swept by a hail of bullets from massed machine guns across the canal the 7th Durhams, pioneers of the 50th Division, who had been also 'much worried by our own howitzers firing short during the night', fell back in disorder to higher ground. At the same time the line had been breached at Eterpigny itself, where a post of the 2nd Middlesex, actually on the damaged bridge, was overwhelmed in the mist.

Now began a furious battle. The companies of the 2nd Middlesex strung out along the river, refused to retreat and German infantry swarmed round them in ever increasing numbers. Eventually ten tattered and bleeding men emerged from the smoke-shrouded ruins of Eterpigny, cutting their way through the encircling enemy – the remains of 'C' Company.

Limping back, they came up with the retiring 7th Durhams. Captain A. M. Toye, who commanded the destroyed Middlesex company, was able to bully, persuade, and inspire seventy of the pioneers to turn on their pursuers. The Germans seeing a line of men sweeping purposefully towards them with fixed bayonets discreetly fell back and went to ground. The pioneers then got down to their accustomed drudgery – digging trenches from which they maintained a resolute fire.

Notwithstanding the stubborn efforts made to hold the Somme crossings, the fact had to be faced that the Germans were over in overwhelming strength and the position was in danger of being carried. The 2nd West Yorkshires hurrying to counter-attack the enemy bridge-head at Eterpigny, were brought to a dead stop by the concentration of machine gun and rifle fire from the masses of Germans on both sides of the river. The 5th Durhams sent up to attack the same bridge-head, clambered over old wire entanglements under attacks from six aeroplanes but by a miracle escaped unscathed.

The Durhams rallied retreating troops and formed them into a line. But after a respite of a couple of hours a Durham officer remembers, 'the Germans crossed the Somme in hordes and pushed back the thin British line'. The attack had a certain professional fascination for this officer.

> It was extraordinarily interesting to watch the Germans working up to and around our flanks. They seemed to come down the hill at the far, or east, side of the Somme, at first in twos and threes followed by larger bodies such as platoons. Then, after crossing the Somme canal, they worked their way forward in small groups till they had accumulated the required number of men at a certain point. They fired white flares to show where they had got to, and gradually they made their way to within two hundred yards of us.[58]

The Germans penetrated well past the Durhams on both sides and a message was sent to brigade headquarters reporting that they were in danger of being cut off. The reply was 'a definite order not to withdraw but to stay and fight it out'.

The 1st Sherwood Foresters were, at the same time, obeying a similar order in their position covering the bridges at St Christ. Having successfully shot down all attempts to carry the bridges from the front they were now being outflanked by Germans pouring over the captured bridges to the south. Directly behind them shells were blasting the village of Misery and tall columns of brown smoke marked the blazing ruins of Marchelepot.

From nine in the morning until six in the evening the battle swayed to and fro with the British troops gradually being consumed. A company of the 5th Green Howards refusing to retire from the flank of the steadfast Foresters was the first to be over-run. Eighty men of the Worcesters dug positions on Hill 102 under a Green Howards officer and engaged stray parties of Germans trying to infiltrate. From all along the front which the 8th and 50th Divisions were trying to hold came repeated demands for small arms ammunition from the hard-pressed infantry.

By evening it beçame obvious that it was no longer feasible to fight it out on the Somme canal-river line. The commanding officers of the 5th Green Howards and the 4th East Yorkshires made their own decision and fell back to Misery. The Foresters, still in position at St Christ, received the order to retreat about an hour earlier. Surrounded as they were, they had to mount virtually a full scale attack to the rear to break out. The 2nd Devons, who had also remained immovable all day had to do the same.[8]

Unhappily, the order to retreat never reached the 2nd Middlesex, who maintained their dogfight until eleven out of the sixteen platoons in the battalion had been wiped out. The survivors retired under a covering party commanded by the C.O., Lieutenant-Colonel C. A. S. Page. The 8th Division historian describes the scene:

> At 7.15 p.m. he [Page] sent off Major C. D. Drew and the adjutant with half the party to a covering position. The remainder he sent back in batches up the trench. Finally Private Burgess the C.O.'s servant and Private Allen of 'D' Company were left with the C.O., each firing rapid to cover the retirement and helped also by a single Vickers gun under Captain Robertson, M.G.C. At 7.25 p.m. when the light began to fail, the C.O. sent back his comrades and, after a final five rounds rapid, the last of the two hundred he had fired himself, followed them up the trench. The Germans occupied the trench about three minutes after Colonel Page left it and sent up Very lights. . . .

The retiring troops in the area were now directed to form a line along the long railway embankment just in front of Misery. The 6th and 8th Durhams were already in position there, and had been in action for some time. So confused had the situation become that parties of friendly and enemy troops were completely intermixed. As early as 1730 the Germans had come on in three waves against the railway embankment but fell back having suffered 'heavy loss by

Lewis gun and rifle fire'.[2] Welcome reinforcement by a cavalry machine gun squadron and forty corps cyclists gave further teeth to the defence. It was obvious, however, that the railway embankment was merely a temporary rallying point.

A controlled withdrawal along the whole of the Fifth Army front was now essential if it were not to be dispersed and destroyed in detail. Although its left flank had not been severely attacked that day, the enemy had arranged a mass of artillery in 'a great half circle' at Péronne and blasted back the 66th Division at Biaches adding an even more menacing threat of encirclement to the troops holding the river line. Biaches is only two and a half miles from Eterpigny.

To the south, XVIII Corps was still bedevilled by the confusion of coming partly under French orders and by the lack of artillery. The divisions of this formation, each around one thousand strong, were being concentrated to fill any gap between the British and French armies. Against them, too, the Germans had used massed machine guns to clear a path for their assault troops. An officer of the 2/5th Gloucesters, holding the village of Breuil, estimated that thirty machine guns were concentrated opposite his battalion. They opened fire in the morning with a barrage lasting an hour and continued firing with varying severity all day while the attack went on. Heavy bursts of shellfire were also directed on the village, but the Gloucesters, having the shelter of substantial cellars, were in a position to give as good as they got and took a particular delight in sniping mounted orderlies arriving at a German headquarters about seven hundred yards north of the village. The Gloucesters confidently expected to hold out indefinitely when, 'At 5 p.m. we suddenly saw the English troops on our right leave the canal and go back in streams.' Despite this the Gloucesters continued to hang on in the face of concerted attacks from Germans who had crossed the canal, until they finally received orders to retire, their commander adding charitably: 'No doubt the people on our right had received the same message; that is why they went back.'

With justifiable pride the same officer wrote later that his men carried out their withdrawal under covering fire, and claimed that 'we were the only troops that I saw that used covering fire'. One platoon did 'a bit of a charge' and 'scattered the Germans like blazes' while another officer, running up to warn a group of French soldiers that they were walking into the enemy, discovered that they were Germans. The result: 'I captured a hun captain, sergeant and batman, with some important maps.'

Gough and Watts had had an anxious telephone conversation about XIX Corps during the late afternoon. Both knew what it would mean to send troops who had fought all day on a night march of four or five miles to a rear position. But there was nothing else to be done.

Inevitably under the conditions some orders failed to arrive. The 5th Durhams had settled down 'realizing that in the morning we should be surrounded and overwhelmed'. Their only orders had been to stay and fight it out. At dusk they had directed the fire of close support field guns on large enemy formations and added their own small arms fire for good measure. As the darkness gathered patrols thought they detected a further massing of the enemy. Another request for shell fire was made by light signal to the artillery liaison officer at brigade headquarters. There was no reply from the artillery man. There was no reply from anyone. A worried company commander learned to his dismay that a platoon of the 7th Durhams on his immediate right had received orders to withdraw. The officer commanding the platoon offered to stay on and fight it out with the 5th Durhams – 'a singularly brave thing to do' – but a more practical view of the state of affairs was taken and two officers were sent off to find brigade headquarters.

As the officers climbed from their trench the click of a rifle bolt sent them diving for a ditch with their hands on their revolvers. The click turned out to be yet another party of the ubiquitous 7th Durhams. Farther on there was another click and another dive – this time it was a platoon of Northumberland Fusiliers boldly coming up to cover the retirement of both battalions of Durhams. The Durhams did not need telling twice. In single file they marched down the road, their nerves in that dangerous forward area as taut as drumheads. 'It is extraordinary what a noise three or four hundred men make on a still night, however hard they try to move quietly,' wrote one officer.

Later, a German patrol actually crossed the path of the hushed, breath-holding files. Rifles and revolvers were silently raised. The Germans, perhaps thinking it wiser not to see anything, crept steadily on their way and not one shot was fired. Then, to their horror, the leading British officers suddenly realized that they had taken the wrong road at a junction and were advancing steadily toward an enemy-held village. 'Quickly we halted and went back whispering "about turn" to each man as we passed him, till we got to the road junction . . . where our guide had gone astray. Then we got hold of the halves of the battalion, as it were, and pulled them behind us along the right road. We got away without a shot having been fired at us.'

Not all the British soldiers who fought that day fell in when their units marched back. Some men could not be roused or would not be roused. They just sat there hungry, weary, and numb, unable to endure the thought of yet another long march. 'Some were all in. Others had just given up.'[18] This is not altogether surprising. Remember that most of them had been fighting and marching without proper food or rest for five days. Remember, too, that the vast majority of private soldiers were ill-educated and, without their officers and NCOs, literally didn't know where they were in broad daylight never mind at night. Until they had joined the army most of them had not even left their home towns.

The troops who could summon up the energy to join the retreat had their own problems. The War Diary of the 8th Durhams records: 'The night was one of bright moonlight and the withdrawal was made across very difficult country with much barbed wire and derelict trenches to be crossed. The withdrawal to the new line was not completed until 3 a.m. on the 26th owing to the tired condition of the men, difficulties of terrain and the necessity for concealment of withdrawal.'

The Durhams halted in some old trenches near Ablain-court where rations were issued. Then because the trench was not fire-stepped they got to work building fire positions. This labour went on slowly, the men working in a dream, being 'very fatigued with the last four days of continuous work'.

The Fifth Army rearguards crept, marched, and sometimes crawled away from their adversaries. The lucky ones were the worn battalions in XVIII Corps who found French troops packing the villages in the rear and who, to one eyewitness, appeared 'very fine men and very much for it [action]'.

The six divisions of XIX Corps now held the entire front of the Fifth Army although they were now little more than outsize battalions, very much intermingled. The 24th Brigade for example, had under its command, apart from its own battalions, the 150th Brigade (50th Division) now formed into a composite battalion, plus two other battalions of the 50th Division. Its immediate neighbour in the Third Army, VII Corps, consisted of tired troops of the 9th Division (in which the South African brigade had been reorganized as a composite battalion) a dismounted cavalry brigade, and the 21st Division, formed into a single brigade with eight machine guns. But the 35th Division (originally formed as a Bantam formation of men under normal height) was now in action under its command. For the moment, but for the moment only, Byng's right flank appeared secure.

It was in the centre of the Third Army line that the real danger lay. The movement of German reserves down the long straight road that leads from Cambrai to Bapaume assumed the momentum of a juggernaut. Steadily their numbers grew until on the 25th a massive assault force had been assembled and some seventeen divisions were sent crashing into the fragile British defences strung together across the heart of the wasteland of 1916. Brutally the attack hammered back the 19th and 51st Divisions directly in their path.

Lieutenant-General Sir George Harper, the obstinate, white-haired commander of IV Corps, was 'much shaken' by the plight of the renowned 51st which he had once commanded (and which still carried the nickname of 'Harper's

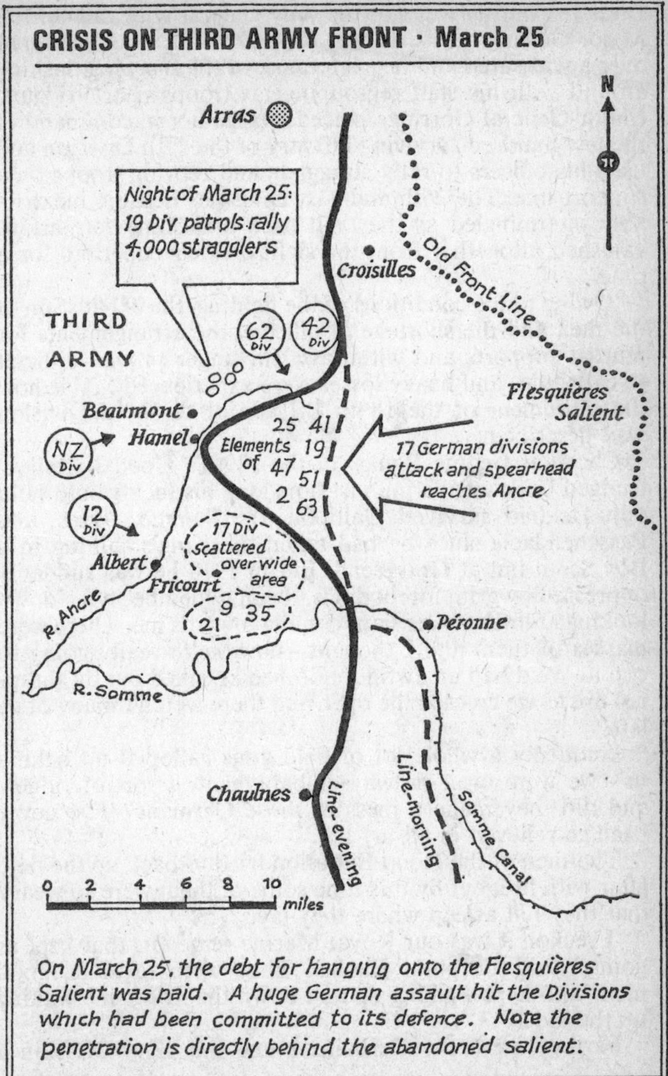

On March 25, the debt for hanging onto the Flesquières Salient was paid. A huge German assault hit the Divisions which had been committed to its defence. Note the penetration is directly behind the abandoned salient.

Duds').[3] And he was not the only general with difficulties. Major-General Robertson's 17th Division was scattered over a wide area and he spent most of the morning dashing around with his staff regrouping his troops near Fricourt. Major-General Gorringe placed a brigadier in command of the few hundred surviving infantry of the 47th Division and used his officers to rally stragglers and retiring troops on a support line. The 25th and 41st Divisions became inextricably intermingled as they fell back and some formations vanished altogether from the sight of their superiors for a time.

'Owing to the conditions of the fighting, the exhaustion of the men and the shortage of officers, the arrangements for mutual supports and withdrawal in stages proved difficult to carry out, and heavy losses were experienced . . .' is how the retirement of the 189th Brigade of the 63rd Division was described.

Corporal George Banks, of the 189th's Hood Battalion, trudged back wondering just how long his luck would hold out. He had survived Gallipoli, the Somme, Arras, and Passchendaele since he had taken the King's shilling in a Boy Scout hut at Gravesend. But in 1918 he was suddenly oppressed by grim forebodings. 'I can remember lying down looking at lines of Germans coming towards me. There were masses of them and I thought – now we're really going to cop it. We'd had an awful lot of men knocked out by shrapnel fire as we crossed the open and there weren't many of us left.

'Suddenly a whole lot of field guns galloped up behind us – we were on a railway embankment, a sort of ridge – and did they make a mess of those Germans? I've never been so relieved in all my life.'

The men of the Hood Battalion tried to back up the field guns with fire, but by this time some of them were so weary that they fell asleep where they lay.

'I reckon it was our Royal Marine sergeants that kept us going,' said Corporal Banks. 'They were regulars, good men, who kept walking up and down the firing line waking up the lads.'[71]

Farther north the Germans found the 42nd Division a

tougher enemy than its worn comrades and particularly Lieutenant Gale and his machine gunners dug into position with the 10th Manchesters. They had a totally open field of fire and let the Germans come well within range before letting fly with belt after belt from their Vickers. 'In spite of their casualties, wave after wave came on,' Gale wrote, 'and the slaughter was horrible.

'Eventually, with incredible bravery, some succeeded in reaching us, and then to my amazement these magnificent Lancashiremen rose up to a man and with rifle butts and, in some cases, bare fists, they attacked the Germans. The enemy wavered and then fled.'[19]

In all the 10th Manchesters beat off eight mass attacks by the Prussian Guard that day. Gale's guns each fired twenty 250 round belts in their support. The water in the barrel cases boiled.

The 42nd held the northern buttress of a zone about to be further strengthened as the 62nd joined it in the line. Eleven miles to the south, the 35th Division was fulfilling a similar role, as has already been described, and by evening another fresh division, the 12th, was advancing to support it, guided by the glare from the blazing ruins of Maricourt.

CHAPTER TWELVE

PANIC POINT-TO-POINT

Much criticism has subsequently been levelled at the general and staff officers who controlled our armies in the First World War. And unquestionably they did on occasion make appalling blunders; British lives *were* thrown away stupidly, and opportunities *were* overlooked. Unquestionably, some of these officers were inflexible martinets or, worse, obsolescent planners. But on this bitterly cold night of 25 March they were magnificent.

The Third Army was retreating, jamming the few routes that led from the devastated zone. Units were lost. Advancing reinforcements clogged the roads. But in the midst of this seething, apparently aimless mass of humanity, small groups of haggard staff officers strived to restore some sort of order.[70]

Headquarters officers of the 19th Division were formed into parties, given military policemen and orderlies, and sent to cross-roads between Gommecourt and Colincamps, some seven miles behind the lines that had been held at the beginning of the day.

They stopped all stragglers, regardless of their units, formed them into detachments and marched them to an assembly point behind the line to be held the following day. There the men were to be fed and, if necessary, rearmed and supplied with ammunition. By dawn, more than 4,000 of all ranks of various divisions had been collected. Six hundred of them actually belonged to the 19th Division.

Many other stragglers found themselves back in the line that night. Officers of the 41st Division collected 'several hundred' men at posts near Achiet-le-Grand. A single company of the 12th Green Howards, managed to swell its ranks to nine hundred men by the same method.[2]

Nonetheless, many stragglers fell into the hands of the

Germans, who were still pressing diligently forward during the night. The wretched condition of the men and the hodge-podge mixture of their units, gave the Germans the impression of imminent British collapse. An officer of the German 49th Infantry Regiment noted in his diary: 'If it goes on like this, in fourteen days we'll reach the sea.'[35]

Few men on either side would have predicted that night that another twenty-two years would lapse before that dream would come true.

Despite the improvisations of the staff officers and their desperate rallying of scattered troops, gaps existed in the British front. It had been hoped to form a new line along the river Ancre but enterprising patrols of the German 24th Division had already pushed across it and other Germans were across the river near Beaumont Hamel. The British army was being driven back to the line it had held before the Somme offensive of 1916. Well might another German author write: 'The sun of Germany's victory was high in the zenith on March 25 . . . .'[14]

The Germans, however, could not fully exploit the new situation. They were tired and haunted by the dismal aura of the old battlefield. Their communications were stretched to the limit and their guns were unable to keep pace with the forward troops. Had they been in a position to press on during the night who can tell what might have happened? As each hour of darkness passed, however, their chances of success diminished. Heading towards the most vulnerable and fluid part of the front were the men of the New Zealand Division with the 4th Australian brigade not far behind. By dawn the vanguard of the New Zealand Rifles was deploying for action.

Streams of lorries had shuttled the Australians from the quiet front in the north, dumped them, and set off on the return journey for more reinforcements. The Australians, confident to the point of cockiness, and not without reason, were ready to march to any danger point at a half hour's notice.

When the enemy came on the following day he found the British once again prepared to renew combat. In the Third Army area the Germans met with varying fortunes. Brigadier-General H. D. de Pree of the 189th Brigade, described an attack on the front of the neighbouring 2nd Division: 'The attack must have been carried out by a very large force, as it stretched as far as the eye could see and came on in two or three lines. It was preceded by patrols, and each line appeared to consist of battalions with a wide interval between them, some moving in a scattered irregular crowd, others marching in fours down a road, as suited them best.'[39] British 18-pounders opened heavy shrapnel fire on the oncoming waves. The Germans went to ground and contented themselves with dribbling men forward in small numbers. Through no skill of their own the Germans had more luck between Hebuterne and Gommecourt, now blackened ruins on the edge of the moorland of the old Somme battlefield. At midday the 4th Australian Brigade was informed that German tanks or armoured cars had broken through between the two villages. The brigade was ordered to do its 'utmost to block the roads' and to intercept the enemy armoured vehicles. Brigadier-General C. H. Brand, the grey-haired commander of the 4th Brigade, mounted his horse and, looking like a Tartar chief in his shaggy sheepskin jerkin, galloped off to reconnoitre while his excited battalions formed up in haste.

Fast as the Australians were, however, they could not match the speed with which the report of a German armoured breakthrough travelled throughout the troops in the rear areas. By now every village behind the lines was packed with transport from the retiring divisions. Literally thousands of horses and their vehicles, plus scores of lorries, were parked in an area of a few square miles. At news of the tank attack many commanders of transport columns decided that the time had come to pull still farther back. Without waiting for orders they backed their horses between the shafts and set off. The civilian population added to the confusion, some of them abandoning half-eaten meals in their haste.

The historian of the 47th Division reported candidly: 'All transport, including the 47th Division Ammunition Column, moved back with or without orders, and for a time complete chaos existed. It was said that the orders had been given . . . by spies dressed as British staff officers.'[34] The records of IV corps Heavy Artillery also mentions 'a sort of panic' which 'had undoubtedly come over many troops in the area Souastre-Hénu (some miles behind the line).' Somewhat pointedly the records add: 'The heavy artillery was not involved in this except for a few battery waggon lines which retired to the rear.'

The 13th Australian Battalion forcing a passage through the swarming, retiring masses, was warned by 'staff officers retreating in great haste' that enemy armoured cars were not far behind. Such officers occasionally received the impolite attention of the troops. A car containing nine red-tabbed officers speeding down the road in indecent haste received a volley of abuse from the 'Diggers' going in the opposite direction, although says the Australian Official History, 'Doubtless they were merely hastening to establish a headquarters farther back.'

Convinced of the impending arrival of the armoured cars, the Australians used a commandeered lorry to block the road, the men taking cover in the ditches. They waited. Suddenly, there was the sound of engines and the ominous clank of metal on metal. Throats tightened and nervous fingers slipped off safety catches.

An alien column of strange vehicles appeared in the distance, and without pause slowly lumbered towards the barricade. The lead vehicle, a car, was bright red and the others were grey and strangely shaped. The Australians were puzzled but then so, obviously, were the drivers of the machines when they caught sight of the Australians huddled in the muddy ditches. The drivers spoke – in *French.* Suddenly the Australians comprehended; these were the men from the French Agricultural Corps, and their bizarre machines of war were ploughs they had rescued from the hated Boche. The disgusted Australians lowered their rifles and crawled from the ditches. For years afterwards the French ploughs were believed to have been the cause of what someone described as the 'great Pys to Pas point-to-point', when every carthorse in France tried to act like a Derby winner between those villages.[7]

The truth was quite different. A number of British artillerymen had formed mounted patrols in order to scout targets for themselves. A group of these had spotted strange tanks moving into the Hebuterne area and reported them as possibly German. Immediately some intrepid gunners of the 19th Division artillery ran out a number of pieces to deal with them but nothing appeared.

The sharp-eyed patrol was not mistaken, however. What they had seen, in fact, were new British whippet tanks returning from a foray in which they had taken some prisoners.

This was unknown to the Australians who were even more scornful of the alarm when their brigadier appeared once more on his chestnut charger to inform them that he had just ridden unscathed through Hebuterne and hadn't seen a single German. As the Australians marched up they learned that the Germans had been stopped on the other side of Hebuterne by scattered posts of the 19th Division. No further attacks were made that day and when the Germans did try again they found themselves faced not by exhausted remnants but by four well-fed, full strength battalions full of fight.

What had been the most dangerous spot on the front of the Third Army now appeared to have been sealed. From left to right the 42nd and 62nd Divisions, the 4th Australian Brigade, and the New Zealand Division formed a stout barrier behind which battered units could rally, rest, and reorganize. A certain stability was appearing in the British front. It was at this moment on 26 March that General Foch took a hand . . . the day of the fateful Doullens conference. At 1100 Haig met all his army commanders, with the exception of Gough who was now technically under the command of Fayolle and his French army group. It was made clear at the meeting that Haig wished to cover the vital rail and supply centre of Amiens at all costs. Since he was about to meet the British and French government representatives and urge that the French should use their reserves to maintain the Allied line, he could hardly advocate giving up one of the major cities of France.

At the inter-Allied conference, both Foch and Pétain made their feelings clear to Haig. Pétain sneered at the

British for having run away like the Italians at Caporetto (in itself a highly debatable remark) and when the Fifth Army was mentioned declared: 'Alas, it no longer really exists, it is broken.'

Foch interrupted him and in an impassioned outburst stated that the fight in front of Amiens would have to be carried on and 'we must not now retire a single inch'.

The meeting concluded with the first steps being taken to make Foch the supreme commander. Everyone wholeheartedly agreed that there would be no more retreating and that all efforts would be made to hold the line as it was. Foch promptly gave orders to Pétain to bring up further reserves to take over from the Fifth Army and immediately set off to see Gough in person. But certain events had already occurred that all General Foch's posturing could not alter.

During the early hours of the morning General Byng had passed on orders received from Haig that 'no retirement is to be made unless the tactical situation imperatively demands it'. Somehow General Congreve, commanding the key VII Corps now forming the right wing of the Third Army at its junction with the Fifth Army, got it wrong. Just how has never been satisfactorily explained.

An instruction phoned to his divisions after receiving the orders began as follows: 'VII Corps will fight today on the line Albert-Bray [Bray was on the north bank of the Somme] in order to delay the enemy as long as possible without being so involved as to make retirement impossible. Retirement, when made [note the phrase] will be to the north of the Ancre [running at right angles to the Somme at Albert], which will be held as a rearguard position, all bridges being destroyed after the crossing.' The retirement of divisions from the right was ordered and the routes to be taken, were listed.

Written orders issued by Congreve later (although not explicit) made it clear that the corps was intended to retire. The responsibility for conducting this retreat fell upon the commander of the 35th Division, Major-General G. M. Franks, who had been placed in charge of all troops on the corps front. Dutifully, as the German attack developed during the day, his units fell back towards the river and at 1500 Congreve was informed that the withdrawal was in full swing. About this time, doubts began to set in at Congreve's headquarters. A message from the Third Army headquarters repeated the instruction that there should be no retirement unless absolutely imperative. Other orders followed thick and fast.

Shortly after 1500, Congreve phoned the 35th Division and ordered a halt to the retreat. A telephone message direct to the division from Third Army at 1600 said specifically; 'The position at Bray is to beld with the utmost determination.' This was repeated in written orders which arrived from Congreve at 1818 hours. By then it was too late. Immediately on receipt of his orders, Major-General Franks set off by car to see whether halting the retirement was practical. It was not. Two of his brigadiers made it quite clear that the troops had been too far committed to retirement and the commander of the remains of the 9th Division agreed with them. There is little doubt that the men on the spot were right for by 1830 nearly all the British troops were already across the Ancre. The best Franks could do was to order them to try to hold the high ground on the 'enemy side' of the river, near Morlancourt and despite the protests of their brigadier, two battalions were despatched on this hopeless mission.

Confusion followed confusion. Immediately further orders arrived cancelling this movement. A breathless staff officer managed to halt one battalion as it was crossing the river (it was actually moving over the bridge) but the other had vanished into the dusk. After locating the German advance guards the battalion dutifully opened fire but mercifully, at this point, an indefatigable messenger arrived with the order to retreat. About 0100 the bewildered infantry trailed back across the bridge, reeling drunkenly from fatigue and sheer frustration.

Just how serious the situation had become was not obvious to the Fifth Army for the best part of the day. It had problems of its own. According to orders, it too was falling back to the line which would stretch ten miles from Bray, where it would link up with the Third Army, to Rouvroy in the south. There it hoped eventually to have the French come into the line alongside. Until they did so it counted upon the four depleted divisions of XVIII Corps, which had been remustered and reorganized, to cover any gaps. They did not have to wait long for battle to be resumed.

Then, as now, the Santerre was a plain dotted with villages – tiny clusters of houses surrounding the inevitable tower or steeple. On 26 March most of these picturesque villages became the scene of bloody clashes. The Germans recommenced hostilities between 0800 and 0900 with, as one battalion put it, 'first M.Gs and snipers at 250 yards, then rifle grenades, then 5.9s and 4.2s'. The British replied as best they could, although the XVIII Corps units were still without their artillery, still supporting the gunless French formations.

At the little village of Le Quesnoy, about one hundred men of the 61st Brigade held fast all day, relying mainly on two Lewis guns and their rifles to hold off two German battalions backed up by cavalry. When the unit fell back at dusk and made their way through the surrounding enemy only nine other ranks and two officers were on their feet.

Farther north, the Germans ran into stubborn defences and savage counter-attacks. The 1st Royal Fusiliers held out until mid-afternoon before slipping away from Chaulnes but the 9th East Surreys were not so fortunate. Almost 250 out of the 300 men were killed or wounded and the remainder were surrounded and captured.

More than a month later, Major C. A. Clark, M.C., who had commanded the East Surreys, described the end of this action in a letter sent from a prisoner of war camp.[66] Remember that these men had been in more or less continuous combat since 21 March. After being surrounded as they tried to sneak away, the East Surreys settled in some old communication trenches and used their rifles until ammunition ran out and the Germans were able to close in.

> They then charged and mopped up the remainder [wrote Major Clark who already had twelve wound stripes]. They were infuriated with us. I am afraid I presented a curious looking object at this time, my cloth-

ing had been riddled with shrapnel, my nose fractured and my face and clothing smothered in blood. . . .

Some splendid cases of heroism have been brought to my notice. A Lewis gunner of 'A' Company was seen to have been shot through the chest, but he continued to work his gun alone. I have been trying to get his name but there is some doubt as to his identity.

I witnessed the following: Two men serving a Lewis gun were doing excellent work when they were blown over by a shell, their gun destroyed and they were badly bruised and shaken, but with scarcely a moment's hesitation each picked up a rifle and continued firing until both were killed by machine gun fire. There are many other such cases.

Private Boylan, many years later, recalled walking back with a small group of British prisoners: 'I well remember that our corporal and our sergeant were made to act as stretcher bearers for carrying wounded Germans. We also saw hundreds of our own men who had been killed in action and had their boots removed. The Jerries liked the British boots. I swapped mine for a loaf of bread plus a pair of German boots. My jerkin went for another loaf.'*

North of where the Surreys were cut off the British were, at least in theory, supposed to enjoy the support of their own artillery. In the middle of the afternoon, however, the XIX Corps 'heavies' appeared to change sides and blew their own men out of the important village Raincourt. As the British fell back in disorder the enemy pushed his machine guns into the adjoining hamlet of Framerville. While a staff officer tried to rally as many men as he could, other officers of the 39th and 50th Divisions led adjoining counter-attacks. The War Diary of the 7th Durhams recorded: 'A and B Companies ordered to attack Framerville while 5 N.F. [Northumberland Fusiliers] attack left of the village. The companies forced their way through the village twice but owing to the commanding position held by the enemy with M.Gs it was impossible to remain.'

In this attack, it was reported later, battle crazed infantry-

*Personal recollection and correspondence.

men had burst into the church tower of Framerville and hurled a German machine gun crew out of the windows.[58] All the same, Framerville had to be given up, and our troops withdrew to the south of it. Despite occasional clashes and isolated casualties, the retirement to the new line seems to have been conducted comparatively successfully. In places, the retreating troops obscured their movements by deliberately firing hutted camps and wrecking anything that may have been useful to the Germans. In one camp they encountered unexpected opposition.

'It was here,' wrote an officer, 'that an old sapper was found in the act of locking up a shed in which an engine pumped water to supply two tanks and about 100 feet of horse troughs. The old man intended to join our retreat. As he showed great reluctance to break his engine I smashed its important part with a hammer. When I saw him he was looking at the damage and muttering. "There'll be trouble over this".'[58]

Obviously the new tactics demanded by open warfare had not yet been fully appreciated by everyone in the back areas. The infantry were the quickest to improvise, their tutor being grim necessity. A small party of the 8th Durhams comandeered an old farm cart while the rest of the battalion was digging trenches in front of Rosières, and returned triumphantly with 20,000 rounds of rifle ammunition and a number of Lewis gun pans they had scrounged.[63]

In Rosières itself, Brigadier Clifford Coffin, now commanding all the infantry of the 8th Division and attached units, ensured there would be no failure of communications this time by concentrating the headquarters of all three brigades in the same place west of the village.[8]

While these very practical steps were being taken the Corps Commander passed on the following message: 'Under instructions from the French Commander-in-Chief [i.e., Foch] to Fifth Army, the XIX Corps will maintain at all costs the line we are now on until the arrival of French troops who are on their way to relieve us. For this purpose every available man will be put into the fight and the Corps commander looks to all ranks to make one more supreme effort and maintain to the last the magnificent fighting qualities and endurance already displayed throughout the battle.'

After nearly a week of such fatuous instructions the order could have had little effect upon those who received it. Yet, for once, there was good reason to call for a supreme effort. General Watts knew what none of the men settling down in the crude trenches of the Rosières line knew. At 2100 he had received news of the calamitous and erroneous retirement of the Third Army on the opposite bank of the Somme. When the enemy attacked the following day it would not be a head-on collision only facing XIX Corps. The Germans could not help but strike too at the left flank of the Fifth Army which was now well in front of its neighbour. Worse still, many bridges had not been destroyed (a situation arising, it may be recalled, from the new army boundary arrangements which failed to ensure that both river banks were under the same commander). Under the circumstances it would appear that to try to hold the existing line in such circumstances would be fatal. Even another night retreat, with all it entailed and inflicted on the exhausted troops, might be better Watts argued in a long telephone conversation with Gough. But it was not to be. Instead Gough dipped into his last-gasp reserve. Six Lewis guns, 300 men, and a Canadian motor machine gun battery were despatched to help support the threadbare Irish regiments of the 16th Division on the threatened flank.

Why did Gough hesitate to make arrangements for a further retreat? The answer may be because earlier in the day he had been roundly abused and insulted by the very man who had been appointed to save the situation, General Foch. Just as Foch's inflexibility had led to confusion north of the river (mainly because he had no real knowledge of the form of warfare now developing) his rigidity now led to similar confusion in the south.

Foch had driven to see Gough straight from the conference at Doullens. Foch's knowledge of the battle was almost entirely second hand, simple because Gough, the man who knew best, was not there – he had not even been informed of the existence of the conference. Gough knew only that he was to receive Foch in his headquarters at Dury that afternoon.

In Gough's own words, Foch was immediately 'peremptory, rude and excited in his manner'.[28]

Melodramatically the French commander wanted to know what Gough was doing at his headquarters? He wanted to know why he was not with his troops in the fighting line? And why the British weren't fighting as they had done at Ypres in 1914? Gough, fiery enough when need be, temperately explained that he was obeying orders to meet Foch, that the situation could not be compared with 1914, and that he was fighting a rear-guard action according to previous instructions. He then expected Foch to depart from his discussion of personalities and to ask questions of a more pertinent nature. They were not forthcoming.

'He did not inquire into the position of the Fifth Army, nor their strength or condition,' wrote Gough. His sole advice was: 'There must be no more retreat, the line must now be held at all costs.' Then Foch spun on his heel and walked out of the room back to his car.

If Foch's display was puzzling, his implication that Gough lacked guts was offensive. 'Those who fought under him constantly wished he had less,' commented the Australian Official History. Even so, insults and abuse can sting, and it may well be that Gough's conduct of the battle in the next two days was influenced by the effect of Foch's words and behaviour. Having been ordered not to give up ground Gough would do everything he could to obey orders.

Neither could Congreve, whose obscure orders that day had caused a crisis, be accused of any lack of courage. In fact, he was a holder of the Victoria Cross, won on one of the darkest days of the Boer War when he received multiple wounds while trying to rescue guns from the enemy.

But physical bravery is not necessarily enough. These commanders had endured a grinding mental strain probably equal to the physical ordeal of any infantryman. (For Congreve there may have been an added strain. The previous day his headquarters had been situated at Corbie where, in 1916, he had attended the funeral of his son, Major William

Congreve, V.C. Now General Congreve had to face the fact that his son's grave might soon lie in enemy-held territory.) Moreover, bombings and frequent enforced moving of HQ could only add to this strain. Congreve, in fact, had a nervous breakdown after the battle and was obliged to leave for home. Pointedly enough, on the day of the muddled orders, he had once again been in the process of moving his HQ, this time to the chateau of Montigny. The evening was bitterly cold and the wind shivered through the trees chilling the new spring buds. Desks, typewriters, map boards, and other office equipment were piled in the gloomy, deserted corridors. Congreve had temporarily established himself at a table in a corner of a large room, and had spread out a map which he tried to read by candlelight. At his elbow was his chief of staff, Brigadier Hore-Ruthven. He too wore the dark red ribbon of the Victoria Cross, won in a clash with Dervishes in the Sudan in 1898.[60]

Dedicated, loyal, and brave, these men, at fifty-six and forty-six, were classical Victorians, the epitome of the Imperial Age. Retreat was anathema. To have retired in error must have been traumatic.

That night Congreve and Hore-Ruthven were still poring over their map when a small convoy was challenged at the gates of the chateau grounds. After a pause, it drove through the trees and up to the main door. There was a trampling of heavy boots, the sound of hearty voices with an unmistakable twang, and the door opened. The candlelight flickered over the radiant-sun badge of Australia. Major-General Sir John Monash, the burly, shrewd commander of the Australian 3rd Division, had arrived with picked members of his staff. Within a very short time Congreve had established Monash in another room in the chateau.[47]

At midnight, two more visitors arrived – Major-General E. G. Sinclair-McLagan, commander of the 4th Australian Division, and his chief of staff. The roads behind them were packed with columns of troops who had jettisoned their packs and greatcoats in order to make better speed. Fearful French peasants who came out of their homes to watch the Aussies, were jovially assured by the cocky Diggers that there was nothing to worry about now. With the arrival of the men from the new lands, a new spirit began to warm the cold night.

CHAPTER THIRTEEN

A GERMAN CALLED JOHNSTON

Amiens. Veterans knew the old city well. For three years this important road and rail centre had served as an arsenal for the attackers, as a capital for the brasshat bureaucracy, and as a haven for the war weary. On the night of 26 March much of Amiens was in ruins. Hundreds of houses had been damaged by shellfire, many were ablaze. Those civilians who had not already fled the city, had taken cover in the ruins. Sparks drifted through deserted streets where but a week earlier whores had solicited their soldier clients by the light of tiny torches. Notices bluntly warned that looters would be shot. Philip Gibbs, sheltering in the cellars of the Hotel du Rhin with a group of war correspondents, listened nervously to the steady crash of bombs from German raiders. When he left in the early morning he stumbled over the body of a British officer, killed as he had knocked at the door of the hotel. Men and horses lay in the agonized postures of death along the Street of the Three Pebbles, and elsewhere throughout the rubble-strewn town.[23]

To the north, Albert (which was just as familiar to the veterans) was already in enemy hands and equally a shambles. Unsuitable for defence, it had been abandoned by all but a few stragglers, mostly old soldiers on the scrounge – looters if you like. But when the Germans did enter the streets these boozy old reprobates opened fire on them and had to be subdued. The 2nd Naval Infantry Regiment claimed the capture of Albert after overcoming the uneven defences of 'a few drunken Englishmen'.

By the following day, the 27th, there were a few drunken Germans in Albert too. Drunks reeled about wearing comical civilian hats. A lieutenant in a marine regiment confessed in despair to a passing infantry officer that he could not get his men out of the cellar they were ransacking

TABLE III XVIII Corps, *Lieutenant-General Sir Ivor Maxse* Front: Nine miles. Artillery: 411 guns (incl. 129 heavies.)

61ST DIVISION	30TH DIVISION	36TH DIVISION	3RD CAVALRY DIVISION*
182 Brigade	21 Brigade	107 Brigade	6 Cav. Brigade
2/6 R. Warwicks	2 Wilts	2 R. Irish Rifles	3 Dragoon Gds.
2/7 R. Warwicks	2 Green Howards	1 R. Irish Rifles	1 R. Dragoons
2/8 R. Worcester	17 Manchesters	15 R. Irish Rifles	10 Hussars
183 Brigade	89 Brigade	108 Brigade	7 Cav. Brigade
9 R. Scots	17 King's	12 R. Irish Rifles	7 Dragoon Gds.
5 Gordons	18 King's	1 R. Irish Fus.	6 Inniskilling Drgns.
8 Argylls	19 King's	9 R. Irish Fus.	17 Lancers
184 Brigade	90 Brigade	109 Brigade	Canadian Brigade
2/5 Gloucesters	2 Bedfords	1 R. Inniskilling F.	R. Canadian Drgns.
2/4 Ox. and Bucks.	2 R. Scots F.	9 R. Inniskilling F.	L. Strathcona's H.
2/4 R. Berks	16 Manchesters	2 R. Inniskilling F.	Fort Garry Horse
Pioneers	Pioneers	Pioneers	*Stationed near Athies
5 Cornwalls	11 S. Lancs	16 R. Irish Rifles	under Army command

The German forces opposing the XVIIIth Corps were the IIIrd Corps (113th, 88th, 28th, 6th, 206th, 5th, 23rd divisions); the IXth Corps (50th, 45th Reserve, 231st, 5th Guard, 1st Guard divisions) and part of the XVIIth Corps (10th Reserve and 238th divisions).

without bloodshed. Their merriment was short-lived. According to Rudolph Binding, 'The troops which moved out of Albert . . . cheered with wine and in victorious spirits, were mown down straight away on the railway embankment by a few English machine guns.'[5]

Drunk or sober, the German attackers were now coming up against the fresh, aggressive British reinforcements. At least 15,000 rounds of small arms ammunition were fired by 'A' Company of the 9th Essex in one early morning clash, ground to within twenty yards of them being strewn with enemy dead.[57] From the well-sited, deep dug positions of the Arras bastion, to Dernancourt not far south of Albert, the British line was gradually hardening. Although the 31st Division was pushed back near Courcelles-le-comte, its artillery caught two German battalions on an open airfield, and almost wiped them out. The Guards Division, on the right, established communications with the 42nd and 62nd Divisions, both strong formations, which in turn linked up with the 4th Australian Brigade and the New Zealand Division. Farther south, the 12th Division extended its right to meet the 9th and 35th Divisions, while behind them the rest of the 4th Australian Division were now in the process of relieving exhausted divisions and racing to the danger area created by the mistaken retirement of VII Corps the previous day. There scratch formations and dismounted cavalry fought for time. As the cavalrymen were mostly well-trained regulars, whose units had not been decimated to the same extent as the infantry, they gave the Germans a great deal more trouble than might be expected from their small numbers. With these reserves now in action the Third Army might feel more confident in the outcome. The outlook for the Fifth Army was less hopeful. Its left was now about six miles in front of the Third's right. And General von Brauchitsch, commander of the German 1st (Konisberg) Division, was soon appraised of the fact.

When the commander of the 3rd Grenadier Regiment, a major with the unlikely name of von Johnston, phoned the news that his frontal attack was held up he was told to switch his line of advance ninety degrees south and cross the Somme into the Fifth Army area at Cerisy and

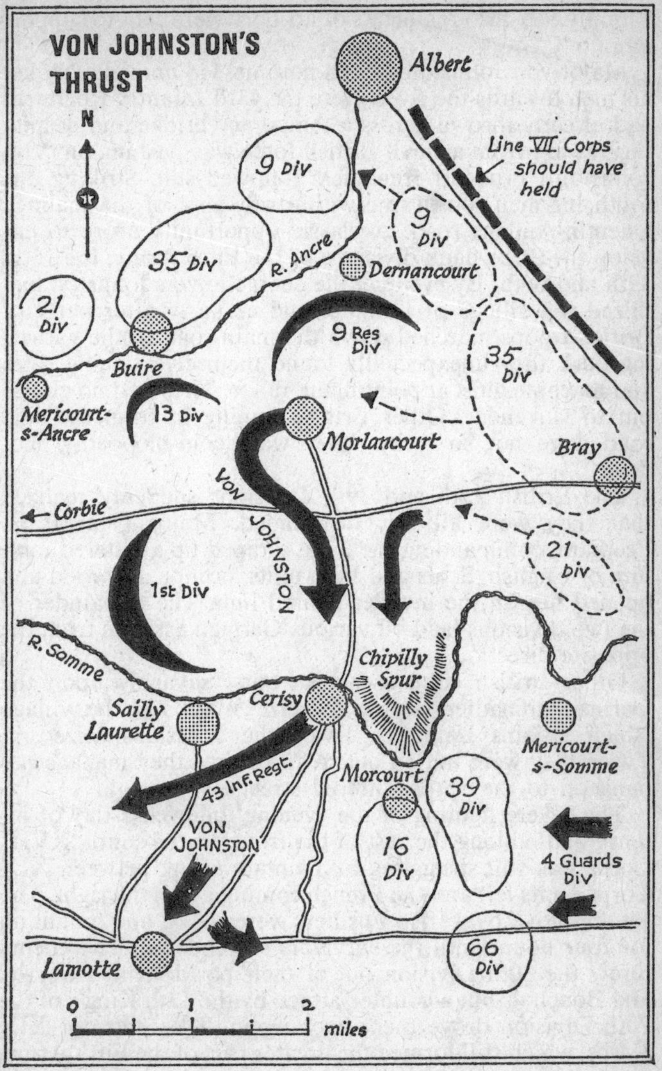
VON JOHNSTON'S THRUST
N
Albert
Line VII Corps should have held
9 Div
9 Div
35 Div
R. Ancre
Dernancourt
21 Div
9 Res Div
35 Div
Buire
Mericourt-s-Ancre
13 Div
Morlancourt
Bray
VON JOHNSTON
Corbie
21 Div
1st Div
R. Somme
Chipilly Spur
Cerisy
Sailly Laurette
Mericourt-s-Somme
43 Inf. Regt.
Morcourt
39 Div
VON JOHNSTON
16 Div
4 Guards Div
Lamotte
66 Div
0
1
2
miles

Chipilly.[4, 20] Two regiments of artillery were sent to support him.

Major von Johnston wasted no time. He immediately led his men towards the river. Here the 43rd Infantry Regiment had already thrown across a temporary bridge and despite furious fire from a small British force was pushing on. Von Johnston's Prussian grenadiers followed suit. Striking due south his men soon came within rifle shot of the main St Quentin-Amiens road. A classic opportunity arose to envelop the three flank divisions of the Fifth Army, the 16th, 39th and 66th. By evening, the energetic von Johnston had seized the village of Lamotte and as party after party of British troops marched down the main road in the gathering dusk they unexpectedly found themselves facing rifles and machine guns at point blank range. They had no choice but to surrender. Other British coming in from the side road were not so lucky – they were cold-bloodedly shot down.

The British 16th and 39th Divisions suddenly realized that they were all but surrounded. Major General E. Feetham, commanding the 39th, scraped up a tattered mixture of English, Scots and Irish units, occupied a wood and opened fire on the invader behind him. The remainder of the two divisions held off various German assaults from the opposite direction.

Other British counter-attacks burst savagely upon the German grenadiers trying to seize Warfusée, the village which adjoins Lamotte. Twice the Prussians seized it. Twice they were hurled out. A third time they managed to hang on to the corpse-littered streets.

The severe fighting of the evening followed a day of intense battle along the rest of the front. In the south, XVIII Corps was still struggling to maintain a link between XIX Corps on its left and the French coming up on the right. The 1st and 9th Royal Irish Fusiliers were cut off and fought on for four hours until the survivors surrendered. The enemy threw the 30th Division out of their positions at Rouvroy and Bouchoir but a counter-attack by the 12th King's of the 20th Division drove them back again. The centre of XIX Corps, which still formed the greater part of the Fifth Army, was held mainly by the 8th and 50th Divisions and gave hardly any ground at all.

The 8th Durhams in front of Rosières, received orders at 0430 to wire their defences. They replied that this was impossible. There was no wire available. As if in reproof for this failure to obey orders, British shells continually 'fell short' on their positions. Just before 0800 a large force of Germans was seen leaving the village of Meharicourt just in front of Rosières.

The Germans were so confident that at one point they advanced to the beat of the drum.[18] The tattoo continued until they were well within range. Immediately all the rifles and machine guns of the waiting British opened up and much to everyone's surprise the British artillery joined in on the right side at the right time. The first two waves of the attack were wiped out and the drums were heard no more. A third wave, however, pressed on and penetrated the trenches of an entrenching battalion which fell back taking its neighbours, the 6th Durhams, with it and forcing the 2nd Northants and the 1st Worcesters to conform.[8, 64] Now the wisdom of keeping a close grip on the battle showed itself. At Brigadier Coffin's orders, the 1st Sherwood Foresters immediately counter-attacked, along with three companies of the Durhams. Those Germans who survived the counter-attack scuttled back to Meharicourt and the British re-occupied their trenches. The German infantry showed little inclination to renew the battle, and during the whole of the afternoon the greatest danger came from artillery – German *and* British.

In the sector held by the Northants there was at least one happy man. He had arrived from Boulogne the previous day where he had been serving as a bayonet-fighting instructor at the famous 'Bullring'. Not unnaturally his comrades, who had been in the thick of it for days, didn't hesitate to pull his leg. Where had he been they wanted to know? Wasn't it a pity he couldn't dodge the war any more? But they were glad to see him for now that he was at the front the rest of them could go home and he could settle the Germans single-handed. The man took his ribbing non-commitally. Outside Rosières the next day, to the astonishment of the rest of his company, this much-mocked sergeant leaped from his trench and proceeded to give a dazzling exhibition of bayonet work on an unfortunate group of Germans who had tried to rush the position. There were no more jokes as he jumped, without comment, back into the trenches; the sergeant retained the respect of his fellows until he was killed later in the war.[18]

The Germans did not make another serious attempt to break through at Rosières until 1745 when they advanced in waves on a 500-yard front. Once again they were driven back by blistering machine gun and small arms fire. By nightfall they still had not penetrated the village, and the flat fields to the east were covered with their dead and dying.

North of Rosières a more threatening situation had developed as pressure on the flank divisions grew. Proyart, a vital road junction, was lost and a breakthrough appeared likely. As every other unit was either in close action or under attack, the 2nd Devons and the 22nd Durhams, were sent on a route march of five miles to deliver a counter-attack. This they did so efficiently that the 4th Prussian Guard Division, which had already been attacked from the air, fell back 1,000 yards. Prisoners were taken and the counter-attacking troops dug in to bolster scattered detachments of other divisions. Another crisis arose at Harbonnières three miles north of Rosières when, due to a misunderstanding of orders, the 149th Brigade fell back about 1300 and the Germans poured into a widening gap.

By 1500 the triumphant Germans were swarming in ten long waves across the field towards Harbonnières intending to roll up the defending line from its left. Suddenly from over the crest of a low ridge ahead of them appeared a straggling line of running men. When three hundred yards away the men went to ground and loosed a hail of bullets into the mass of Germans. Machine guns joined in from their flank, enfilading the now wavering ranks in field grey. Enemy sections trying to set up their own guns fell dead on their weapons. British artillery zeroed in accurately on the rear ranks.

The long lines of attackers lost all semblance of order and

fell back in confusion, officers and NCOs shouting conflicting orders, laden men stumbling into smoking shell holes, goaded by the lash of shrapnel bursting over their heads. The lucky ones among the laggards were taken prisoner and hustled to the rear. The unlucky ones were bayoneted or shot at point blank range. The rest reached cover and lay down to fire back and ask themselves where these berserk British had sprung from?

The answer lay with the much criticized British generals. Riddell, riding a lumbering artillery 'hairy' he had 'borrowed', had rallied his three battalions and ordered every signaller, sanitary man, clerk, cook, and headquarters officer into battle.[58] Coffin, with a firm grip on the battle at Rosières itself, had detached the last reserve of the 8th Division, the hardfighting Foresters, to cover the right flank of Riddell's counter-attack. The Foresters had tramped along parallel to the line of battle listening to the rising pandemonium and wondering what they would find when they got there. Augmented by a crew from the 15th Field Company Royal Engineers, with an assortment of weapons, they were also joined by the so-called 'specialists' of the 24th Trench Mortar Battery, hastily buckling on pouches and belts. They had been told to abandon their Stokes guns for the time being and fall-in with rifle and bayonet.[8]

On the far left of the gap, the survivors of the Lancashire Fusiliers, Manchesters and East Lancashires were prodded and cajoled on to exhausted legs by senior officers, ordered to fix bayonets, pointed towards the enemy, and pushed and led forward. Dumbly they obeyed. Near Warfusée transport men and details of the 6th Durhams, under an anxious lieutenant called Tyerman, were suddenly told to march to Harbonnières.[2]

Had the Germans known it, this was the last of the British reserves. There was now nothing of any consequence behind the left of the Fifth Army, until one reached make-shift detachments dug in before Villers Bretonneux. The worn-out 61st Division backed up the rest of the line.

The batmen, bandsmen, and brigadiers, who charged shoulder to shoulder with the infantry at 1500 on the afternoon of the 27th did more than inflict severe casualties on the enemy – they may well have prevented the Germans from creating a breach which would have led certainly to the fall of Amiens and possibly to the breaking of contact between the French and British armies. Had the gap of the afternoon remained unsealed, a flank attack across the Somme at Cerisy would have isolated at least three divisions and possibly trapped the forces holding Rosières. As it was, the Germans found themselves battling hard to hold their own. Framerville was re-entered. Vauvillers was recaptured. The scratch battalion of Lieutenant-Colonel Little saw the furious battle for Vauvillers and as the British fell back (they were running out of ammunition) opened a withering flanking fire on the German pursuers.

Every British soldier and every British bullet now counted. About fifty men of the Tank Corps appeared humping Lewis guns removed from their abandoned machines. They went straight into action opposite Framerville. Even skeleton formations raked up reinforcements for the menaced area.

That night the Fifth Army could claim to have done well. At Rosières it had not budged. On its flanks it had been pressed back but to no great depth. Yet in spite of all its efforts it was in greater peril than before. The Third Army, by 28 March, lay farther than ever behind the exposed left flank of the Fifth Army. On the Fifth Army's right, the French had been driven back nearly fifteen miles in a single day. The key town of Montdidier, with its network of railways and roads necessary for the rapid distribution of reinforcements, was in the hands of the enemy. Thus the ten divisions which now comprised the Fifth Army, having done all they could to obey Foch's command to hold fast, lay in a salient in the German lines, holding a front of nearly twenty miles.

A messenger arrived from Haig's headquarters that afternoon to reward Gough for his doughty services. He was to be relieved by General Sir Henry Rawlinson. Sir Hubert would be given another job after the handover of commands, but in the meantime he would just have to carry on as best he could.

That night the destiny of the thousands of men, guns, and material in the area of the stricken and almost trapped army, was resolved by the most primitive of instincts . . . self-preservation. The troops of the 16th Irish division (so roundly condemned by Haig earlier for 'giving way immediately the enemy showed') were the first to take steps to extricate themselves as German artillery and infantry poured into the open flank. For the Irish to remain where they were meant capture. To strike south-west, where spasmodic sounds of battle still rumbled, meant almost certain ambush. The most promising line of retreat lay through the German 'ocupied' zone on the other side of the river. The enemy had now driven so far to the west that a backwater had been created behind the battle front, used only by enemy troops in transit and by supply trains. Forming up in columns, the weary Irish marched first to Mericourt on the river bank; their patrols reported it to be strongly held by Germans. Quietly they directed their steps down the tow path towards Cerisy itself. German sentries on a bridge near the village were disposed of in a bloody brawl and the Irish battalions remustered on the other side of the Somme behind German lines. They marched cautiously on through German territory until finally, by eliminating more bridge sentries near Sailly Laurette, they recrossed the Somme and made good their escape.[30]

While the Irish sought their salvation to the north of the Somme, the three brigadiers of the 39th Division elected to head south. Two officers crept past scattered German posts to inform divisional headquarters, from which the brigades were cut off, that they would start the retirement at 0200. To everyone's dismay divisional headquarters ordered the brigades to stand fast; a counter-attack was to be made to clear the Lamotte road and open a line of retreat. It was with undisguised relief that a countermanding order was received shortly afterwards suggesting that a retreat south might, after all, be in order. The brigades didn't give anyone the opportunity of changing his mind again.

In the meantime, the commanders of the 8th, 50th and 66th Divisions had been holding a council of war at Cayeux, about four miles from Rosières. They were agreed.

If they stayed where they were they would be cut off. At 0100 a call was put through to Watts, at XIX Corps headquarters. Watts referred the matter to Gough, who was roused from his bed. Gough was already aware of the threatening situation having discussed it with Watts earlier. But Gough had his orders; reluctantly he dismissed the idea of retreat. 'I had been ordered by Foch to hold ground at all costs until relieved by the French, and I was still anxious to comply with these orders if there was any prospect of French relief being in sight . . .' Yet the only help on its way to the trapped divisions was the exhausted 61st Division. In vain had its officers protested that the men were unfit to march more than two miles. Fifth Army headquarters said it would provide them with buses – not a difficult task in view of the small numbers involved.

But even as these buses, jammed with khaki figures slumbering among their arms, were rumbling through the moonlight, Gough decided that enough was enough; whatever his personal fate might be, he would not leave his men to be slaughtered. Foch was called from his bed by telephone and, testy though he was, made to see the consequences of leaving the Fifth Army where it was. The order to retire was sent out at 0330.

The headquarters drama was lost on the men holding the line at Rosières. The 8th Durhams had sent out patrols to cover its front, according to normal military practice. Rations had arrived. And the officers had done their best to keep up the spirits of the men. The War Diary recalls, 'The greatest difficulty by day has been lack of orders, and by night to keep the troops awake, as everyone was worn out by the recent strain and heavy fighting. . . . The night passed without incident but, owing to the impossibility of allowing the troops to sleep, dawn found a very weak and tired battalion awaiting the enemy attack.'

Mortars, 5.9s, and heavy machine guns opened up as retirement from the pocket began at 0800. 'The troops were dazed and weakened by their long period of fighting without rest,' wrote one officer in his diary. 'There was no sign of panic and any attempts to withdraw were quite orderly, and the men obeyed willingly when ordered to return to position. But they appeared to have lost the sense of reasoning and it was difficult to make them understand.'[28]

General Gough himself wrote: 'Our retirements were usually made at a slow walk [the Germans] following at a few hundred yards at the same pace, and halting when the British line halted and turned round.'

Despite the numbed condition of the troops, the impossible was accomplished although hesitation in giving the order to retreat meant some units had to leave their wounded at regimental aid posts to be taken prisoner.

An attempt to halt on an intermediate position was impractical, however, as the German turning movement, driving in the 39th and 66th Divisions made itself felt on the sides of the pocket.

At noon the 61st Division had attacked, as ordered, from Marcelcave. At first they made good progress, but were driven back gradually by machine gun fire. An aircraft of 82 Squadron reported as early at 1115 hours (just as the 61st was forming up): 'Our troops seen advancing north taking up positions 500 yards north of Marcelcave station in three lines . . . Large number of troops retiring from Bois de Pierret [on the vulnerable flank of the 61st] in good order. Many enemy seen in the open east Lamotte. Dropped eight bombs and fired 400 rounds on them, these troops in thick formation. . . . Dropped message on three batteries south of Villers Bretonneux aerodrome and on two batteries at Bois de Hamel, giving information and position of enemy. The batteries had only one or two men per gun but they halted and went into action.'[49]

When the 61st Division fell back, these threadbare batteries were insufficient to stop the Germans pushing in the left of the pocket faster than the troops at the tip could withdraw. This ugly situation was resolved by a counterattack led yet again by the indefatigable Riddell, still riding his lumbering artillery 'hairy',[58] and by the commander of the 50th Division, Major-General H. C. Jackson. Riddell was lucky enough to come across a pioneer battalion wolfing down a hasty meal in a sunken road, and Jackson urged bands of stragglers into action with his hunting horn.[28] The Germans were sufficiently startled to halt at least for the time. But the rest of the day became a grim ordeal. The narrow area to which the retiring divisions were confined was completely exposed to German fire. As is not unusual in a retreat, there was confusion and tragedy. The 8th Durhams, who had been at the tip, tried to withdraw in artillery formation, but suffered severe casualties 'including many killed' as they made their way back.[65] The commanding officer of the 6th Durhams, Lieutenant-Colonel F. W. Robson, M.C., was killed. The 2nd West Yorkshires never received the order to retire at all and finally decided to make their own way back. Their commanding officer, Lieutenant-Colonel A. E. E. Lowry sent back the survivors of his battalion in scattered small groups. When it came his own turn, his group ran head on into a German machine gun crew. There was no option but to put up their hands. The 2nd Middlesex too found themselves without orders but led by Colonel Page, who had covered the retreat of his battalion only a few days previously, they cut their way out.[8] The 150th Composite Battalion remained in action until about 1630, anxiously watching the fighting roll farther and farther past their flank. It was then that a solitary cyclist was seen pedalling furiously towards them, vanishing from time to time in the smoke of bursting shells. Finally he arrived panting. The order he brought was straight forward: 'You will proceed to Moreuil.' They did not need telling twice and set off immediately to this haven in the rear.[68]

The withdrawal of the Fifth Army on the 28th succeeded mainly because the troops were willing to use their last reserves of strength to march out of the trap. Their disjointed counter-attacks were just enough to persuade the enemy to advance with caution. The artillery retired by batteries, a mile at a time, holding off their pursuers with shrapnel. The RFC joined in with relentless air attacks. At the same time French cavalry arrived, screening the French infantry now taking over still more of the line. The villages in fact, were so jammed with French troops that the exhausted British had to tramp still farther back before they could rest. A late afternoon drizzle was a gratuitous addition to the discomfort. It was not until late at night that the last of the infantry battalions were able to find billets. The Rosières pocket – which could have been as disastrous as the Falaise pocket of 1944 was empty. The Germans had missed the boat.

The 8th Durhams recorded that its strength at the end of the day was twelve officers and 150 men declaring gratefully that at 2200 'the 149th M.G. Company fed the battalion in pouring rain.'

So much for conditions south of the Somme.

The Australians who came into action that day north of the river, subsequently remarked that although they were aware of some fighting going on in the south that day, they had no idea of its extent. They understood, and the rumour persisted throughout the night, that the Fifth Army had been pierced and many men cut off.[3]

One can understand the Australians' suspicions. When their advance guard had reached the Somme bridges the previous day, they found them guarded by drunken soldiers. The Australians were appalled – unquestionably discipline had disintegrated among the British forward troops. Disgustedly the Australian commander posted his own guards and set off to reconnoitre. By the time he returned half of his own company were drunk as well.[52] Fortunately the Australians were prepared for business as well as pleasure.

CHAPTER FOURTEEN

COMPANIES OF CHILDREN

While the Fifth Army struggled out of the Rosières pocket, and the Third Army's line grew slowly firmer, another blow fell on the beleaguered British. The German 17th Army was hurled at Arras on 28 March. Seven German divisions attacked four British. But this time the British were well prepared and, above all, well supported. This time the British had a Green Line to fall back on that really existed. This time there was no fog to add to the confusion. This time the attack was confined to a narrow front which the British knew well. This time there was no Colonel Bruchmüller to direct the German guns. 'Apparently the artillery had not been sufficiently effective,' Ludendorff wrote in his memoirs, adding: 'The vitalizing energy which emanated from Colonel Bruchmüller was lacking. This is another instance of the decisive influence of personality on the course of events in war, as in life generally.'

The attack was a blood-clotted failure. It had a sobering effect on the German infantrymen. The 247th Reserve Infantry Regiment thrown back near Albert was convinced that in their own sector the great offensive was petering out. 'We were told as a consolation that yesterday at Arras we had begun a new attack,' wrote their historian on the 29th, 'but news of its results was not forthcoming . . . rumour trickled through that it had been a complete miscarriage.'

The historian was somewhat erroneous in his judgement, for it was only the first phase of the offensive launched on 21 March that was now dying down. The British troops in the line were less credulous than the doleful historian; they were no longer easily deceived. Corporal Banks, standing with the survivors of the Royal Naval Division Hood Battalion in a village square behind the lines, heard the sole

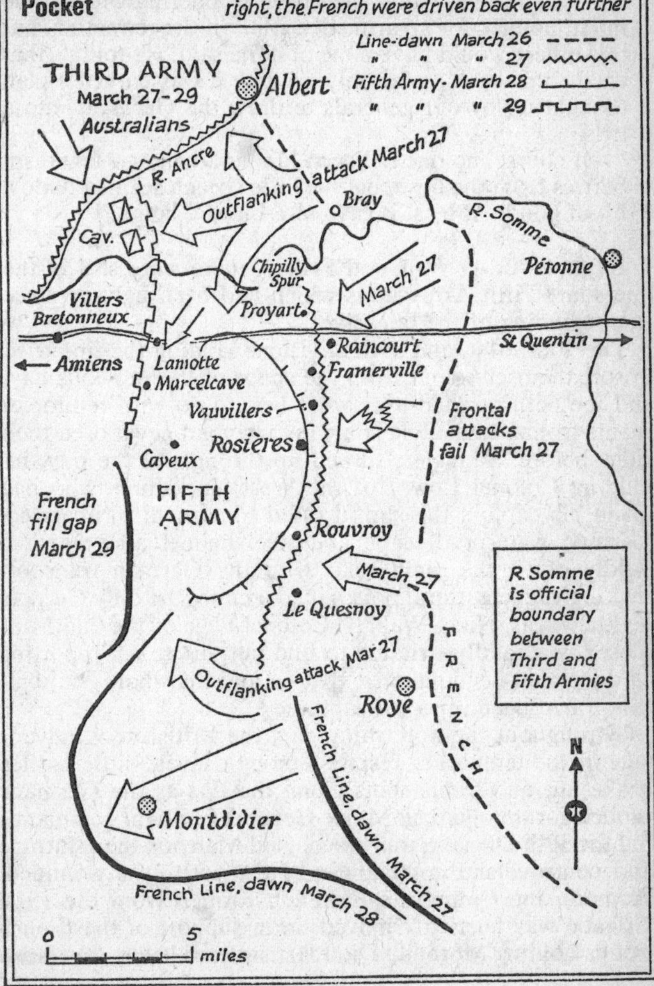
FOCH'S FOLLY
The Rosières Pocket
Ordered to stand fast at all costs, the Fifth Army obeyed for 2 days. On its left flank the Third Army fell back more than 6 miles. On its right, the French were driven back even further
Line-dawn March 26
" " " 27
Fifth Army - March 28
" " " 29
THIRD ARMY
March 27-29
Australians
Albert
R. Ancre
Outflanking attack March 27
Bray
R. Somme
Cav.
Péronne
Chipilly Spur
March 27
Villers Bretonneux
Proyart
Raincourt
St Quentin
Amiens
Lamotte
Marcelcave
Framerville
Vauvillers
Frontal attacks fail March 27
Rosières
Cayeux
French fill gap March 29
FIFTH ARMY
Rouvroy
March 27
R. Somme Is official boundary between Third and Fifth Armies
Le Quesnoy
FRENCH
Outflanking attack Mar 27
Roye
French Line, dawn March 27
N
Montdidier
French Line, dawn March 28
0
5
miles

surviving officer of his company call the men round him.

> A few of the Old Sweats like myself – though we were only youngsters really – had been wondering whether we might not ask for an armistice after all the retreating, but this officer would have none of it, he said. He told us that we'd come back so far only because it was part of a plan thought up by our generals to draw the Germans into a trap.
>
> Of course, no one believed him and he got a few raspberries from the boys, but his little speech seemed to do a bit of good. At least it gave us a bit of a laugh.[71]

As dawn broke on Good Friday, there were still in the line some Fifth Army units which had been fighting since the beginning of the offensive.

The 20th, 61st, and 39th Divisions holding the line tried to sort themselves out from the chaos of the previous day, and the 66th puzzled over what best to do with reinforcements from a tunnelling company who had never used their rifles before. Stragglers turned up throughout the day, including Colonel Lowry of the West Yorkshires who had given his captors the slip, dressed himself in a 'liberated' German waterproof cape and steel helmet and marched boldly down the main road with the German transport making vague guttural noises if spoken to (the only German he knew was 'Nicht Wahr!') Colonel Page of the 2nd Middlesex was mildly irritated to find out, on at last reporting to divisional headquarters, that he and his whole [sic] battalion had been reported captured.[8]

Throughout the dull, rainy day, the British took advantage of the temporary respite although savage little battles broke out at various spots along the line as the Germans probed for an opening. Major-General Feetham commanding the 39th Division was killed. Neil Malcom, the saturnine and controversial commander of the 66th, was wounded. At noon the Composite Battalion formed from the 151st Brigade was hurriedly moved up in support of the French troops holding Moreuil. The 151st suffered heavy casualties from shelling and indirect machine gun fire. The Green Howards and East Yorkshires of the 150th Composite Battalion became involved in a struggle for a patch of woodland and complained of the French troops giving way.

Dead beat as they were, the survivors of the long retreat were ruthlessly thrown into battle for the next three days. On the 30th the Germans came on again, making heavy probing attacks. An officer of the 61st Division saw British front line troops streaming back near Hangard and went down to inspect the supporting troops. 'It was a curious line . . . within half a mile of us were Gloucesters, Royal Berks, and Oxfords, Warwicks, two squadrons of yeomanry and the servants and staff of the Fifth Army Infantry School.'[58]

A counter-attack in this area led by a brigadier of the 66th Division who scraped up all the troops within sight, gave the Germans a considerable fright. 'It was wonderful to see the lines, hastily got together, advancing under a perfect hail of machine gun bullets and shrapnel,' wrote Lieutenant-Colonel Little who took part. The indefatigable colonel was most disappointed when the attack was stopped short of some German guns which had been blazing away over open sights.

Not far from this scene, the infantry of the 8th Division (now commanded by Brigadier Grogan, as Brigadier Coffin was 'on the verge of collapse' from lack of sleep and want of food) were incredibly once more on their way back to the line after a brief rest.[8] Despite this almost robot-like obedience to orders, it was only a matter of time before the soldiers of the Fifth Army would have to be relieved. '. . . it was clear that some of the depleted divisions now in the line were not really in a fit state for further stick and could not be trusted to maintain their positions against enemy pressure' wrote the commander of XIX Corps.

Lieutenant-Colonel L. J. Morshead, twenty-eight-year-old commander of the 33rd Australian Battalion coming into action alongside the 12th Lancers supporting the shaken 39th Division near Hangard Wood commented: 'On reaching the wood we found the whole front line garrison withdrawing . . . although there was no hostile fire and no sign of any kind of attack. I met two brigadiers and a battalion commander . . . informed them what was happening and asked them [to] get their men back to the line at once. The cavalry commander also helped by sending a squadron dismounted to re-establish the line. The infantry went forward with the cavalry but in a reluctant manner. During the whole time we were going forward men were constantly leaving the line.' Of the Lancers, a fresh unit, Morshead had only praise. Like nearly all the reserves coming up he did not appreciate the unparalleled strain to which the Fifth Army had been subjected. By this time the determination of the troops varied according to their experience during the previous week.

Some were simply incapable of further effort without rest. Some achieved miracles. The Germans burst through the 2nd Devons at Moreuil soon after 0100 on the 31st, but by evening were thrown out of the wood by the 2nd East Lancashires and the 2nd Royal Berkshires. The 150th Composite Battalion, having taken part in a successful counter-attack with the French the previous evening, when seventy prisoners were captured, fought out of a German pincer movement at great cost.

As late as 1 April elements of the 20th and 8th Divisions were still in action, but these were the final flickers of resistance squeezed out of the Fifth Army by the staff.

The following day the Fifth received its *coup de grâce* – not from the Germans, but from its own high command. From now on even its name would be obliterated. Under Rawlinson (he had taken over on the 28th) it would be called the Fourth Army. Gough had already been given his final insult. Invited to dine with Haig on Good Friday he had been told that he and his headquarters were required to supervise the digging of a trench line from Amiens to the sea.

'It may be necessary,' wrote Haig 'for me to hold such a line if the French do not hold on and allow the enemy to interpose between the British and French Armies.'

In the event, Gough did not suffer the indignity of becoming an officer in charge of an army of navvies. Instead, within days he experienced the ultimate humiliation of being sent home on half pay – an unjust fate for a man who had held an army together under the most trying circumstances and who had never ceased to fight courageously.

As the weeks went by, rumours about the Fifth Army began to drift back to England; lurid, and for the most part untrue, many of these reports were coloured by scenes well behind the lines of both the Third and Fifth Armies. Few of the reports appreciated the conditions under which the battle was fought – conditions which reduced crack units to grimy, battle-harassed scarecrows. The Guards Division, for instance.

'As the Guards were more or less stationary throughout this period,' says their historian, 'there was little difficulty in providing rations, forage and ordnance stores, although the issue of the latter was naturally confined to essentials, and the appearance of officers and men somewhat ragged and woebegone at the end of their ten days' fighting.' Major C. H. Dudley Ward, of the Welsh Guards wrote in his diary: 'I have men now who are ragged about the trousers to the extent of indecency and many have their bare toes sticking through their boots.' How much worse then for those men who had marched back and forth and dug trenches without number for days on end? A younger gunner officer of the 25th Division recorded on 1 April: 'You should have seen us when the retreat ended. No one had washed or had boots or clothes off for the past week, and we were all in a most awful state of dirt and unshavenness. The men were smoking the last of the many boxes of Coronas that the quartermaster-sergeant lifted from the Bapaume canteen before the Boche reached it.'[27]

The horses were in an equally bad state, not having had their harness removed for days, and a long string of animals unfit to pull guns or wagons trailed behind batteries on the move. As a wet week drew on, these convoys began to resemble circuses on the move with men in sou'westers, cloth caps, and gumboots or waders.

Guy Chapman, moving up behind Bucquoy with the 13th Royal Fusiliers, described 'the first serious evidence of how badly hit the army was . . .'

It was a matter of atmosphere rather than of obtruding

fact. We had often seen roads packed with stationary transport interspersed with worn infantry but at those times there had been an alertness and an order within disorder. Now the drivers seemed listless, unwilling to help themselves, until shouted on by impatient officer. . . .

The road was ankle deep in creamy mud, through which laboured small infantry drafts led by worried subalterns.

The privates were nearly all children, tired, hardly able to drag their laden shoulders after their aching legs. Here and there an exhausted boy trudged along with tears coursing down his face.[11]

The reinforcements from England that might have averted the crisis had they been made available earlier in the year, were now on the move. By 4 April a total of 101,000 infantry reinforcements had arrived in France. Contrary to an undertaking given in Paris on 14 January, all lads of eighteen and a half who were considered to be trained were included. An Australian noted: 'For two days companies of infantry have been passing us on the roads – companies of children, English children; pink faced, round cheeked children, flushed under the weight of their unaccustomed packs, with their steel helmets on the back of their heads and the strap hanging loosely on their rounded baby chins.'[3]

The atmosphere in which the youngsters arrived was ominous. They could hear the thump of heavy guns in the distance, and feel the menace throbbing in the damp air that hung over the countryside.

Throughout the battle the German divisions had made excellent use of their artillery and its thunder still continued to blast sections of the British line. Regimental commanders had developed an efficient technique by which they retained a small group of 5.9s or minenwerfers under their direct control and were thus able to concentrate shellfire on points of resistance.[18] The farther the advance penetrated the devastated area, the more difficult it became to sustain this tactical advantage and in the end it petered out. A quarrel over priorities broke out, some commanders wanting to get more guns forward across the smashed roads of the battle area, others insisting that fewer guns but more shells were the real answer to the problem. By the time agreement had been reached the front had coagulated and the British artillery was too strong to be overwhelmed without classic blasting. To some extent this was now possible, thanks to the efforts of sixty German railway construction companies who built, repaired, and restored communications behind the front.

On the foggy morning of 4 April a barrage of an intensity reaching almost the proportions of 21 March fell upon the British 14th Division which had recently come into the line outside Villers Bretonneux. Guns of three enemy divisions blazed away for more than two hours and storm troops swept back the stunned defenders. The light infantry regiments forming the 14th had been in the front line on 21 March and had fought non-stop until relieved on 26 March, reduced to sixty-two officers and 1,476 men. In the intervening week its ranks had been filled with any men available and it was too much to expect such raw units to hold. The 8th King's Royal Rifle Corps and the 7th and 8th Rifle Brigade of the 41st Brigade fell back 'precipitately'; all efforts of the officers of the supporting 43rd Brigade failed to halt them. Later, when the Australian 15th Brigade moved up, its officers were ordered to stop all stragglers and 'compel them to fight'. About 500 men of the Rifle Brigade were thus re-organized and rearmed.[3]

Fortunes fluctuated throughout the whole of that confused day. The invaluable cavalry once again came to the aid of the infantry, the 6th Brigade approaching at a squelching canter through the sodden fields and going into action dismounted.

Australian officers suddenly discovered that their men were human too. The 9th Brigade, holding the area immediately in front of Villers Bretonneux, had been heavily attacked on the right of the 14th Division. A soldier of the 35th Battalion tramping back with a mud-choked rifle slung on his shoulder explained apologetically when stopped by an officer: 'We've been in five days without a spell. He gave us a lot of gas shell,' [the man was carrying his respirator in his hand], 'and we are pretty well done up.'

Two Australian officers found that although it was easy

TABLE IV VII Corps, *Lieutenant-General Sir Walter Congreve* Front: Seven miles. Artillery: 433 guns (incl. 150 heavies).

9TH DIVISION	21ST DIVISION	16TH DIVISION	39TH DIVISION (in reserve)
26 Brigade	62 Brigade	47 Brigade	116 Brigade
8 Black Watch	12/13 N'thumberlands	6 Connaughts	11 R. Sussex
7 Seaforths	1 Lincolns	2 Leinster	13 R. Sussex
5 Camerons	2 Lincolns	1 R. Munsters	1 R. Herts
27 Brigade	64 Brigade	48 Brigade	117 Brigade
11 Royal Scots	1 East Yorks	1 R. Dublin F.	16 Sherwood F.
12 Royal Scots	9 KOYLI	2 R. Dublin F.	17 KRRC
6 KOSB	15 Durhams	2 R. Munsters	16 Rifle Brigade
South African Brigade	110 Brigade	49 Brigade	118 Brigade
1 SA Regt.	6 Leicesters	2 R. Irish	6 Cheshires
2 SA Regt.	7 Leicesters	7 R. Irish	4/5 Black Watch
4 SA Regt.	8 Leicesters	7/8 R. Inniskilling F.	1 Cambs
Pioneers	Pioneers	Pioneers	Pioneers
9 Seaforths	14 Northumberlands	11 Hampshires	13 Gloucesters

The forces opposing the VIIth Corps were the XIIIth Corps (3 Marine, 54 Reserve, 27th, 107th and 183rd divisions) and the XXIIIrd Corps (79th R., 50th Reserve, 18th, 9th Reserve, 13th and 199th divisions).

to halt parties of men who had joined the withdrawal, the moment they left them and moved to another group, the first party would carry on with its independent withdrawal. Some of the junior officers of the 33rd and 35th Australian battalions 'would not heed' the order to halt, despite the desperate plea of their seniors.

Rumours of spies abounded. An Australian lance-corporal shot dead a man wearing a British officer's tunic and a private's cap when the latter failed to convince the NCO of his authenticity. From subsequent inquiries there seems little doubt that the officer was from the 7th Queen's.

At 1600 the Australian 36th Battalion, in reserve just outside theatened Villers Bretonneux, noticed a stream of retiring British troops, some of them without arms or equipment. An attempt was made to halt them but they were beyond the limits of their endurance. The Germans, they said, were 'coming on in thousands'.

Fortunately, Brigadier-General E. A. Wood, the stout, red-faced commander of the 55th Brigade, had more success in rallying three companies of the 7th Queen's who had broken after being caught by an intense barrage while forming up for a counter-attack. Stumping about in a great-coat and waving a walking stick, he managed to instil confidence into the shaken troops. When a messenger arrived to say the Australian 36th Battalion was about to counter-attack he had no difficulty in persuading the Queen's to join in on their right. The 6th Londons, vanguard of the 58th Division, now on its way, had already acquitted themselves well, and although they had been retiring slowly and in good order, willingly reversed their tracks and formed a solid second wave.

Now it was the turn of the 9th Bavarian Reserve Division to run, although some stayed and took a heavy toll of the khaki waves sweeping towards them. The counter-attack gradually came to a halt, and the Germans brought up a battalion of the Guards Ersatz Division to back up their line. As the Australians went forward in front of Villers Bretonneux, their compatriots farther north (and the dismounted cavalry with them) were 'retiring in perfect order as on an Aldershot field day'. At just that moment the mounted 17th Lancers appeared and rode forward through the retiring troops. The Lancers, sent up by the 7th Cavalry Brigade, could see no sign of the enemy but were delighted to note that their own appearance had acted as a signal for the Australians and the others to turn about. The Lancers' commander, Lieutenant-Colonel T. P. Melville, galloped his horse to a quarry, climbed up the steep bank and looked over. A sinister sight met his eyes. 'It looked as though the whole German army was advancing unmolested in extended order across the plain,' he later recounted, 'while on the road itself [to Amiens] masses of troops marched in column on route.'

The men of his regiment, who had been hoping for the opportunity of a glorious charge, were easily converted to a more realistic frame of mind. Their pennanted lances were stacked, horse-holders were told off, and Hotchkiss guns hurriedly unlashed from the pack horses. Fire was held until the Germans made a target that could not be missed. Within a matter of minutes another reinforcement arrived on the scene, banging and clattering over the broken roads. The appearance of three ugly mud-splashed cars of a Canadian motor machine gun battery was not as romantic or colourful as that of the Lancers, but the weight provided by their Vickers compensated for their aesthetic shortcomings.

That attack on Villers Bretonneux was swamped by a hail of machine gun fire and although the Germans had advanced some two miles or so (driving the French to the right of the town even farther back) they gained no more ground from the Australians during the night.

Three more hammer blows were fended off by the British the next day. At Colincamps, New Zealanders and Australians dealt summarily with a Bavarian and Wurtemberg Division, one battalion commander refusing artillery support in a message which stated: 'They are about 150 yards in front of me but don't worry we can kill them as fast as they come.' From Albert the Germans advanced against the 12th and 63rd Divisions. Minor penetrations were achieved but these were quickly snuffed out and prisoners and machine guns captured.

Surprisingly, it was on the front of the Australians at

Dernancourt that the only German success of the day was recorded. In a thick fog, the 50th Prussian Reserve Division surged over the railway embankment where they had been help up a few days previously and broke through the front of the 12th Australian Brigade. Not since the worst days of the Somme had such a heavy bombardment fallen on entrenched Australians, according to veteran eye-witnesses. After fighting fiercely all day, the Germans reached maximum penetration of about 2,000 yards.

It had been a revealing day for the Australian 4th Division. Their gunners had been shocked to see bewildered, officerless infantry and pioneers passing back through the batteries. When a colonel ordered them to return to the line they asked: 'But where are we to go and what are we to do?' Worse still, the defence had been overcome at what should have been one of its strongest points and two batteries of four machine guns each had been overwhelmed. For days afterwards men talked of the sacrifice of the 24th Company of the 4th Divisional Machine Gun Battalion. Returning wounded told of hearing drawnout bursts long after the breakthrough. No one doubted that the crews had fought to the last.

The truth was less dramatic; the guns in fact, had been captured without firing a shot. Four of them, in a quarry, had not even been mounted for action. Orders that the guns were not to be exposed during daylight, lest they should attract the attention of enemy shells, seem to have been obeyed too literally – especially as a warning to expect an attack had been issued the previous night. As it was, the Germans by-passed the quarry unseen, and when the Australians ran to mount their guns they found themselves covered by a line of Germans standing on the rear edge of the quarry. The other battery of four machine guns was also captured without firing a shot, the enemy taking it from the rear. No one even bothered to escort the Aussie prisoners. The way back was pointed out and they went . . . with their hands up. There was no option.

McLagan, the commander of the 4th Division, sounded anxious when he reported that night to General Congreve, still Corps commander after nearly two weeks of terrible strain. 'I don't think, if we are hammered by artillery, that we shall be able to hold the line,' he told the old warrior. Congreve's reply was reassuring. Congreve felt that the Germans were unlikely to be able to renew the attack, which, despite everything, had achieved only limited success. Besides, where would the enemy get fresh divisions? They too must be feeling the strain.

Congreve was right. Many of the German divisions which had been the spearhead of the offensive had suffered heavy losses and a consequent drop in morale. In particular, the arrangements for the evacuation of wounded had been inadequate. Ludendorff himself confirmed this in his memoirs. The arrangements 'had not sufficed at all points, although they had been carefully examined by the Director of Medical Services before the battle'. Ludendorff complained too that 'the numerous slightly wounded made things difficult by the stupid and unsatisfactory way in which they hurried to the rear'.

In that desolate land ravaged in 1916 by battle, devastated in 1917 as the Germans fell back, and now scourged again so that barely a building remained undamaged, these 'numerous' lightly wounded went through hell. Sergeant Renn, who took part in one of the attacks at the beginning of April, was among them.

His company had been called out in a rainstorm from their billets in captured British tents on a pitch dark night. Three men promptly took the opportunity to desert. When the rest marched off to assemble for the assault the rain stopped and the sky cleared to leave an indelible picture on Renn's mind.

'Great white clouds came driving across the sky, and let the moon occasionally peer through. These clouds were coming from the sea. We marched through villages. Fitful gleams of moonlight lit up the fields. I kept dreaming about the sea towards which we were perhaps going. What did it look like?'

The poet of the night became a very practical soldier the following day when he realized that he was one small frightened part of an attack mounted by about three divisions. With the eye of an expert he took in the scene as dawn broke. The three rows of batteries to the left of the road; the short thick guns, the long thin ones, the heavy mortars. Transport men lounging and watching carelessly knowing they were not going to be risking their lives – not that day. Then the objectives and the landmarks, the field of winter corn, the wood that changed colour in the middle from olive green to chalky green.

Renn's company was in the vanguard and suffered heavy casualties from well-aimed rifle fire. A shell burst within a few yards of Renn and blasted a piece of shrapnel through one of his feet. He limped back and found his comrades; one, an orphan, shot through the stomach, now sure to die unmourned; another with a hole in the front of his helmet, lying as the bullet had killed him propped on his elbows; a third, blinded, lay unseeing on his side, one arm clumsily outstretched.

More of Renn's wounded comrades lay in the makeshift hospital in an old woollen mill, gazing with hurt eyes at the blood-spattered doctors working feverishly in the glare of a carbide lamp to cut, sew, and bandage those with a chance; hopeless cases died alone and untended in the inky shadows.

The next morning Renn set off through the waste land, helped by a young soldier with a bullet in his calf, while he in turn tried to assist an officer with a shattered arm. They walked all that day. Renn spent the night in fever and delirium then set off again the next day begging food from hospitals, trying in vain to get a lift on hurrying ammunition lorries. Only when the young soldier stood in the road and refused to move did the wounded trio eventually shame a driver into giving them a lift to St Quentin. It had taken them nearly three days.

The high losses in specially trained storm troops such as Renn's machine gun company were eventually to restrict German aspirations. Ludendorff had relied on the cream of the army to smash the British; the losses in numbers could be counted, the losses in quality were incalculable.

Now convinced that he would not be able to penetrate the junction of the Allied armies, the First Quartermaster General put into operation phase two of the operations designed to destroy those he considered his most dangerous adversaries. Strangely, it was the apparent determination of the British politicians, rather than their soldiers, which made the greatest impression on Ludendorff. In his memoirs he frequently expresses positive envy of the single-minded will to win of Lloyd-George who (apart from refusing to introduce conscription into Ireland) 'shrank from nothing'.

The only surprising thing is Ludendorff's surprise. Anyone reading the British newspapers in 1918 could deduce that the government was resolved to win. Dramatic measures were announced to economize on the use of coal, gas, and electricity.

> 'The regulations will mean that [from April 2] entertainments will close at 10.30 p.m. no shop window lighting, no food to be cooked or hot meals served in any hotel, club or restaurant or boarding house at 9.30 p.m.' The lights in public dining rooms were to be put out by ten o'clock each night. A new Manpower Bill was rushed through 'which it is understood will raise the military age from 41 to 50. . . . Orders have been issued for all Grade 1 men in the Royal Ordnance Factories to be released for the army.'

The newspapers carried other stories. Steve Donoghue's win at Windsor on Mr M. S. Joel's Polyorama. (There was a full programme and the jockey listings included a young man called Piggott – father of a famous son.) The sporting columns concentrated on 'How Chelsea won the Championship'.

These stories served to conceal the war weariness, the despair and grief of Britain. In France, however, they could not be concealed. Those officers and men who had survived the battles of the previous days looked pityingly at the raw recruits, now pouring into their battalions. Lieutenant-Colonel Lowry of the 2nd West Yorkshires, was assigned 700 of them, mostly boys of eighteen and a half. The 2nd Middlesex were in a similar plight.[8] Every survivor in the 8th Division (which had suffered 5,000 casualties, mostly infantrymen, in the March offensive) was put to work helping absorb and instruct the replacements. Similar problems faced the 50th and 51st Divisions, now being directed to the north to take over a quiet sector of the line so they could reorganize and train their drafts.

The 8th Durhams had moved by bus to Bethune where they welcomed a 'good keen draft' of 160 boys under nineteen on 5 April. After fairly blunt questions about the boys' training it was wisely decided to set up a basic Lewis gun school for their further education.[63] For the 800 reinforcements sent to join the 4th Green Howards at Locon, just outside Bethune, the area had an aura of history. The signposts in the district pointed to Festubert and Givenchy, to Neuve Chapelle and Cuinchy. When most of the reinforcements had been schoolboys, the picture papers had been full of dramatic scenes of the actions fought there in 1915. The bones of many of the British soldiers who fought those actions lay even at that moment mouldering in the mud of a no-man's land which had hardly changed in the years since this particular part of the front had lain quiet. But was it a British front?

It came as a distinct shock to many of the newly arrived troops to discover that this legendary British battlefield was mainly garrisoned by men in drab, greenish grey uniforms. The soldiers of Britain's oldest ally had been in France for many months, although few people in England knew of them. The presence of the Portuguese, however, had not gone unnoticed, by the German General Staff.

CHAPTER FIFTEEN

MEET GENERAL BUMFACE

Jan Smuts had given the clearest possible warning. In his capacity as a member of the War Cabinet, he had advised Lloyd George in February that the part of the front held by the two Portuguese divisions in France was vulnerable – highly vulnerable. General Sir Henry Horne, commander of the First Army, holding the threatened sector, had earlier made a similar observation. As a result of further inquiries, Haig decided to take what can only be described as a calculated risk. He expected that the Portuguese would undoubtedly give way, but speculated that as long as the British divisions on their flanks held, other British divisions in the main defensive positions along the rivers behind the Portuguese would be able to link with those standing fast and surrender only ground that was of little significance.

General Horne remained unhappy about the situation. Lieutenant-General Sir Richard Haking, commander of XI Corps, in which the Portuguese were serving, was even more anxious. Representations were also made by the commander of the neighbouring XV Corps, Lieutenant-General Du Cane. He and Haking regarded the presence of the Portuguese as an invitation to trouble. (Other officers regarded them as a dangerous joke. 'This is General . . .,' a senior British officer told Philip Gibbs about this time, adding as they shook hands, 'We call him old Bumface.' The Portuguese General, he hastened to add, did not speak English.)[22]

The unreliability of the Portuguese was mainly political. Unrest at home, lack of sympathy with the war (it was very difficult to explain to simple peasants that their presence in France rose from the necessity to use the Atlantic ports in the battle against the U-boats), and a wide social gap between officers and men, had led the Portuguese to a state

Fifth Army
(Red on Yellow)

III Corps
(Red, White, Black on Blue)

VII Corps
(White on Blue)

2nd Cavalry Division
(White & Red on Blue)

18th Division
(Black on White)

24th Division
(White on Red)

30th Division
(White on Black)

36th Division
(Red on White)

50th Division
(Red on White)

58th Division
(White & Black on Blue)

bordering on mutiny. On 8 April, as it happened, a battalion refused to march up to the trenches.

That did it. Haking and Du Cane immediately reiterated requests that the 50th and 51st Divisions replace the 2nd Portuguese Division which had all its brigades in line with a brigade of the 1st Portuguese Division in reserve. Request granted.

Unfortunately, the move was more easily planned than done. The commander of the 51st Division was Major-General George Carter-Campbell. He had taken part in a bloody assault at Neuve Chapelle in 1915 as an infantry officer; he had seen his brigades cut to ribbons only two weeks previously. Carter-Campbell knew what his youngsters might have to face in the line and begged for time to let them at least fire their newly issued machine guns and Lewis guns. He was given a day's respite. The 7th Argylls were willing enough but noted gloomily that they had only nine shovels for the whole battalion. The 50th Division, with memories of the Somme battle still fresh in the minds of its officers, also asked for a day in which to reorganize. Relief of the Portuguese was postponed from the night of the 8th of April to the night of the 9th. By this time it was too late.

What had become the accepted preface to a big German attack occurred on the night of 7 April and the early morning of the 8th. A colossal gas shoot was unleashed on the British front, 40,000 mustard gas shells being pumped into Armentières alone. The drenching of the Flesquières Salient just before the offensive on 21 March was immediately recalled and veterans may have thought they detected a familiar taste in this vintage barrage. They were correct. Colonel Bruchmüller was on the scene.

The area chosen for the attack was flat, covered with farms and had the narrow rivers Lys and Lawe, partly canalized, running behind the front line at a distance of from two to four miles. Other small streams and canals criss-crossed the area along with an abundance of ditches and hedges in the small fields. Under normal circumstances its muddy clay would have made it unsuitable for the movement of large bodies of troops, and certainly for guns and transport; that may be why Haig was not unduly perturbed.

The spring, however, had been dry and to make matters worse British engineers had achieved considerable success in repairing and improving the drainage. But other things distracted Haig's attention. He had a near fixation that the enemy would strike hard at Arras again, and maintained a powerful force there to deal with such an offensive. For the moment Ludendorff held the initiative. With a huge front to guard, one that had been subjected to fearsome blows and which was still not stable, the British commander-in-chief bore a responsibility of unprecedented weight; any decision he might take could have a vital significance on the outcome of the war. It was wiser for Haig to be a counter puncher. Nor was his burden lightened by uncertainties about the willingness of the French to hurry to his aid. In any event, whatever the reasons, whatever the pressures, Haig did not properly read the sinister message in the gas tinged storm clouds gathering over the valley of the Lys.

General Von Quast, commander of the German Sixth Army, had no doubts about the outcome of the impending battle. Nor had Ludendorff. Both had been rushing preparations with one specific aim – to relieve the Portuguese before the British could. Bruchmüller, supervising the artillery preparations, informed them that all would be ready for 9 April. The giant offensive of 21 March, had been code-named 'Michael'. The unsuccessful attack on Arras of 28 March had been 'Mars'. Now the Germans would launch what had originally been designated 'George'. 'George' had been conceived as a counter-measure should the British attacks from Ypres continue in 1918 (surprisingly, perhaps, a project Haig actually contemplated). Preparations for 'George' were continued by the Germans during the early months of the year, but in a modified form which led to a teutonically untypical touch of humour – the code name was changed to 'Georgette'.

First indications that there was anything other than mustard gas in the wind came for the 50th Division on 7 April. The first battalion was moved by train from Bethune to an unfamiliar region a few miles north. New recruits, with their nice clean untorn uniforms, were told to forget about having unit flashes sewn on their shoulders and to look to their equipment instead. The move caused considerable confusion as the battalion settled into its billets. Platoon officers tried to sort out who was who. New drafts failed to recognize their own company commanders. When the heavy gas barrage came down on the night of the 7th some units needlessly stood to arms in the early morning 'just in case'.

But 8 April passed quietly. Mist and gas hung over the fields and the long lines of breastworks that served in place of trenches. (It was not practical, in most places, to dig with water so close to the surface.) The young lads of the 51st and 50th Divisions wrote home that night, that they were 'going up the line' the following evening. With no small pride and with kits packed neatly beside their beds, they lay down to sleep.

Nine hundred guns and howitzers awoke them before the dawn. At 0415 Bruchmüller's batteries unleashed their fury on a ten-mile front from Bethune to Armentières. At periods in the next four hours, the infantry of fourteen divisions surged forward behind a screen of strong patrols and battle groups.

Five of these divisions (three in the first line and two in support) struck the British 55th Division, holding the slightly higher ground near Bethune. Two divisions (one in the first line and one in support) attacked the 40th Division holding a group of villages south of Armentières (where it had been sent to *rest* after its trials on the Somme). Seven divisions (four in the first line and three in reserve) smashed into the Portuguese.

As predicted by Haig, the British flanks held – at first. As predicted by everyone, the Portuguese were overwhelmed. Some Portuguese, in fact, surrendered before the actual assault commenced, preferring to risk German POW camps than the fire curtain that ravaged their lines. Some literally ran for their lives, even removing their boots to achieve greater speed. Some, however, fought back bravely when shadowy figures loomed through the flame-slashed mist. The remnants of one Portuguese battalion held out until 1100 when they ran out of ammunition and made a last stand with the bayonet. There were other isolated attempts to delay the enemy but at 1340 the commander of the 2nd Portuguese Division reported 'Whole of division either lost or scattered'.

Two battalions of cyclists were rushed in. They ignored the fleeing Portuguese and fought desperately for time against swarms of Saxons and Bavarians. The 50th and 51st Divisions, who had been put on 'one hour's notice to move' were marching hurriedly to their aid. The 50th had already suffered its first casualties, although these might well have been avoided had the corps commander anticipated the depth of Bruchmüller's barrages. This time the shrewd old gunner had included the villages, towns, and roads behind the lines within his plans; and he reaped a grim harvest. For nearly three years the villages had survived in this quiet area of the front, their populations gradually drifting back, and life going on virtually as normal within a few miles of the front line. Security was taken for granted; a tragic error in war. With a narrower front to concentrate fire on than that attacked in the south, Bruchmüller could pay attention to the rear communications.

Among the first places to be hit was Estaires, the key town at the junction of the Lys Canal, the Lawe, and the Meteren Beque. In their billets there, the officers of the 6th Durhams were hurriedly packing to leave when, with a crash and a roar, a heavy shell plunged through the roof and exploded. Five were killed outright, including Captain Aubin who had rallied the battalion when it was ambushed on the Somme, and Lieutenant Tyerman who had led his transport details in the counter-attack at Harbonnières. Eight other officers were wounded and the companies marched through the smoking, dust-filled streets led by only five officers. By 0900 the battalion was in action and had lost Captain Cardew, the other hero of the Somme ambush.

The 5th and 8th Durhams had moved off at about the same time as their sister battalion amidst similar scenes of terror and destruction. Bruchmüller had placed barrages on the approach roads and continued the fire at a great intensity for much of the morning. The village of La Gorgue, a couple of miles from Estaires, was ablaze, flaming timbers crashing into the street, and debris cascading down unheard above the shell bursts. Transport drivers trying to get their ammunition limbers up to the battalions on the other side of the canal were forced to use minor routes. Patrols of the XV Corps cyclists now began to return, sweating and panting with some sort of picture of the state of the Portuguese. A lone British interpreter reported to the 8th Durhams HQ that the Portuguese were retiring in haste; then appeared a British liaison officer with a similar report; then more reports from the cyclists said the Portuguese were retiring in groups of a dozen or so.[63]

What effect this panic would have on the young British troops in the midst of the chaos no one could guess. The battalion's companies had set off independently to try to reach positions already reconnoitred across the Lys. At last a message was received from the vital defence work at Le Marais. One of its three strongpoints had been over-run, the report said, but the others were holding out and heavy casualties were being inflicted on the enemy. Some retreating Portuguese Lewis gunners had been rallied and had joined in the defence of the position.[65] The amateur warriors, it seemed were learning fast.

The battle in the centre now began to develop in much the same way as on 23 and 24 March except that instead of trying to hold the line of the Somme, the 50th and 51st Divisions were endeavouring to hold posts on the east bank of the Lys and the Lawe.

On the wings two completely different pictures emerged. The British right flank division (the 55th) had been badly mauled in one of the worst of the Menin Road battles the previous September (it took part in three assaults during Third Ypres) and had also suffered heavily in the German counter-attack at Cambrai. According to notes found on German officers, the 55th was 'below the average quality' and fit only to hold a quiet sector of the front. The Germans' information was out of date for the division had been nursed carefully by its commander, Major-General Jeudwine, and had enjoyed two months of rest and training; furthermore it had been in the area for seven weeks and knew it well.

As the battle sections of the 4th Ersatz Division scrambled forward in the mist, the carefully sited machine guns of the 4th Loyals and the 4th King's Own ripped into the attackers. Shells rained down in answer to SOS flares. When Germans penetrated the maze of forward keeps, sunken roads, and breastworks, other units of the 55th filtered back by different routes and bombed and bayoneted them. Haig later recorded his admiration for the spirit that inspired a pillbox machine gun crew to unheedingly keep up a galling fire on the enemy to its front while the rest of the garrison were using their revolvers to shoot down Germans who had penetrated a rear compartment.[29] When a forward field gun was damaged it was not abandoned. Although the crew had to use a pick-axe to open the breach after every round, they kept it in action at close range.[14]

Pulling back its left flank (where the Portuguese had retreated) to link up with the oncoming brigades of the 51st Division, the 55th took an unparalleled toll of its attackers. It captured 100 machine guns and even a band that was to have played the victorious Germans into Bethune but had carelessly strayed into some wired-in defences. The southern buttress of the defence was solid. To the north it was a different picture.

The 40th Division, on the left flank of the disintegrating Portuguese Corps, had been hurled into the breach when the 59th Division was smashed on 21 March and had suffered more than 4,000 casualties during the fighting up to 30 March. It had then been sent by lorry to the quiet Bois Grenier sector south of Armentières. When a single German division attacked it frontally, the forward troops gave a good account of themselves, but when elements of two German divisions (who had penetrated the Portuguese front) came in behind them, the position became desperate. Support machine gun positions were particularly vulnerable to attack from the rear. In fields dotted with cosy names, such as Streaky Bacon Farm, Tram Line Avenue, and Windy Post, the 18th Welch Regiment and 13th East Surreys were butchered by a hail of bullets from all directions. At noon the dishevelled figure of the commanding officer of the 20th Middlesex appeared to report at the HQ of the 13th Green Howards that his battalion had been all but annihilated and that Germans were even then threatening Red House Post well in the rear of the Green Howards.[68] As the day progressed the right brigade of the 40th Division was battered back to right angles from its original front, and the 34th Division sent its reserve brigade to bolster the flank and protect its position in Armentières, which had not been directly attacked.

The key aiming point for the German attack in this sector was the bridge at Bac St Maur across the Lys. Here three companies of the 12th Green Howards and a pioneer unit made desperate efforts to hold a position east of the river, even though they had suffered seriously from the terrible barrage laid down on the Armentières road when they had marched up from reserve. Slowly, remorselessly, fighting sometimes with bayonet, they were driven back by an enemy who attacked 'in great strength and with many light machine guns'. The Green Howards were forced back across the river, covered by nineteen men under Second-Lieutenant Champney who kept a Lewis gun in action until the enemy were within twenty yards of him and he fell riddled with bullets.[68]

While this savage action was being fought, two companies of Royal Engineers were frantically trying to destroy the vital bridges. As far as the main bridge was concerned they were successful; it was detonated in the face of the Germans racing to seize it. Other engineers supported by 100 reinforcements under Lieutenant-Colonel W. E. Brown of the 18th Welch, were hacking madly at ropes of a floating foot bridge. There were three of these footbridges and they were now surrounded by splashes from German machine guns established in houses overlooking the crossings. First one was destroyed, then a second, now stained with blood as well as water. As Brown and his scratch party made for the third bridge they were met with machine gun fire – from both sides of the river.

There was no lack of initiative and courage on the Germans' part. An officer of the 22nd Infantry Regiment, Lieutenant of Reserve Imiolcyzk, had led a party of soldiers across the bridge at Bac St Maur and established a firm foothold on the far bank. Other troops were hastily diverted to support him.*

Immediate steps were taken to eliminate Imiolcyzk's bridgehead. A brigade of the 25th Division (the 74th) was loaded into buses and rushed to the threatened area. The brigade had been carefully placed to support either its own division, holding Plugstreet Wood on the left of Armentières, or the 34th Division holding Armentières itself, and its sudden move left the front north of the city very weak. As it was, the 74th's counter-attack (supported by the 12th Green Howards and some Engineers) foundered. Lieutenant Imiolcyzk was proving a stubborn customer; and his penetration was a drastic threat. The bridge he had seized at Bac St Maur pointed directly at the line of heights, less than nine miles away, which protected Poperinghe and the vast dumps lying behind Ypres. If this high ground were to be seized the whole of the British Second Army, plus the Belgians, was in danger of being cut off. Further reinforcements were sped towards the danger spot.

While these events had been taking place, a grinding struggle was being fought to prevent the Germans from seizing the crossings farther south. From Bac St Maur the Lys runs south-west and then, just beyond Estaires, the Lawe canal and river wind away due south. The Germans were driving against both faces of the rough open 'V' formed by the two rivers. Before them lay the battalions of the 50th Division, roughly in position along the Lys, and the 51st, coming into action along the Lawe.

Despite their lack of training the young troops of these hard-pressed formations provided stubborn opposition under heavy shelling which was maintained for the best part of the day. The 8th Durhams' HQ, having virtually been blown out of one position, and with most of its orderlies killed, was functioning again in a house in the important village of Lestrem by 1700. Half an hour later the steady tempo of the enemy artillery increased together with the chatter of their machine guns; shortly afterwards a runner arrived with the

*Imiolcyzk's regiment was leading the assault of the 11th Reserve Division and support came from the 10th Ersatz Division.

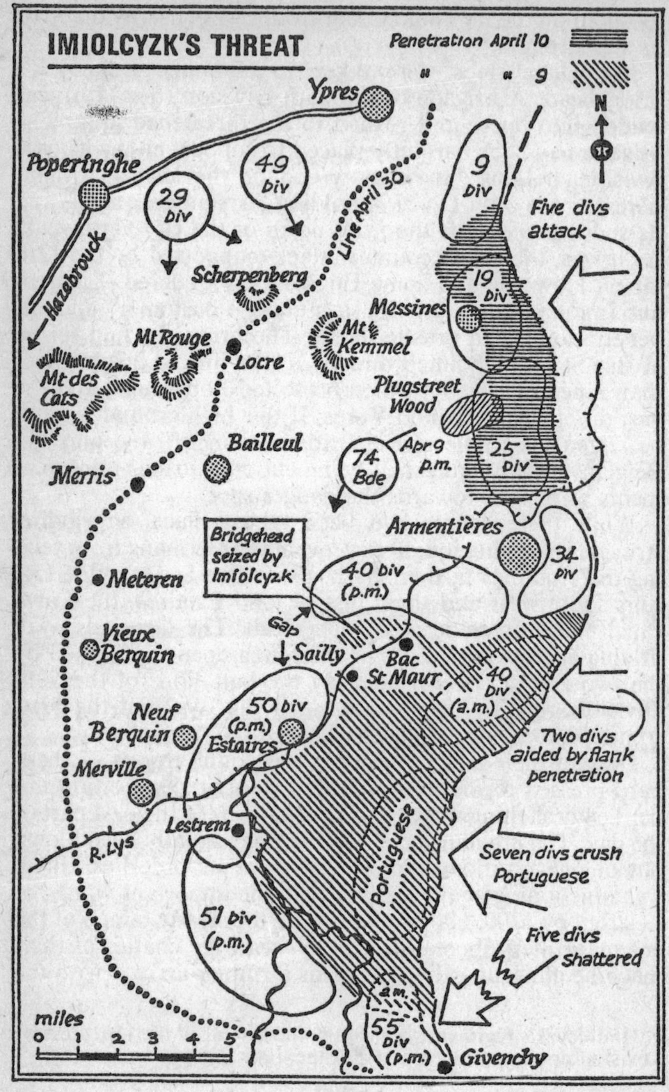
IMIOLCYZK'S THREAT
Penetration April 10
" " 9
N
Ypres
Poperinghe
49 Div
29 Div
Hazebrouck
Line April 30
9 Div
Five divs attack
Scherpenberg
19 Div
Messines
Mt Rouge
Mt Kemmel
Mt des Cats
Locre
Plugstreet Wood
Bailleul
74 Bde
Apr 9 p.m.
25 Div
Merris
Armentières
Bridgehead seized by Imiolcyzk
40 Div (p.m.)
34 Div
Meteren
Gap
Vieux Berquin
Sailly
Bac St Maur
40 Div (a.m.)
Neuf Berquin
50 Div (p.m.)
Estaires
Two divs aided by flank penetration
Merville
Lestrem
R. Lys
Portuguese
Seven divs crush Portuguese
51 Div (p.m.)
Five divs shattered
a.m.
55 Div (p.m.)
miles
0 1 2 3 4 5
Givenchy

news that a small force of the enemy had crossed the canal at Lock la Rault, about a mile away.

Greatly weakened by the fighting of the afternoon (which had raged unceasingly since about 1400) the Durhams ordered up their last reserves – three platoons. Cut off from communications with their own brigade headquarters they were happy to make chance contact with the 153rd Brigade and were even more pleased when two kilted battalions turned up at a cross-roads in their rear with orders to dig in on the western bank of the river. The Highlanders willingly joined the counter-attack but the forward rushes became slower and slower as the massed machine guns on the other bank lashed the attacking troops with bullets and finally forced them to a halt. The Durhams and the men of the 6th Black Watch and 7th Gordons crawled back to cover as best they could. Their commanding officers, staring through binoculars at the smoke-wreathed battlefield concluded that those few Germans who had crossed the canal were either dead or wounded and held a conference to decide on the best course of action. No sooner had this been agreed than orders came for the Black Watch to move into reserve, and for the Gordons to march to a village on the right flank. As the Highlanders moved off into the night the Durhams were left to hold an awkward salient with their sadly depleted battalion. It was not to be long before they met the Highlanders again.

On the right of the Durhams, the survivors of King Edward's Horse, the Corps cyclists, were similarly pleased to see the 5th Seaforths and the 7th Gordons come into action alongside them, while still farther south, the 154th Brigade came into line beside the victorious troops of the 55th and hung on determinedly, closing the gap left by the Portuguese.

Farther north, the 5th Durhams were firing from the houses of Estaires, harassing the Germans who had managed to get a foothold at the Pont Levis bridge for a brief time. Between Estaires and Bac St Maur, the 150th Brigade had destroyed the footbridges at Sailly but their charges had failed to blow up the road bridge properly. As if drawn by magnet, squads of German infantry rose at intervals from the ruined houses on the east side of the bridge and tried to rush it. The defence held firm. By nightfall the approaches were littered with dead and wounded and smashed equipment; not a single German had crossed.

As darkness deepened (and as 6,000 Portuguese prisoners were marching to cages behind the German lines) the 50th and 51st Divisions were facing seven German divisions whose sole mission was to seize the river and canal crossings – at any price. The terrors of the night began to equal the horrors of the day.

At 1400 the 74th Brigade repeated its counter-attack of earlier in the day. Charging out of the darkness towards Bac St Maur, which was in flames, the British drove the surprised and exhausted Germans to the river. Then the enemy, who had wasted no time in throwing over his own bridges, regrouped and swept into the attack again; the 3rd Worcester, 11th Lancashire Fusiliers, and 9th Loyals suddenly found themselves fighting for their lives, and being driven relentlessly back as the morning mist began to rise.[59]

Just after midnight, there had been great activity in the flat fields outside Pont Riquel, where a garrison of the 8th Durhams covering the bridge was holding out in sandbagged houses and breastworks on the east side of the Lawe. One after the other, German 77s were wheeled and heaved into position while infantrymen helped point out the dim outlines of the strongpoints.

At 0130 hours harsh voices bawled orders and salvo after salvo of whizz bangs tore into the British posts. Men not killed outright found themselves assailed by grenades and rifles at close quarters the moment the barrage ceased. The enemy had penetrated the posts and the defenders then hurriedly tried to destroy the bridges. As had happened many times before, the demolition charges did only a partial job and small arms had to be used to drive back the enemy trying to cross on the wreckage. As dawn broke the 6th Black Watch once again arrived in support of the Durhams, its troops now dazed and red-eyed from constant marching and fighting.

CHAPTER SIXTEEN

PLUGSTREET REVISITED

Unpleasant and vicious though the night attacks on the First Army had been, more menacing events were building up on the Second Army front. At 0300 a stupendous bombardment fell on the six-mile front between Frelinghien and Hollebeke. 'Georgette's' twin had been delivered. Some twenty-four hours after the assault on the Portuguese had drawn reserves to the threatened area south of Armentières, the Germans attacked in the north. The storm troops appeared through the mist about 0530. The attackers were opposed by the weakened 25th Division, already minus a brigade, the 19th Division which had been smashed up during the retreat across the old Somme battlefield in March, and the 9th Division which had suffered heavy losses at the same time. Their ranks filled with boyish recruits, these formations had been sent into the line again, the 19th arriving on the night of 7 April. The 1st and 2nd Australian Divisions, from whom the patched-up formations had taken over, were shocked by the appearance of some infantry units. 'Thin ranks had been expanded by a flood of very young recruits who, to the harder (and older) Australians, appeared as mere children, pink-cheeked, soft-chinned, giving the appearance of being dazed by the grim conditions into which they were suddenly plunged', wrote an observer.[3] The Australians noted that one brigade, for example, lacked many of its Lewis guns and all of its light trench mortars when it arrived. Other British units 'showed some disorganization . . . due to their recent losses' and were 'still deficient in certain equipment'. Some of these deficiencies had been corrected by the time the Germans attacked, but there was no time for the 'children' to acquire the experience needed to hold a defence system which, although strong, with many pill-boxes and belts of wire, was essentially built for a veteran garrison.

Gradually the whole of the front line north of Armentières was forced back across the ancient tangle of trenches and charred tree-trunks of Plugstreet Wood, where the 10th Cheshires and 1st Wiltshires contributed still more bodies to ground that had surfeited itself with corpses earlier in the war. Many of the supporting British batteries were situated in the wood, which lay just over a mile behind the line, and as the withdrawal continued gun crews with teams and tractors were trying to haul their pieces out of the swampy ground. Some died in the attempt. At least three tractors were needed in one case before a gun-carriage could be moved and a number of guns had to be abandoned.

Steadily the Germans pressed up the slopes of the Messines Ridge (which had been captured less than a year before and where the yawning mine craters on the reverse slopes were still objects of wonder). Both the 25th and the 19th Divisions had taken part in the original battle of Messines and now their gains were being relinquished by the same divisions in practically the same area. The anonymous rubble that was Messines fell in the afternoon and the reconstituted South African brigade, some 1,300 strong, mostly recruits, was sent to counter-attack. They went over in the evening light and were driven back by every machine gun the Germans could bring to bear. The urgency to get up reserves to replace those which had been sent south now became acute. Any man who could march and hold a rifle was sent towards the front. There was said to be even a platoon of town majors led by an ASC colonel.[30]

As the second half of 'Georgette' thrust back the weakened divisions north of Armentières, and as the attacks were continued to the south, the town gradually became an irregular salient outflanked to a depth of three miles on the Plugstreet side and nearly seven miles in the direction of Bac St Maur. The salient was about four miles across. In this cauldron the 34th Division was exposed to anything the enemy cared to fire in its direction but was not assaulted frontally. The commander of the 34th, Major-General C. Lothian Nicholson, had suggested as early as the previous evening that a retirement might be started rather than allow his division to be surrounded by default but he did not get the order until 1000 hours the following morning. Wearily the garrison slouched back through the deserted streets, still spattered with yellow stains from the gas bombardment; they straggled across the main square with its handful of trees still holding up splintered branches, past the twisted gas lamps, and down the main road towards the Pont de Nieppe, the main bridge out of town. Units of the 40th Division also penned in the salient made their way back over a railway bridge after the commanders of four battalions had conferred.[68]

North of Armentières, the 51st and 50th Divisions were still desperately trying to hold the river-canal line. Attack and counter-attack continued the whole day and the hoarse, rasping chatter of machine guns never ceased in the streets of Estaires. There were plenty of town boys among the young British troops and house-to-house fighting was something that they could comprehend, bloody though it was. They burst in the doors of abandoned homes, clattered upstairs and set up their machine guns at the bedroom windows, blazing away under the gaze of solemn family portraits of the late owners. Riddell sent in the 6th Northumberlands to eliminate Germans who had formed a bridgehead at the Pont Levis end of the town. By 0930 they had almost succeeded; then the weight of German fire from across the canal sent them scrambling back over the piles of broken bricks and plaster to less exposed positions.

At 0830 the Germans under cover of heavy machine gun fire drove the defenders from the shambles which now constituted Lestrem. In the smouldering wreckage, amid shapeless piles of collapsed sandbagged strong-points, the assaulting troops of the 8th Bavarian Reserve Division frantically tried to find cover. Runners were dispatched with urgent requests for reinforcements but before these could arrive a hail of machine gun bullets swept the Bavarians, a shower of Mills bombs landed with ear-splitting cracks, and through the drifting smoke scattered groups of panting figures in helmets or hatless, in kilts or in puttees, fell on them with bayonets. The remnants of the 8th Durhams had hastily reorganized, and attacked in conjunction with the 6th Black Watch. By 1130 Lestrem was again in British hands.

Close combat of this kind is costly and as the day wore on, the 50th and 51st Divisions were whittled away. Yet, their line (stretching now for nearly nine miles along twisting canals and rivers) remained firm. Had fresh reinforcements been available, it might have been possible to exploit the situation. As it was, the only reserves on which the two raw divisions were able to draw were their own indispensable pioneers, the 8th Royal Scots and the 7th Durhams.

Two brigades of the 29th Division had been taken straight from the line at Ypres, and sent in buses to points behind Estaires. The crisis at Bac St Maur, however, had caused them to be diverted in that direction. As the staff car with the famous red triangle pushed through crowds of refugees, the 29th's commander, Major-General D. E. Cayley, noted the rage of the fleeing French against the Portuguese and 'on more than one occasion saw unfortunate soldiers of that nation being violently assaulted by women'.[24]

Other divisions were on their way to the beleaguered front; the 31st, the 33rd, the 61st, two brigades from the 49th, and even the 5th Division fresh from Italy. A list of these reinforcements may sound formidable, but there would still be only fourteen British divisions to face almost double that number of Germans. Moreover, with transport difficulties, these units were filtering into the line piecemeal. This the Germans knew well and their efforts to break through the flimsy forces facing them were redoubled.

By 2100, on 10 April 'the situation became very obscure on the 51st Division front and stragglers in large numbers were arriving'. Eventually a joint headquarters was established by officers of the 8th Durhams, the 6th Black Watch, and the 7th Gordons – 'in order that there might be complete co-operation between units'. Some iron man then formed the 51st stragglers into an extended line and led them forward in the 'very dark night' and placed them in position to await further attack.[63] Haig had issued an order to his armies that day which began, 'All armies will hold their ground and will employ all their resources to stop any advance on the part of the enemy.'[3] No one could say that the men tenaciously clinging to a front some twenty miles long had not done their best to obey.

In his memoirs Ludendorff pays tribute to the staunch defence of 10 April. 'Towards Estaires we did not penetrate far enough, but stuck fast in the Lys position; towards the Lawe also, our progress was but slight. The enemy's machine guns continued to give our infantry much trouble; it should have grappled with them more vigorously. . . .'[45]

This criticism is hardly fair on the German soldiers who once again showed ferocious determination in the attack. By stubborn erosion of the divisions in front of them, they had presented Ludendorff with the opportunity to destroy the British Army, or at least a large part of it. The German forward troops were now within ten miles or so of Hazebrouck, a town of some 13,000 people, and an important railway centre for the whole of the British northern front. Furthermore, enemy intelligence officers had now established that the formations before them had, with one or two exceptions, been through the great Somme battle only a fortnight before. German intelligence noted one other thing; French reinforcements were being moved forward very slowly.

At first Foch seems not to have realized the danger. Haig's appeals for him to take over part of the British line in the south, so that reserves could be transferred to the north, fell on deaf ears. Foch preferred to keep one of his two French reserve armies near Amiens, while the other was concentrated near Beauvais. Perhaps Foch feared that the stroke on the Lys was a feint and that Ludendorff, who still had fresh divisions in reserve, was preparing to strike elsewhere. If he allowed his reserves to be drawn north he might be taken by surprise in another sector. Only as the battle intensified did the little old artilleryman arrange for his two reserve armies to form up where they would be better placed to intervene. As a gesture, however, he ordered the French 133rd Division by rail to a position near Ypres.

It was somewhat inaccurate of Haig therefore to state in his Order of the Day on 11 April that, 'The French Army is moving rapidly and in great force to our support.' The famous order of 11 April, issued to all units of the British Expeditionary Force also declared, after stating Haig's admiration for the troops now in action: 'There is no other course open to us but to fight it out! Every position must be held to the last man; there must be no retirement. With our backs to the wall, and believing in the justice of our cause each one of us must fight on to the end.'[62]

For many the end had already come. Others were so heavily committed to battle that they had little time to reflect on such inspired messages – even if their commanders had seen fit to distribute them. In many cases the message was not delivered for days after it was issued; in some cases it was deliberately withheld. At a battery of the 25th Division, which had headed north from the Somme battle looking forward to a 'rest home', it was handed to the officers without comment. 'Little was said. Resignedly we prepared for a fight to the finish,' wrote a subaltern who had ridden towards the growing thunder of the guns that day counting the number of dumps blazing on the Flanders plain.[27]

Captain Essame, still adjutant of the 2nd Northants stationed near Villers Bretonneux, thought the order added to general uncertainty and confusion of the situation. 'For the first time, so far as the fighting troops were concerned, the idea began to spread that there was a possibility that we might lose the war,' he wrote later. 'Morale in some of the units which had been involved in the retreat had deteriorated. . . . Possibly this order may have been necessary, but to many who had fought in the March retreat its tone was insulting. It infuriated my own commanding officer who refused to publish it to the troops and said that if the morale of the higher command was low, his at least was not.'[16]

A Royal Fusilier is reported to have commented acidly, 'What ruddy wall?' after hearing the message read out, and a number of troops in quiet areas laughed out loud. Not everyone reacted so cynically. The Australian official History records: 'The issue of this appeal has been criticized as unnecessarily alarming. Among the Australians, however, it had precisely the result intended – that of stinging them to the highest pitch of determination.'

In the event, the men holding out on the damp Flanders battlefield sensibly relied more on their rifles than on Haig's promises and exhortations. The fact that the weather cleared slightly (apart from the perpetual mist there had even been occasional snow showers) was of more help, enabling the Royal Flying Corps to intervene in full strength and leading to a number of flights over the battle area involving scores of aircraft.

Now in their third consecutive day of non-stop battle, it was obvious that the exhausted 50th and 51st Divisions could no longer maintain their extended line. The troops holding Estaires had been withdrawn at 1800 the previous day in order to avoid being buried under the ruins of the buildings, and all the ensuing morning they had been pushed steadily back. Coming into action north of the town, the 29th Division soon found itself involved in a fire-fight. Its troops had occupied many of the small farms scattered over the area and 'The day opened in perfect stillness and dense fog, but out of the fog arrived the Boche with trench mortars and machine guns mounted on lorries. Every farm was subjected to intense fire at close range,' reported an officer of the 1st Border Regiment.*

Slowly the 29th fell back, the 1st Border and other troops in their vicinity being encouraged and inspired by the sight of the commanding officer of the Borderers, Lieutenant-Colonel J. Forbes-Robertson, riding a borrowed horse between strongpoints and posts. His own charger, an old dun mare, he regarded as too valuable to risk; as far as his own skin was concerned, he seems to have given it little thought.[24]

There were effective counter-attacks and minor successes for the British but hard as they fought the Germans were not to be denied. In the 50th Division area, criss-crossed with streams and canals, each of which had various locks, drawbridges, and footbridges, the fighting became extremely confused. Cut off in a sharp salient the 5th Green Howards held on too long, were all but surrounded and those who could were forced to fight their way back in small, independent parties – the wounded had to be left behind.[68] The 6th and 8th Durhams, fighting side by side, found their numbers dwindling as the line they were expected to cover grew longer. Germans penetrated the

*Captain J. C. Ogilvie.

gaps and threatened to cut them off. One by one the Durhams destroyed bridges over the twin canals and withdrew fighting to Merville, where they attempted to maintain contact with the Black Watch on their right and with the rest of the 51st Division on the other side of the canal complex.[63]

'The situation was reported to Brigade headquarters and reinforcements to fill the gap between our right flank and the canal were urgently required as the enemy was working through this gap and it was feared he would manage to capture Merville,' says the War Diary of the 8th Durhams. 'The enemy repeatedly attacked our position which was subjected to the most intense hostile machine gun fire but was repulsed.'

A brave attempt by a group of Highlanders to enter the line and close the gap ended in hopeless slaughter – 'Owing to all approaches being covered with machine gun fire, they were almost all casualties en route' wrote the historian of the Durhams.

As the battle raged, the first reinforcements trickled in behind the 51st Division. The 5th Cornwalls came into the line not far from where the battalion had first been stationed on its arrival in France in May 1916. 'But the whole of the draft (more than 400 men had just joined the battalion) were youths without any experience of real warfare and the change, practically from the barrack square to the firing line against a well-trained, war-bitten enemy was a terrible experience,' wrote the Cornwalls' historian.[69]

The Cornwalls found themselves hampered by large numbers of stragglers, not only Portuguese but from British regiments as well. By early evening these youngsters were fighting hard to make contact with the troops on their flanks.

Heavy explosions were heard spasmodically during the night of 11 April as the British blew up bridges over the network of canals and rivers. Occasional bursts of machine gun fire and the crack of grenades marked clashes with adventurous German patrols. In the darkness the British officers once again tried to sort out the many stragglers. One officer scraped together enough men of the 150th Brigade to form a weak battalion. Lieutenant-Colonel Forbes-

Robertson collected the survivors of his own battalion and the 1st Lancashire Fusiliers who had lost their entire headquarters staff and most of their officers. By the light of burning farmhouses Forbes-Robertson led a total of 150 men to a group of cottages on the outskirts of the village of Bleu and prepared them for the morrow.[24] Elsewhere artillery brigades were asked to spare any available officers to command the leaderless infantry of the 51st.[3]

In Merville, depleted platoons guarded the bridges of the various canals and gradually withdrew at about 0100 with German patrols close on their heels; soon the splintering of glass and battering down of doors told the familiar story of looters at work. After a hard day's fighting the victors were taking their reward. All that night the drunken shouts of German revellers enjoying the contents of the wine cellars of Merville could be heard by the exhausted remnants of the 50th Division huddled outside the town. Not far from Merville small groups of Highlanders clashed continually during the night as they sought to creep through the encircling enemy. Behind the exhausted divisions in the line there were now only a few Royal Engineer companies holding strategic villages. Obviously the Germans would exploit the situation; in the dawn two fresh divisions came into the attack while elements of others came into action farther north.

The commanders of the riven 152nd and 153rd brigades had spent the night in a humble village, a joint headquarters they shared with a forceful Australian gunner officer. At daylight bullets ripped through the lath and plaster walls of one cottage headquarters and upwards through the ceiling. They could have come only from close range. One of the Highland brigadiers, although lame, crossed the road smartly and, tapping on the window of his fellow brigadier, reported laconically, 'It's time to be going.' He was right. At that very moment the Germans were setting up another machine gun on the road a few yards away. The Australian gunner officer hurried back to get the lame man's walking stick and left by the front door as the Germans were entering by the back.

Farther north a dangerous situation developed as the 31st

Division and the hotchpotch of units near Armentières were driven back. Lieutenant-Colonel Seton Hutchison, commanding the machine gun battalion of the 33rd Division (newly arrived at Armentières), set off that morning at the head of cyclist patrols and met a number of British troops in 'precipitate retreat without officers, saying they had orders to retire'. Immediately he pedalled to the rear and hitched a lift on an ambulance to divisional headquarters where he obtained permission to rush his guns into action. Hutchison overcame the objections of an obstructive transport officer by stunning him with a blow from his revolver, commandeered the necessary lorries, and drove recklessly with eight machine guns and their teams to form a solid line of resistance. No troops were allowed to retreat past these determined machine gunners on pain of being shot. Any officer who hesitated was immediately relieved of his command by the ruthless Hutchison. [33, 38]

Just as had happened during the Somme retreat, communications now began to collapse. No one at higher headquarters knew exactly where the fighting line was and, indeed, whether or not the weakened divisions were still in action or had been destroyed. Only the comparative slowness of the German advance indicated they were encountering opposition. The 4th Guards Brigade located the whereabouts of the advancing enemy by the weight of machine gun fire which met their patrols spreading out in line beyond the Nieppe Forest. The brigade was being sent up independently to form a barrier on which the forward troops could retire and, under an accurate bombardment from German guns, directed by a mass of observation balloons, found cover by fortifying scattered hamlets and farms.

On the right the first troops of the 5th Division were arriving; at Hazebrouck itself the first train loads of Australians were pouring in battalion by battalion and moving to positions already reconnoitred by their own staff officers. While these reserves were formed into a rearward line of defence, the enemy presssd forward against the weary remnants of units which had now been fighting for three days.

As the German transport became more organized the

weight of shell fire increased. Clusters of 5.9s began to drop at short intervals around an advanced dressing station set up in the village school at Vieux Berquin. The houses around the school were demolished first. Then the school windows were blown in, scattering glass and dust over the forty stretcher cases and the many lightly wounded packed into the classrooms. As no ambulances could approach, the RAMC major in charge organized a series of stretcher parties and the wounded were carried, through the barrage, to Strazeele station nearly two miles away. All arrived safely and, as the last of the stores were packed, a fastidious RAMC orderly produced a brush and swept out the largest classroom. This bit of swank was nullified shortly afterwards when a 5.9 fell directly on target and obliterated the school.[24]

The severe fighting as British reinforcements arrived, although disjointed, paid dividends. By packing troops on the northern flank near Ypres, the withdrawal of the British line was gradually being halted and to the south where the 55th Division stood fast, the Germans had virtually been stopped. The fluid area in between these points, where the Germans had made their deepest penetrations, now formed a long salient and was subjected to heavy flanking fire that caused heavy losses in the enemy attacking columns. On the 12th it dawned on Crown Prince Rupprecht that he was unlikely to achieve the hoped for breakthrough. In fact, his troops were stranded in a precarious position. To draw back would be to admit failure. The only hope was all-out attack. During the night the crack Alpine Corps began to move up.

CHAPTER SEVENTEEN

VORWARTS – AND BACKWARDS

As the Germans grouped for a new line of attack, the British defensive barrier grew in density. The outsize 5th Division advancing through the Nieppe Forest was able to relieve the fragments of the 50th Division (including the 149th Brigade reduced from 1,700 strong to 200 men). The other division which had borne the brunt of the fighting, the 51st, was relieved not only by the 61st but by the 4th also, coming up from the Arras front.

Farther to the rear, the 8th Australian Battalion detraining at Hazebrouck, waited shivering for its transport and cookers to arrive. They noted the red reflection of burning villages on the skyline and commented on the strange absence of noise, except for a British 60-pounder firing at intervals. Cautiously the companies advanced through deserted villages and barren fields, with patrols ahead and platoons at fifty-yard intervals with connecting files.[3]

Ahead of them in the darkness, the 2nd Royal Fusiliers and the 2nd South Wales Borderers, having fought all day, suddenly found themselves isolated. It was decided that at a chosen time the order 'left turn' would be sent down the trenches and thereupon every man would rise and follow the man on his left. Soon a long line of shadowy figures, with an officer's servant and a rifleman as scouts and the two commanding officers heading the column, was wending its way through country occupied mainly by Germans. The column made it unscathed and even survived the dangerous experience of being challenged by the Australian sentries. Other units were less fortunate; a detachment of Lancashire Fusiliers fought a bitter night battle until they had exhausted their ammunition and withdrew in the confusion taking their wounded with them.

At first light the battle increased in ferocity. The forward

TABLE V GHQ Reserve Divisions placed at the disposal of Gough during the battle.

20TH DIVISION*	50TH DIVISION†	8TH DIVISION‡
59 Brigade	149 Brigade	23 Brigade
2 Scottish Rifles	4 Northumberlands	2 Devons
11 KRRC	5 Northumberlands	2 West Yorks
11 Rifle Brigade	6 Northumberlands	2 Middlesex
60 Brigade	150 Brigade	24 Brigade
12 KRRC	4 East Yorks	1 Worcesters
6 Shropshires	4 Green Howards	2 Northants
12 Rifle Brigade	5 Green Howards	1 Sherwood Forest
61 Brigade	151 Brigade	25 Brigade
12 King's	5 Durhams	2 Royal Berks
7 Somersets	6 Durhams	2 East Lancs
7 Cornwalls	8 Durhams	2 Rifle Brigade
Pioneers	Pioneers	Pioneers
11 Durhams	7 Durhams	22 Durhams

*Under command XVIII Corps as from 1 p.m. 21 March

†Under command XIX Corps as from 3.30 p.m. 21 March

‡Under Command XIX Corps as from 1 p.m. 22 March

marching Australians met pathetic groups of elderly refugees left behind in the villages when the more robust inhabitants fled in the first panic. Behind the refugees came the bedraggled, mud-covered stragglers of the British divisions. After them came machine gun bullets. From their support positions the Australians were able to watch the desperate resistance put up by companies of the 4th Guards Brigade which had been isolated by the German advance. Captain Tom Tannat Pryce, who had been involved in the savage house-to-house fighting the day before, held out for ten hours with only forty men left in his company. When the Germans brought field guns to within sixty yards of the trench he was holding, Pryce promptly led his handful of 4th Grenadiers in a bayonet charge that drove the enemy back. When he had only seventeen men left and the last cartridge had been fired he led his little band in yet another bayonet charge and was killed.[31, 60] A full company of the 2nd Irish Guards pushed stubbornly down the road to aid the Grenadiers but were forced to take cover by remorseless machine gun fire; one NCO and six men returned to their battalion that night.

The 3rd Coldstream, fighting on the right of the brigade, held out all that day against the German 35th Division. Two companies were practically wiped out and a solitary guardsman, the sole survivor of a platoon, held off single-handed a mob of Germans for twenty minutes before he was killed by a stick grenade.

Fighting stubbornly alongside these famous old regiments, those humble maids of all work – the divisional pioneers – proved equally tough customers and the Germans were forced to bring up mortars and literally blow the 12th KOYLI out of their position at close range. The pioneers retreated across open fields, where, the watching Australians reported, 'a tremendous number were scuppered'.

The resistance in the centre of the line was matched elsewhere, and although heavy attacks were made on Bailleul, only three miles from the vital hills guarding the flanks of Ypres, the total overall advance was less than half a mile and the elements of four battered British divisions were clearly unbroken. An infuriated Ludendorff, concerned with reports that the II Bavarian Corps headquarters was out of touch, relieved its commander at once. Further attacks, after strong artillery preparations, were to be made the next day.

Ludendorff must have realized with a growing sense of frustration that part of the failure was his own. Had he used his reserves earlier to exploit the weak front before Hazebrouck the attack might have carried there; but now the Australians and strong British formations were waiting for him. Alternately, he might have used these same reserves to smash through to the heights beyond Bailleul but here also fresh British troops were gathering and behind them the French 28th and 133rd Divisions were committed to the defence.

Nevertheless another battering attack was delivered early on the 14th. An amazed Australian corporal looked out of the farm where he had established a Lewis gun post and saw 'miles of infantry' marching over the countryside, with officers on horses riding up and down the columns. It was impossible to miss, even at long range. Seven brigades of artillery landed shells among the massed troops but throughout the day the Germans pressed forward wave on wave. The Australians held their fire until the range was sometimes as short as thirty yards. One German officer, shot down twice, got unsteadily to his feet and was heard plainly to shout 'Vorwarts! Vorwarts!' before being shot down a third time. The bodies of his men lay in a long row beside him. Four machine guns of the 95th Machine Gun Company, having been installed in the line during the night, found themselves with magnificent targets and an almost unlimited supply of ammunition. By mid-afternoon all movement in front of them had stopped and that evening they held fire while enemy stretcher bearers cleared the fields in front of their position.

The British did not have it all their own way. A forward German field gun near Merris knocked out six machine guns one after the other. Nevertheless the German losses were beginning to affect morale, even among officers.

A battalion of the German 141st Infantry, held up in front of the Nieppe Forest, recorded: 'The enemy is strong while our little handful is exhausted.' After an attack on Caudescure, a hamlet in front of the forest, the commander of the 22nd Reserve Infantry Regiment stated bluntly that it was useless to attack again without the total destruction of the village by artillery. Previous attacks had been broken by a hail of small arms fire from the windows. Caudescure remained untaken.

At this point, a personally signed order from Hindenburg ordered Rupprecht to concentrate on the right wing of the attack and to 'push on against the heights'. The Kaiser went so far as to call at the headquarters of the Sixth Army, with the same message. Whether inspired by this or not, the Alpine Corps and two other divisions forced their way into Bailleul after Wytschaete was lost by the British, recaptured, and lost again. Once more the luckless 59th Division bore the brunt and its 176th Brigade fought its way out of Bailleul when in danger of being surrounded. The following day the Germans seized the village of Meteren on the right of Bailleul after surrounding two companies of a New Zealand entrenching battalion. Efforts by a Royal Engineer unit succeeded in helping one company escape but the other was captured *en masse* – the largest haul of the New Zealanders taken by the Germans during the war.

These advances could be measured in hundreds of yards, however, and they cost thousands of lives Ludendorff could ill spare. Opposite Ypres itself the Germans could measure an advance in miles and without serious casualties. But this was of little comfort for the British positions on the hard-won Passchendaele Ridge had been held only by outposts since the night of 12 April. On the 15th the elements of five divisions holding the line outside Ypres trailed back over the greasy duckboard tracks, past the loathsome stagnant pools, the rusting wrecks of tanks, the still unburied bodies. Four out of the five divisions of the withdrawing troops had participated in the gruesome attacks to seize this unspeakable wilderness, and now the survivors of the earlier disasters covered in two nights the ground that had taken them three months to win. Plumer, so long the custodian of Ypres, had withdrawn the garrison from the sullen Salient to release further reserves for the battle to the south. The Germans were welcome to the Salient and its gas drenched marshes, its blackened, cracked pill-boxes, its pulverized villages and obliterated woods.

Although contemporary writers referred to Ypres as 'sacred ground' and to the surrender of this stagnant death trap as near blasphemy, the troops themselves were delighted.[23] Their commander may have paid lip-service to the tragedy of relinquishing what had been so dearly won, but they knew also the withdrawal would, by shortening the line, release troops desperately needed elsewhere. It also removed a tempting target for a major German assault (which in fact the German Fourth Army had actually been preparing). The preliminary barrage fell on empty positions and it took superhuman effort to heave the guns and ammunition forward again.

The reserves created by quitting the Passchendaele bulge were sorely needed. Once again, as had happened in March, Ludendorff rained a series of furious blows on the battle area. An enormous barrage fell between Merris and Meteren on 17 April but obviously had not been thoroughly registered. The Germans were shooting at 'pretty well everything marked on the map, farms, crossroads, villages, even some hedges'. The barrage missed the main defences and when it lifted British, Australian and French troops (two battalions of the Chasseurs Alpins had come into the line) poured a withering fire on the German assembly positions. South of Merris, the Australian 3rd Battalion could see German officers leaping in and out of their trenches trying to persuade the men to follow them. They had little success and when they did it led to slaughter. The German 23rd Infantry Regiment, a Silesian formation, noted that 'enemy machine guns from the flank had mown down whole ranks'.

After this failure to deepen the centre of the penetration, the Germans swung south to Bethune on the 18th, once again preceding the attack with a prodigious barrage. By this time the redoubtable 55th Division had been replaced by the 1st Division and the enemy penetrated hitherto impregnable defences. But the regular battalions of the 1st quickly recovered and the Germans were thrown out, although it was some time before a bloody struggle for a position known as Tuning Fork Switch was resolved.[1]

Despite these defensive successes, Haig was far from happy. At least seven of the British divisions holding the line on the right flank at Ypres had been reduced to dangerously weak proportions. Plans had already been made for a strategic withdrawal to lines near St Omer and the flooding of the low-lying area near Calais to reduce the front still further. As St Omer lies about twenty-five miles to the rear of Ypres, Foch ignored the suggested withdrawal and reluctantly ordered more French reserves north to relieve the weak British Divisions and maintain the present front.

French cavalry and infantry units also took over the line of hills which dominate the Flanders plain – the hills on which the German High Command had all this time kept their sights. Possession of these hills might provide the spectacular military success needed to create a new political situation. They must be taken. In order, therefore, to draw attention from his real design, Ludendorff prodded once more at an area about which both Haig and Foch felt particularly sensitive.

CHAPTER EIGHTEEN

LOOK NO PRISONERS

Villers Bretonneux had been the target of German guns since the abortive attack at the beginning of April. As the days passed the houses and the woods around it became saturated with mustard gas from the virtually non-stop bombardment. Although there were plenty of deep cellars, it had become impractical to station troops there. The woods, where new buds struggled for life in the uncertain spring, became untenable; in the Bois d'Aquenne, just west of the town, the horses of an entire artillery brigade could be seen lying dead in rows. Around 20 April the shelling of the town itself ceased but the Germans continued to blast the empty woods with gas and high explosive in the hope of catching concealed reserves.[16]

These ceaseless shell-storms formed a sombre backcloth for the young soldiers of the 8th Division, holding the front line outside Villers Bretonneux. Like other divisions cut up in the March offensive, the 8th had been brought up to strength with 'A4 Boys', mostly under nineteen years of age, few of whom had even started to shave. All day, the new recruits listened to the whine and whistle of shells on their way to the rear. By night, strong German patrols ambushed their raiding parties. Old hands noticed that the Germans had ominously refrained from erecting barbed wire in front of their positions, as if they were merely waiting for the order to move forward. It was also seen from aerial photographs that light railways had been extended to within a few hundred yards of the enemy front line.

A sergeant-major of the German 4th Guard Division captured on 22 April confirmed that his division had come into the line for the specific purpose of attacking the following day. That night the British artillery blasted possible forming-up places but the enemy did not come. The follow-

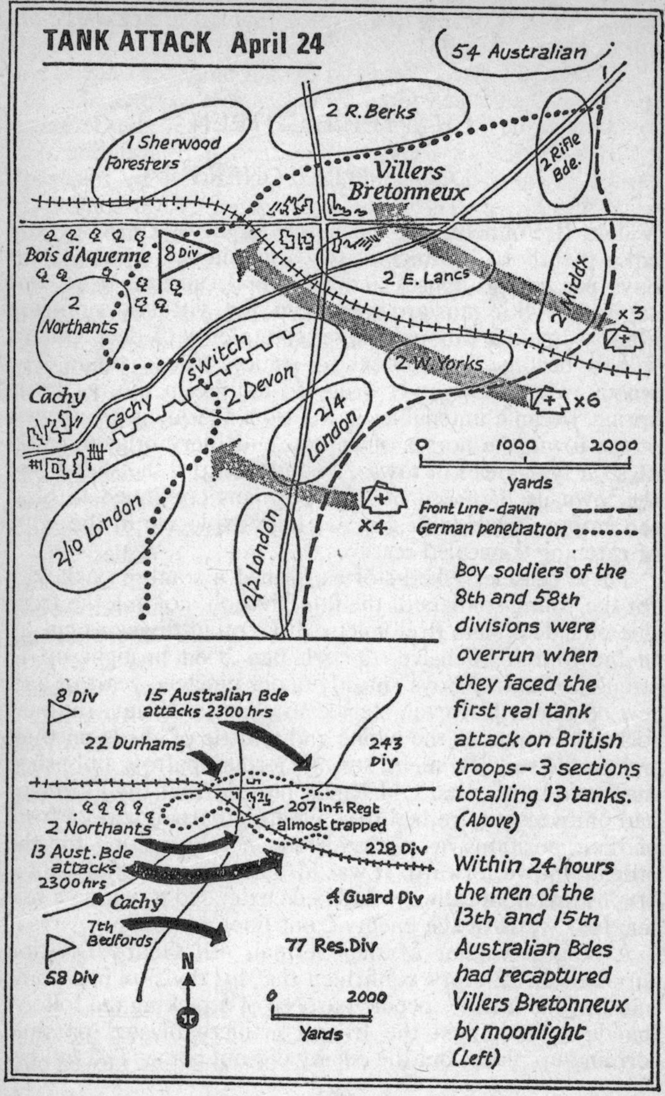

Boy soldiers of the 8th and 58th divisions were overrun when they faced the first real tank attack on British troops – 3 sections totalling 13 tanks. (Above)

Within 24 hours the men of the 13th and 15th Australian Bdes had recaptured Villers Bretonneux by moonlight (Left)

ing day other prisoners confirmed that an attack was due within twenty-four hours.[8]

On the night of the 23rd the British batteries once again hurled heavy concentrations on possible targets, the 18-pounders alone firing 100 rounds each. At 0330 the Germans replied with a super-heavy barrage from guns standing axle to axle in the fields near Marcelcave served by relays of artillery men stripped to the waist. About 0500 some batteries switched targets in the rear, while others fired smoke shells. About 0700 sentries peering from the wreckage of their posts on the front line saw strange, shadowy monsters lumbering out of the fog. Some thirteen German tanks, more cumbersome than the British models, but heavily armed with machine guns and one cannon, were almost upon the British trenches. Immediately rifle and Lewis gun fire was directed on them, but their armour was too solid. Three companies of the 2nd West Yorkshires and two of the 2nd Middlesex were overwhelmed as nine tanks straddled their trenches and poured machine gun fire into them. Some troops surrendered there and then; some fled in a panic through the fog; others fought back and were killed.

An officer with a support platoon of the Middlesex described how he was amazed to find a machine gun raking his trench from close by; any man who put his head over the parapet was immediately killed. When the machine gun fire ceased, this officer put up his head and saw 'An enormous and terrifying iron pill-box bearing down on him'. When this particular tank had passed right above the officer as he cowered in his trench he leaped to his feet and blazed away with his revolver at the water jacket of the rear machine gun, having realized that the rest of the vehicle was invulnerable. At the same time he ordered his boy soldiers to open fire on the supporting infantry, pinning them down. Only when two more tanks arrived was the German 228th Infantry Division able to advance. The Middlesex platoon tried to flee to a nearby railway cutting but nearly all were killed.

South of Villers Bretonneux another German tank clanked up to the headquarters trench system of the 2nd Devons, blew away most of the parapet, and then moved off.

Soon afterwards at least three more tanks overran two companies of the Devons. Others turned north followed by strong infantry formations which enveloped the 2nd Rifle Brigade. This battalion put up a desperate struggle, two companies fighting until they were all either killed or wounded. To the south, the 2/4th London Regiment were also driven from their trenches and clung to a line of shell holes.

German accounts show that the tank break-in created confused dog fights over the whole of the area in and around Villers Bretonneux. Eighty British troops counter-attacking the town, for example, captured twenty Germans; then, were themselves taken prisoner by two companies of the 5th Guard Grenadier Regiment.

The world's first tank versus tank battle was fought that morning when a British 'male' tank hit a German opponent three times with six-pounder shells and forced its crew to abandon it. Two other German tanks retreated under its fire. As he pulled out of action, the commander of the British tank enjoyed the cheering sight of seven small whippet tanks going into action at top speed. They disappeared over a rise where they dispersed two German battalions forming up for an attack. Only three of the whippets returned – with bloodstains on their hulls – but they had suffered a mere five casualties among the crews. German tanks claimed to have knocked out two of the whippets.

In the midst of this confusion, the British field guns gave a dashing display on the correct way to handle artillery in the open. Batteries and sections held on often after the infantry had retired and shot down the attackers with shrapnel. One gun took on a tank at 200 yards' range and drove it off after scoring three hits. Another crew ran their 18-pounder onto the railway bridge at Villers Bretonneux, pulled down the parapet, and opened fire on German troops packed into the cutting below them. It was perhaps this battering by field guns more than anything else that blunted the impetus of the advance and encouraged the remnants of the defending battalions to hang on. Troops of the 15th Australian Brigade spoke with admiration of the gunners firing furiously from exposed positions in the fields.

Not all Australians were as favourably impressed with the British troops. Brigadier H. E. Elliot, the dedicated but somewhat choleric commander of the 15th Brigade, hearing that British troops had withdrawn without orders and sometimes in a panic, ordered that they should be 'rallied and re-formed, as our troops march through them, by selected officers, and on any hesitation to be shot'.[3]

Having had experience of their eccentric commander's orders at Corbie some weeks earlier (when he threatened to hang in the main square any soldier caught looting) the officers of the brigade ignored the order and it was cancelled a few hours later by the divisional commander.

By the time night fell it became clear that the 8th Division (and units of the 58th) had managed to contain the first major tank attack on an Allied army on the Western Front (although tanks had been used in the March attack, the Germans had confined their role to mopping up; on the Lys the tanks merely broke down and jammed roads). The best part of two brigades had been killed or captured and the enemy was in possession of Villers Bretonneux, but they had failed to seize the important positions overlooking the town – positions essential to them if they hoped to push on towards Amiens.

Late in the afternoon Brigadier William Glasgow, of the 13th Australian Brigade, a subtler and less sanguine type than Elliott, arrived at 8th Division headquarters and was told that he would probably have to counter-attack. Setting off to assess the positions at first hand, Glasgow came across the headquarters of the 23rd and 24th Brigades under a high railway bridge in the fields. He found their respective Brigadiers, R. C. Haig and St George Grogan, exhausted by the strain of the day and able to give little information. The opportune arrival of 'one of those efficient young English Regular Army officers' who had just been on a tour of the area, enabled a clearer picture to be drawn and Glasgow motored back to his headquarters meeting his own battalions marching confidently up from the 4th Australian Division's billets in the rear.

Later when Glasgow discussed details of the counter-attack, he bluntly opposed a plan to strike at 2000. This was only a few minutes past sunset and the light would still be good for the enemy machine gunners. When Major-General Heneker, commander of the 8th Division, explained that this was the order of the III Corps Commander, Lieutenant-General Butler, Glasgow burst out, 'If it was God Almighty who gave the order it could not be done in the daylight.' Wisely 'Billy' Heneker, whose sympathy lay with the Australian, consulted his superior who eventually conceded that the Australian brigadier probably had something and the attack was postponed until 2200.

Brigadier Elliot had been equally forthright earlier in the day and wanted to try to retake Villers Bretonneux with his brigade alone. Heneker, aware that the German machine guns would decimate any move by day over the open hillside, vetoed the suggestion and based his expectations on an attack by moonlight – should there be any. In the end it was arranged that the Australian Brigades would attack on each side of the disputed town supported by the two remaining battalions of the 8th Division. As had already been arranged after Glasgow's intervention the time was fixed for 2200. Glasgow's battalion commanders gathered at the headquarters of the Northants in Blangy Wood under a crude tarpaulin and studied newly prepared maps by candlelight. Then off they moved into the darkness to lead their troops over completely strange ground against an enemy deployed in unknown strength.

The counter-attack of the 13th Brigade was one of the finest feats of the war. A German barrage opened as the Australians set off and they then encountered a diagonal belt of barbed wire which threw them off direction. At that moment Villers Bretonneux, which had been burning in a desultory fashion, received the full weight of the British bombardment and burst into vivid flames. Scores of RFC aircraft, specially ordered to add their weight to the attack, dumped bombs on the illuminated target adding to the blaze. With the town thus a fixed landmark, the Australians re-orientated themselves and burst upon the Germans just as reliefs were taking place, cookers were being brought up, and working parties were stringing wire. In a nightmare of tracer bullets, showers of flares, the roar of machine guns, screams, yells, and occasional cheers, battle was joined. To the right of the Australians, the 7th Bedfords and the Royal West Kents also attacked.

The medical officer of the 52nd Australian battalion recorded that, as he crouched behind a heap of mangel-wurzels with bullets whizzing all round, 'A little Tommy corporal came stumbling in, weeping like a kid and holding his arm.' Asked if he was in pain the lad replied: 'This is nothing, Sir, but I can't get the boys to go forward.' He had been trying to lead on a shaken platoon of youngsters. 'Never mind kid,' said a wounded Australian, 'Our boys will hunt Fritz without your kids.'

The 'kids' who made up the two British battalions attacking Villers Bretonneux, were committed against one of the toughest sections of the whole German line. The Northants were stopped by massed machine guns on the railway embankment and the 22nd Durhams struck similar opposition north of the town (where the Germans had been expecting the counter-attack to fall). Complaints by both Australian brigadiers that the support battalions had never left their starting points were subsequently disproved. The Durhams lost nearly 200 men – more than any of the Australian 15th Brigades' battalions – and the Northants lost 285 men including their colonel.

Ironically, the 15th Brigade was fortunate that its commander had been so keen to attack earlier in the day. Unscrambling the complicated arrangements he made took so long that his men set off more than an hour after the 13th Brigade attacked. With their attention distracted by the fighting to the south the Germans were taken completely by surprise and another wild, scrambling struggle ensued in which the Australians used their bayonets with deadly effect and, for at least part of the time, took no prisoners. 'They screamed for mercy but there were too many machine guns to show them any consideration as we were moving forward,' wrote Sergeant R. A. Fynch of the 59th Battalion (himself to die of wounds three months later). According to the Official History: 'Later, as the men tired of killing, prisoners came back in droves.'

The attack of the two brigades had basically achieved

what it had set out to do. Now it was the turn of the Germans to be trapped in Villers Bretonneux and it was due only to the energetic action of a battalion commander of their 207th Infantry Regiment, Captain Teichmann, that some sort of control was restored. The town was then attacked from a different quarter as the 2nd Royal Berkshires and the 57th Australian battalion moved in to mop up. Throughout the early hours of the morning house-to-house fighting continued as the Germans first tried to counter-attack and then to escape under cover of a mist. On the third anniversary of 'Anzac' (the Australian and New Zealand assault at Gallipoli) the gap created by the German tank attack was forcibly closed. The enemy formations fought fiercely throughout the day but their casualties and disorganization were such that the 19th Bavarian Reserve Division had to be used to relieve the assault troops.

At the very moment the Australians and British were driving back the Germans from the approaches to Amiens, Ludendorff returned to his true objective. At 0310 hours another withering artillery barrage crashed down on the front from Bailleul to just short of Ypres. Two hours later the crack Alpine Corps swept round the lower slopes of Kemmel Hill and overwhelmed the forward troops of the French 28th and 154th Divisions. By 1000 most of the 'impregnable' hill's defences were in German hands although a French plane reported continued fighting late in the day. Fortunately, the rest of the chain of heights remained in French hands and a bitter struggle began to regain Kemmel Hill.

Troops of the British 25th Division, rushed up from the rear where they had been enjoying a well-earned rest, went splashing through the Kemmelbeek that evening and fought their way back furiously into Kemmel village where they took 300 prisoners. The village, however, was dominated by the 500-foot hill beyond it and incessant machine gun fire drove back the attacking troops. Within hours the Germans attacked again and pushed back these troops still farther.[59]

On a front of eight miles or so between Kemmel and the boundary with the Belgian Army beyond Ypres there were elements of ten British divisions. The French had four infantry and two cavalry to hold a much narrower and stronger front line along the vital hills. For Foch and the French the loss of Kemmel proved an embarrassing experience. Haig noted scathingly in his diary: 'General Dimitry commanding the French Corps in Second Army had to employ French cavalry to collect the French fugitives from Kemmel, and prevent a rout. What Allies to fight with.'[6] Yet had Ludendorff taken the fleeting opportunity that opened up when the attackers first seized Kemmel, this apparent rout might have been turned into a genuine calamity, for Haig had virtually no reserves. A pause for regrouping, however, enabled the gap to be covered and the battle dissolved into a slogging match during which three more French divisions arrived. As late as 29 April massed regiments of Germans with fixed bayonets charged against the same British units which had been in the line since Kemmel fell. Once again reserves were made available by a withdrawal which still further flattened the Ypres salient much to the chagrin of Foch who regarded the voluntary surrender of one foot of land as a crime.

The assault was extended along both the French and Belgian sectors at either end of the British line. An excited French artillery observer, straining his eyes on the summits, saw German soldiers through a rift in the wreaths of smoke. Winding frantically at his telephone he reported that the enemy had taken the Scherpenberg and Mont Rouge, the hills adjacent to Kemmel in the chain held by the French. The commander of the French 39th Division quickly relayed the report to General Plumer, at Second Army headquarters. Plumer, appalled by the news, and fearing envelopment from the rear, phoned GHQ. Haig at once ordered Lawrence (the chief of staff who had been so unhelpful to Gough in his hour of need) to drive to Plumer's headquarters and warn him to prepare for a withdrawal to the St Omer line they had discussed earlier. Then, after a quick conference with his intelligence chief and his director of transport, Haig also went racing to Plumer's headquarters at Cassel. He arrived about 1300 his mind filled with details of the possible retirement, only to find that the report had been a false alarm. The French still held the two hills and although the enemy had penetrated between them the attack had foundered in a cross-fire of French machine guns. The village of Locre had been entered but the French were resisting fiercely and continued to do so throughout the next day.[14] By that time Ludendorff had decided to call a halt, but his baleful gaze remained fixed upon Flanders which he had always believed was where he would win the war. His mind had been unchanged by recent events. He would create a diversion elsewhere and would strike again at the hills. In the meantime, all troops that could be spared would be withdrawn for training for the next offensive. Ludendorff looked to his resources. His losses were around 500,000 men but still he could count on a reserve of eighty-two divisions by mid-May as the rest of the troops from Russia arrived. This would give him a superiority of twenty-five divisions over the Allies.

British losses during the period of non-stop battle were just over 300,000 although 93,000 of these were missing or prisoner. With fifty-five divisions they had fought off 109 German divisions, and now could depend only on raw recruits from home or the arrival of formations from other theatres of war to make up the deficiency. Of the ninety-nine French Divisions in existence on 21 March only thirty-two had been involved with losses in the region of 92,000, but these casualties could not readily be replaced; the cities and villages of France had already been denuded of men.

Only in the cramped holds of British steamers crossing the Atlantic was there any real hope of substantial reinforcements. A contemporary newspaper carried the headline 'London's Stunning Welcome to U.S.A. Troops' over a picture showing a mass of men marching past King George V and Queen Mary outside Buckingham Palace. By the end of May 120,000 Yanks would be in France and were to be assisted in their training by men who knew something about the business of war – the cadres of the 39th, 66th, 30th, and 34th Divisions. One or two of the latter, perhaps, might have given the Americans a heartier welcome had they arrived in March or April.

CHAPTER NINETEEN

BACK TO SCHOOL

It was May. In England the cricket season had begun; in London, Westminster School lost by 78 runs to 35 to Essex Club and Ground. The Carl Rosa Opera reopened in the capital with *Carmen*, and Harry Lauder raised a laugh in packed houses. Servants were promised 'a new era' with a fabulous standard wage of thirty shillings a week.

But not everyone was left in peace. Certificates of exemption granted men in vital industries could now be overruled because of the emergency; men of fifty-five abruptly found themselves in uniform. The return of recovered wounded was speeded up and in France itself the big comb-out was commenced. Hundreds of men who had been employed on the canals were now available for service in the trenches. (For three years units of the Royal Engineers had worked on barges moving ammunition and stores, or fitted with bunks and medical facilities. It was more comfortable for a wounded man to glide smoothly to hospital on a canal than bump over battered roads in an ambulance but most canals were now in enemy hands.)

Further, as the lines of communication shrank, the Army Service Corps was able to release storemen and drivers, and even the army's jails were emptied. On 18 April, the 8th Durhams received twelve men of the Royal Irish Rifles – all under suspended sentences. Suspended sentences were common because by 1918 some old hands preferred prison to the trenches.

The Durhams were typical of many of the infantry battalions which had been through the thick of the fighting. Towards the end of the month they received a draft of 190 ASC and ninety Royal Engineer other ranks, plus forty-four soldiers described as 'old B.E.F. men of various regiments'. These new drafts sometimes received graphic indications of

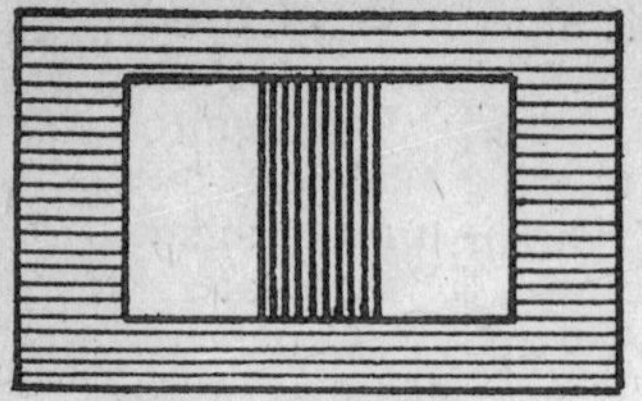

1st Cavalry Division
(Red & White on Blue)

3rd Cavalry Division
(White on Black)

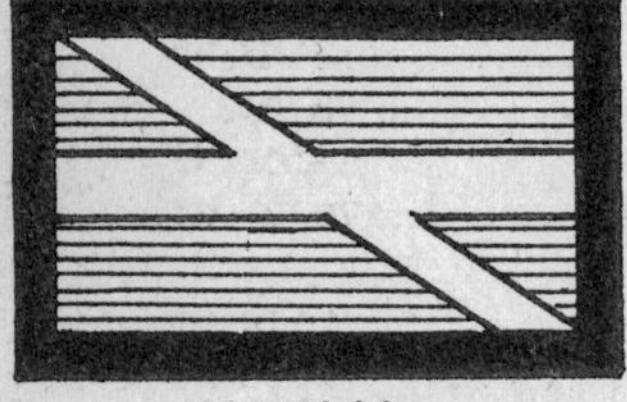

14th Division
(White on Yellow)

61st Division
(Black on Red)

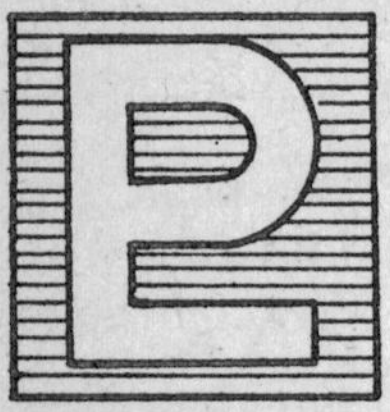

16th Division Transport
(Yellow on Blue)

16th Division (Personnel)
(Green on Brown)

21st Division
(Red on Black)

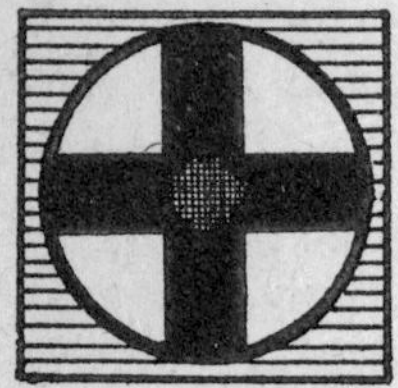

20th Division
(Red, White & Black on Blue)

39th Division
(White and Blue)

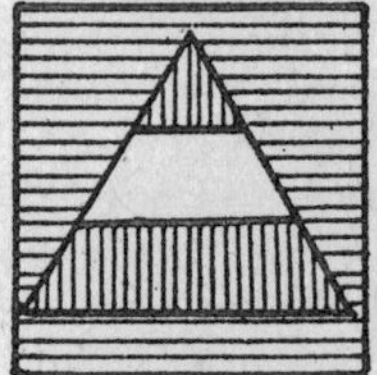

66th Division
(Yellow & Blue on Orange)

what they might expect. Private Frank Bestwick, arriving with a group of eighteen-year-olds bound for the 8th Division, reconstituted after its ordeal on the approaches to Amiens, found himself billeted in a barn with two survivors of the March retreat. 'Both of them ran amok with fixed bayonets the first night I arrived,' he wrote later. 'They were shouting to imaginary Germans "Come on you bastards" and it was with great difficulty that we restrained them – one of them was a full corporal – and got them quiet again. No one got any sleep that night.'[71]

Shortly afterwards a medical officer told Bestwick that he was not fit to go into the line. Bestwick had had most of his lower teeth extracted before coming to France and was not able to hold the mouthpiece of his box respirator. Until he was fixed up with false teeth he would have to wait. He watched his friends march off without him to join the 22nd Durhams, little knowing that he would never see them again. Ironically, they were bound for what Foch euphemistically described as the 'secteurs calmes du front français'. Later, as a Lewis gunner, Private Bestwick (complete with bottom dentures) was to see much fierce fighting, but it is unlikely that it surpassed what his young comrades experienced in the 'calm sectors of the French front'.

Destined for these trenches of tranquillity were five divisions which had seen the worst fighting of the preceding weeks. Three were veterans of the Fifth Army – the 8th (which had losses of 8,600 men since 23 March), the 50th, and the 21st. The others (the 25th and the 19th) had been through the thick of the fighting on the Third Army front; all five had been in costly battles since. As they arrived in the French area 'les Khakis' were carefully indoctrinated. All officers and NCOs down to platoon sergeant level were treated to lectures on 'The French Army and its customs', and 'The commanders of the French Sixth Army', given by a senior officer of IX British Corps.[65] No doubt that gentleman did his best, but one thing he could not easily explain to the troops was that they had come under the orders of one of the most controversial leaders in the French Army, General Duchêne, nicknamed 'The Tiger' (although the words were not spoken with the same affection as when applied to the redoubtable old Clemenceau, who was similarly dubbed).

A French historian described Duchêne, who fancied that he might one day succeed Pétain as Commander-in-Chief, as stubborn and hard. He was detested by his staff whom he terrorized with his bullying. These were not necessarily ruinous qualities for a soldier, but they were hardly calculated to make him the ideal custodian of British divisions whose men were either raw or exhausted.[10]

First to arrive under the claws of The Tiger were the 50th Division. They had a week of drill and instruction, a field day, and a parade ending in a march past at which the corps commander (Lieutenant-General Sir Hamilton Gordon) took the salute. By 7 May they were ordered into the trenches. Hamilton Gordon's surprise at this swift move elicited the comment that with things so quiet the rest and training programme could still be carried on regardless. Hamilton Gordon and his subordinates were further distressed when they saw the line they were destined to occupy. The British generals knew from bitter experience the effects of a German gas and high explosive barrage on crowded front trenches. And the disadvantages and problems of falling back on a river-canal line, with all the bridges to be demolished, as on the Somme and the Lys, were memories a few weeks' old. Yet they were being asked to expose the men to exactly the dangers that they had learned to avoid.

The position allocated by Duchêne for the British corps was the right wing of the legendary hog's back known as the Chemin des Dames, an ancient highway running just below the crest of a long ridge, roughly parallel to the Aisne river and its attendant canal.

In May 1918 the front lay fourteen miles north of Soissons. It ran some seventeen miles west to east until it turned at an obtuse angle and continued for twenty miles straight to Rheims. The plan was for the British to take over the blunt salient caused by the angle, with the 50th Division on the left, the 8th Division to its right, and the 21st Division on the other face of the angle. In vain the British commanders pointed out that to station the bulk of their troops between the ridge and the Aisne would be to court disaster; they would be merely presenting a tightly packed layer of men and guns to German artillery. There would be no escape should a major offensive be launched. The commander of the 22nd French Territorial Division on the left of the 50th, which had been among the first reserves sent by Pétain to the aid of the Fifth Army in March, also complained only to be overruled.

General Duchêne brooked no opposition and some of his subordinates obviously took their cue from him. When Major-General David Campbell, of the 21st Division, told a Frenchman that the position could not be held for twenty-four hours against a major attack he was told haughtily, if erroneously, that it had been held for two years.[14]

Such differences of opinion, happily, were concealed from the British troops marching up in the fine spring weather. And indeed, there was a certain atmosphere to the sector which made the complacency of the French command almost credible. In normal times, thick woods grow in patches on the slopes of the ridge and the fields on the plateaux are worked by peasants. There are cattle and vines and crops. In the early part of the war the area had been the scene of bloody fighting which culminated in the horror of the Nivelle offensive of April 1917 when machine gunners concealed among the rocky outcrops had cut swathes in the attacking waves. A coup by General Maistre had seized the ridge in October 1917 and the French had held it ever since. Peace had again established itself in the martyred landscape. Captain Sydney Rogerson, serving at the headquarters of the 23rd Brigade wrote later, 'The woods had been blasted by the shell fire of the previous year, but now each shattered tree stump had covered its wounds with close foliage. In the shell holes grass had grown and water plants; near the gun emplacements of the reserve line grew lilies of the valley, forget-me-nots, larkspur and honeysuckle. The whole battle area had become a garden fashioned by artillery.'[55] Amid the flowers and tall grass, wrecked tanks and barbed wire rusted undisturbed. Only rare artillery bursts hammered sinister echoes through the sunny calm of these sleepy hollows, but these sounds were not strong enough to reach the ears of General Duchêne, reigning tyranically over his staff in Soissons.

For the younger British troops there was too much to learn for them to be apprehensive. For the veterans of the grey, flat dreariness of Flanders, the change of scenery was welcome and comparisons interesting. The headquarters of the 8th Durhams at Chaudardes, a hamlet in the Aisne valley, actually contained ten civilians and although there were deep dug-outs, the men were billeted in ruined houses 'very comfortable for all ranks.' (It was noted rather casually that the village was 'under direct observation from enemy balloons.)

On 12 May a special brigade school was set up to train the rawest soldiers. As the 8th Durhams had to send 217 men to this school they were much under strength and a company of the 7th Durhams was attached to the battalion so it could take its place in the line. These extracts from the War Diary give a clear idea of the efficiency of the battalion.

> May 13: In order to hasten the training of A.S.C. and I.W.T. [Inland Water Transport attached to the Royal Engineers] drafts it was decided to select the best 25 men from Brigade School and attach them to the company in the front line for a six-day tour of duty, then to return them to the school for further training.
>
> May 14: In trenches Aisne front. A quiet day. Special attention was paid to instructing men in trench routines as few had been in trenches prior to this.
>
> May 15: A quiet day. The trenches were very exposed to view in several places; camouflage curtains were erected and certain trenches deepened where necessary. Maps of trenches were found to be inaccurate so careful reconnaisance was made and accurate maps prepared.

While the men trained, the officers got to know each other. Four of the new arrivals came from the Royal Irish Rifles and a fifth from the Dublin Fusiliers. Captain K. H. Ewing, of the United States Army Medical Corps, quickly learned to weed out the malingerers in the morning sick parade.

South of the river, on the height known as the Bois de Gernicourt, Private Bestwick's former comrades did their best to communicate with the grizzled French Territorials who formed part of the garrison. The Frenchmen painstakingly showed the boys the difference between their own *mitrailleuse* and the Vickers. In reserve, the 6th Durhams even found time to visit 'The Jesmond Jesters', the divisional concert party.

But on the other side of no-man's-land, other soldiers were busy. Troops bustled about the Rue de France and the Avenue Jesse-de-Foret at Ludendorff's forward headquarters in Avesnes. In the streets, strolling placidly with his son-in-law, Field Marshal Hindenburg benevolently responded to the raised hats of the civilians.[10] Ludendorff himself was rarely seen. He had too much to do. Virtually three offensives were in simultaneous preparation, all aimed ultimately at smashing the British in Flanders. The assault on the Chemin des Dames was to be a compelling, massive diversion. Once the ridge was taken his generals had instructions to cross the Aisne and halt on the Vesle which ran parallel to the Aisne some miles beyond it over another ridge. There they were to form a defensive position, in the same way that Hutier, in March, had formed a shield along the Somme. Occasionally a familiar figure was seen in conference with the Prussian master-mind: Colonel Bruchmüller. In Bruchmüller's wake had come trainloads of guns. Laon, a key city in German hands in front of the Chemin des Dames, was well supplied with railways, and the flat fields and orchards stretching out to the foothills made excellent positions for the heavy artillery and the ammunition dumps.

Secrecy, strength, and surprise were the order of the day. At the end of April there were only seven German divisions before the ridge; by 20 May a total of twenty-nine had been concentrated near Laon. The guns (French estimates put them as high as 5,200 including 1,600 heavy and super-heavy pieces, and 800 of the biggest minenwerfers) were moved during the night, hauled into the fields and hidden in camouflaged emplacements or in the undergrowth before dawn. A giant policing operation attempted to secure the area from prying eyes, although few enough French civilians remained between Laon and the ridge. Stations were guarded, and regimental and divisional identification marks removed from vehicles. Creaking joints were oiled, horses' hoofs muffled, and loose equipment and chains secured. That, despite these security precautions, such a massive array could gather unnoticed by French observation planes and unreported by spies seems almost unbelievable; that this vast host could be coiled to spring forward without a hint of its objectives being conveyed to the Allied high command is almost incredible. Yet so it happened.

Foch, it seems, was immersed with his own plans for an offensive to free the approaches to Amiens and restore lateral railway communications. Haig, fearing the resumption of an attack on the Arras-Albert front, was glad to see French reserves gathered there. Pétain, Commander-in-Chief of the whole French front, accepted reports from his intelligence service that all was quiet. Only the junior partner, American military intelligence, insisted that Chemin des Dames was the target for the next blow. No one took the newcomers seriously.[43, 51]

In the trenches before the Chemin des Dames, old hands noted the enemy artillery had become more active and that there was an ominous increase in the number of single shell bursts just as if new batteries were registering. Attempts at patrolling met unusually fierce resistance. If Duchêne ever received these reports he paid scant attention to them. Earlier in the year, when Pétain had issued Directive No. 4 laying down the principles of elastic defence (that is, to hold the front with mere outposts while the main defence belt was pulled out of range of the deep enemy shell carpet), General Roque, a member of the French government, challenged the theory on political grounds. He did this so astutely that Clemenceau was drawn into a clash with Pétain over its viability. Pétain offered to resign, and although he was not allowed to, the damage was done. Generals who did not agree with Directive No. 4 ignored it. Duchêne was among them. To regard the Chemin des Dames as an expendable outpost line and to station his main defences on the south bank of the Aisne could be bad for public morale, he said, taking heed that Foch too was lukewarm about 'la défense élastique'.[10]

The unhappy British generals, unable to influence the situation at a high level, redoubled their patrols. For the men from the brigade schools, this was a chance to put their lessons into practice and they entered into the task enthusiastically. A group of men from the 8th Durhams, stealthily observing a gap in the German wire on 25 May, saw three men coming down a path in the dusk, heading for a listening post. As the patrol tried to cut them off, sixty Germans appeared through the undergrowth and a bomb fight ensued which drove the Germans to ground. Hurriedly the raiders seized a wounded German (he turned out to be a twenty-two-year-old Polish corporal) hurled him bodily over the wire, and retreated with their prisoner under cover of a shower of rifle grenades. A subsequent report recorded with regret that their only casualty '907 Private Carrington' had been left dead 150 yards from the enemy line. The prisoner, from the 4th company of the 444th Infantry Regiment proved most interesting. His division was due to be relieved soon, he said, although he did not know when. Had fresh troops then, arrived secretly in the area? If so, why?

Even as the prisoner was being questioned the 77s and 5.9s were being man-handled into their assault pits. Two million shells were stacked in the shadows. Oblivious of this menace, the French Sixth Army issued an official intelligence message to General Hamilton Gordon; 'In our opinion there are no indications that the enemy has made preparations which would enable him to attack tomorrow.'[14] No indications, indeed. The following night, the British captured a cadet-officer of the 41st Field Artillery Regiment near Juvincourt, a unit which had not been identified on this front previously. Closely questioned he denied all knowledge of attack preparations, but his guardedness left his examiners with an uneasy feeling. On the French 22nd Division's front, a soldier of the 13th Jäger Battalion was less reticent; 'Offensive rations' had already been issued, he stated and Guard units in the line were believed to be the same regiments which had lost the ridge the previous year. The Jäger even gave the hour of the barrage. It would fall at 0200 hours.[10] General Renouard, commander of the 22nd Division, sent for the uncommunicative cadet-officer still detained in the British cage. Without ceremony he was handed over to the Deuxieme Bureau and told that he was to be shot as a spy for giving false information according to the laws of war – unless he was prepared to tell the truth, of course. The frightened cadet told the truth. It corroborated the Jäger's information. Sixth Army intelligence message No. 6335/2 announced that the prisoner had amended his original statement which, added to information supplied by escaped French prisoners, seemed conclusive. Still Duchêne hesitated. A French observation plane reported as late as the afternoon of the 26th that the region of the Ailette stream, which ran through no-man's-land in front of the French defences was deserted. There were no fires, no soldiers, no convoys, no new camps. Was it a false alarm?

On the ground, however, British outposts had noticed that black boards, which they guessed might be used to guide tanks, had been erected in the German lines. Much hammering and banging had been heard in the night. Hamilton Gordon had no doubts. A signal based on the circulated intelligence reports was sent to his divisions; 'The enemy will attack on a broad front at 0100 [the British forces in France, curiously perhaps, still used British summertime] hours tomorrow.'[8] Instructions to man battle stations followed. As Captain Rogerson put it: 'The landscape smiled no longer. It was all a grinning unreality, a mockery. . . .'[55] Resigned to the inevitable, a British battalion which had been through it all before recorded, 'Stragglers posts were established as per instructions previously received.'[65]

In another world, miles away in London, a carefree audience was waiting for the curtain to go up on the 500th performance of 'The Better 'Ole'.

CHAPTER TWENTY

SHOOT THE DEVILS

The beautiful summer evening faded slowly in the soft silence. As the moonless darkness deepened, hoarse orders broke the stillness and British 18-pounders opened a slow harrassing fire on possible approaches to the ridge. From time to time a rapid slamming noise marked the contribution of quick-firing French 75s. Yet from the mysterious area north of Chemin des Dames, now speckled with the flame bursts of searching shell, there came . . . nothing.

Troops stared anxiously over the parapets and through loopholes at the undergrowth of no-man's-land stirring mysteriously in the flickering light of the gun flashes. In deep dug-outs and tunnels, already uncomfortably hot, platoon and company officers assigned their men work to take their minds off impending events; 'Fill those belts'; 'Move that box of bombs nearer the stairs'; 'Check your men's waterbottles, sergeant'; 'Just do as you're told son and you'll be all right.'

At midnight, dozing youngsters were startled by a rolling, rumbling noise and looked anxiously at their superiors. They were reassured. It was only the British heavies commencing their 'counter-preparation'. In the French gun lines there was nervous activity. Duchêne, still not convinced that the enemy was about to strike, had ordered that at the first sign of violent shelling his batteries were to 'respond as vigorously as possible'.[10] Bearded Territorials muttered in low tones and slowly sipped the rough red issue wine; it might have to last some time. To the east, dark-eyed Bretons peered out uneasily from dimly-lit concrete bunkers in the gloomy Pinon Forest. Their unit had not been in serious action since March 1917 but they would soon have every opportunity to rectify this deficiency.

Whatever their nationality or regiment, it proved to have

been unnecessary for Allied officers to glance so often at their watches as the taut, pitiless minutes had marched by. At precisely 0100 watchers in the valley of the Aisne saw the black mass of the Chemin des Dames outlined against a brilliant sheet of lightning as an enormous thunder clap rolled back and forth along the hills. Thousands of shell bursts flamed brightly on the reverse slopes, in the valley itself, on woods and fields, on villages miles to either side and to the rear. Bruchmüller excelled himself on 27 May.

He had massed forty batteries to the mile on the front of the 50th Division and French 22nd Division (compared with the mere 35.6 to the mile which had blasted the Fifth Army on 21 March).[14] Also, instead of concentrating the opening ten minutes upon the enemy artillery, as on previous occasions, he had ordered all weapons to fire gas shells at the highest possible rate at targets dispersed over the widest possible area for the same period. Having created maximum confusion, all guns then switched to a mixture of high explosive and gas shells. Mustard gas, Green Cross, tear gas, and some smoke descended on the Allied artillery, while German mortars stripped barbed wire entanglements with their powerful blasts.

Faced with this lethal deluge, the Allied gunners were hardly in a position to reply 'as vigorously as possible' although with gas masks on, they did their best. For more than an hour German shells crashed onto the British artillery hurling 75s and 18-pounders out of their pits. Timbered emplacements caught fire. Dumps exploded in pillars of flame and smoke. One British battery later reported, 'The enemy's shooting seemed uncannily accurate'.[8] The observation balloons had done their job well.

At 0215 certain Allied batteries reported that the barrage around them was intensifying, and other batteries in the rear (which had been spared until then), suddenly found great gouts of smoking earth towering above them, and shells scoring direct hits on howitzers or high velocity guns. Phase three of Bruchmüller's plan had now come into operation, and groups of his guns were now directing their fire onto selected targets among the opposing artillery, especially the long-range pieces. This tornado lasted well over an hour. Shortly after half past three in the morning, the fire pattern changed again and the Germans began to pound the front trenches with shells and mortar bombs of all calibres.

The ordeal of the Allied infantry now reached its climax. Those in the outpost trenches were caught under collapsing parapets and buried alive in the charred earth. Others cowered in deep dug-outs, their mouths burning from sucking at the mouthpiece of their respirators, saliva bubbling in the tube and fighting back a hysterical urge to tear off their masks and gulp down deep draughts of air. Clods of soil rolled down the stairs and the thudding vibration continued non-stop. Timber supports creaked and cracked showering dust and dirt on their steel helmets. 'The long night was spent forty feet underground, at the hottest time of the year, in stinking overcrowded holes, their entrances sealed up . . . [with antigas blankets] . . . and charcoal braziers [another anti-gas precaution] drying up the atmosphere,' wrote Captain Rogerson.[55]

In the tunnels beneath the Bois des Buttes the 2nd Devons found the heat almost unbearable.[14] Over the Aisne, in Gernicourt Wood, crazed horses bolted with wagons carrying ammunition boxes to the garrison. Ignoring the hail of shrapnel lashing the trees, two conscientious Indian drivers struggled to right their ditched vehicles.[59] By the time Maharaj Singh and Nathan Singh had succeeded in doing this, the quality of the uproar had changed. The assault had begun.

Screened by mist, smoke, and gas the storm troops left their trenches as soon as the barrage switched to the front trenches and crawled as near as they dared to the flaying, sizzling curtain of flying metal. Hauling themselves forward through the undergrowth on their elbows they lay prone, heads down, waiting for the whistles. Opposite the 22nd French division lay the German 28th Division; opposite the 50th, the 5th Guard Division awaited its opportunity to regain the ridge for the Kaiser. About 0345 they got their chance. On a front of nearly forty miles, the advance guards tramped forward over the burned and powdered wreckage of the front trenches. A few marshy places in the bottom of the valley gave the assault troops more trouble than the rifles of the defenders. 'For the second time in the war [the first having been at Messines in June 1917] what had so often been attempted had been achieved,' says the British Official History. 'So thorough had been the preliminary destruction that all resistance was crushed and the infantry had only to advance to take possession of the front position.'

The German 28th Division, scrambling up the steep slopes to the attack, found deranged and tattered figures lurching aimlessly around the devastated area. The remainder of the middle-aged French Territorials seem to have been swept away by the violence of the storm unleashed upon them. Quickly, the 28th ordered regiments to the right and left to penetrate behind their surviving opponents. The 150th Brigade on the flank of the 50th Division was the first to suffer.

The three British divisions had their brigades in line to cover the extended front, with precious little to support them. At the first change in the tone of the barrage, experienced officers leaped into the deadly grey dawn and ordered the men to open rapid fire to their front. Others failed to realize that zero hour was upon them and soon found German grenades pouring into their confined underground shelters. Others tore frantically with their hands at the splintered planks and part-filled entrances to the dugouts. For still others the hissing, roaring, oily-smoked bursts of fire from German flame thrower teams persuaded the trapped men to surrender.

On the left of the 50th Division, the 4th East Yorks were gradually overwhelmed and the 5th Green Howards, who had not been attacked frontally, were ordered to restore the position. The Green Howards pressed forward with great determination into the battle haze and found themselves immersed in a flood of Germans. The last message received from their colonel was that his headquarters staff were fighting all round his command post and that he appeared to be surrounded. Not long afterwards the colonel and most of his men were dead. The 4th Green Howards advanced to try to seal the gap. 'A' Company made a probing counter-attack and was literally swept away by a storm of shells; the survivors of the battalion clung to some houses near Craonelle until their commanding officer was killed and all his men had become casualties. The 150th Brigade no longer existed and Brigadier-General Rees, survivor of both the previous great offensives, was a prisoner.[14, 68]

To the right, German tanks and infantry moved forward up the gentle slope of the Craonne Plateau close behind the shell curtain and hit the 151st Brigade head on. A whole company of the 5th Durhams was captured before it left its dug-outs and was hustled to the rear, through long, hurrying columns of men in grey. Two sister companies trying an optimistic counter-attack ran into an entire German regiment and fell back, fighting for their lives, on a company of the 7th Durhams and two companies of Royal Engineers. The other two battalions of the 151st suffered heavily in the front line and although a number of stubborn strong points took a considerable toll of the enemy the brigade had ceased to exist as an organized formation by 0800. Brigadier-General Martin, another survivor of the Somme and the Lys, lay dead, killed by a shell as he and his old friend Riddell were conferring. Riddell, an individualist, had deliberately refrained from obeying French orders to the letter and had maintained his posts on the forward slope with only skeleton garrisons. His main strength had been concentrated on the reverse slopes where the best part of two battalions put up a defiant struggle, falling back slowly to a switch trench. But by 0600 four captured British tanks, now bearing German markings, were rampaging through the area amid clouds of dust and smoke spouting bullets and shells. The 4th and 6th Northumberlands were annihilated and only four hours after the infantry assault had begun the 5th Northumberlands were the only formed body remaining in the 50th Division. The staff of divisional HQ itself only just managed to escape.

Riddell, wounded by the same shell that killed Brigadier-General Martin, sent the following laconic message to the 23rd Brigade at the height of the confusion: 'Enemy has broken our battle line and is advancing on Ville au Bois.'[8] This was alarming news for the enemy had penetrated the right wing of the division also. Aided by tanks, and under cover of a thick ground mist, the enemy had broken through at the junction of the 24th and 25th Brigades; as early as 0515 strong bodies of storm troops were splashing along the marshy banks of the Miette where it ran into the 8th Division area from no man's land and marked the boundary between the two brigades. Another break-in along the valley of the Aisne meant that the 25th Brigade was effectively surrounded and that the 8th Division was losing contact with the 21st Division on its right.

Just after 0600 a bedraggled pigeon fluttered into the 8th Division headquarters at Roucy on the south bank of the Aisne. Anxious fingers removed the message from its leg:

> H.Q. 2nd Royal Berkshire Regiment, consisting of Lieutenant-Colonel Griggin, Captain Clare, R.S.M. Wokins, Sergeant Trinder, Corporal Dobson, Privates Stone, Gregory, Slee and Quartermaster, surrounded. Germans threw bombs down dug-outs and passed on. Appeared to approach from right rear in considerable strength. Holding out in hopes of relief.

By the time the message arrived, however, its senders had been wiped out. Brigadier-General Hussey, with his staff and a handful of the 2nd East Lancs, was fighting his way back to the river where he proceeded to superintend the blowing up of every bridge within sight. Within a matter of hours he was to be badly gassed and receive a mortal wound.

Despite a resolute defence by the 1st Worcesters in the support trenches, the Germans swept on – the colonel of the Worcesters was killed with his men. Brigadier Haig and his staff fell back, choking from the effects of gas, as the net closed around the 2nd Northants in the front line. Resistance ended soon after. Lieutenant-Colonel C. G. Buckle was killed outside his headquarters in a trench littered with dead Germans. Battle-stained, jackbooted soldiers cast a quick glance into the HQ dug-out and left. Pinned to the wall fluttering unevenly with the concussions of battle was Buckle's last message to his men: 'All platoon commanders will remain with their platoons and ensure that the trenches are manned immediately the bombardment lifts. Send short situation wire every half hour. No short bombardment can possibly cut our wire and if the sentries are alert it cannot be cut by hand. If they try to, shoot the devils.'*

To the left of Buckle's battalion, the 2nd West Yorks and 2nd Middlesex were making a last stand, virtually back to back, supported by a handful of French artillerymen. The ex-British tanks which had created such havoc here too but were knocked out one after the other by the French 75s. This gave the trench garrison a brief respite but in the end only the irrepressible Lieutenant-Colonel Lowry of the West Yorkshires (limping with a bullet in his foot), one corporal of his battalion, and a handful of the Middlesex made their way back.

The third British division, the 21st, lost the eleven companies which were holding the forward lines (for the most part only a few hundred yards deep in front of the Aisne canal).[14] But a considerable proportion of the 21st's artillery escaped destruction and as the Germans tried to come on, the constant crack of shrapnel overhead and the boom of sixty-pounders lobbed into their midst, slowed them down. On the right, the French 45th (Colonial) Division held on at Rheims, and the 21st was able to pivot on the hinge it provided, hoping thus to provide some protection for the retreating remains of the 8th and 50th Divisions heading for the bridges over the Aisne.

As soon as he had been informed of the impending attack, Heneker had pressed for the destruction of the main three-arch stone bridge at Berry au Bac, on the right rear of his division. Permission was refused. Duchêne ordered that no bridges were to be destroyed without direct instructions from Sixth Army Headquarters. To further complicate matters most of the men best qualified to destroy the bridges – the Royal Engineers – had been drawn into the action as infantry. In the end, although thirty-three of the forty-two bridges were destroyed, those which remained gave the Germans an opportunity they were not slow to take.

*This message was found still in position when Buckle's father visited the site after the war.

The bridges had presented a dilemma to the officers controlling the various detachments retreating to the river. No one knew whether or not the French would send up reserves to attack across the Aisne. No one knew how long the surviving bridges should be kept open for our own men making their way back. Individual commanders had to make their own decisions. Lieutenant-Colonel R. H. Anderson-Morshead, whose Devons had been fighting a deliberate rearguard action from Ville au Bois, took it upon himself to cover the large bridge at Pontavert which was being used by retiring troops of both the 50th and 8th. Taking cover in old trenches and ruined buildings, the battalion mowed down wave after wave of Germans trying to crash across by sheer weight of numbers. A more discreet group of the enemy used the diversion to sneak into Pontavert itself and installed itself in houses from which they trained their machine guns on the Devons.

The Devons were now completely cut off but continued to defend themselves tenaciously. Late in the morning a retreating gunner officer and a handful of men reached them and offered to stay and help. Anderson-Morshead realized they had no weapons and ordered them to make their way back if they could. The artillerymen left the colonel sitting in a trench writing out orders 'with a perfect hail of shrapnel falling all round him'. [8, 14]

A mile to the west, headquarters personnel of the 24th Brigade formed a covering party for troops falling back on the bridge at La Pecherie. They too were cut off and when the survivors of the brigade were counted shortly afterwards they were found to number only three officers and sixty-eight other ranks. Toiling up the hillside on the south bank this forlorn band slid into a trench and waited for the next assault. It was not long in coming. The Germans were already over the Aisne in the French sector, as well as at Pontavert, and pushing vigorously along the southern slopes, lapped round the rear of the strongpoints in Gernicourt Wood. Now among tangled branches and fallen trunks (all of which had been liberally splashed with mustard gas) the German bomb and flame-thrower sections sought out the strongpoints of the defenders. Mitrailleuses, Vickers,

Madsens, and Erfurts rasped and rattled as the storm troops closed in. Bearded Frenchmen of the 11th/23rd Territorial Battalion and smooth-chinned boys of the 22nd Durhams shared trenches and dug-outs, tended each other's wounds, and served the same weapons. The 1st Sherwood Foresters pushing forward on the right of the wood afforded some relief but, as the enemy continued to press on at Pontavert and another bridge just west of it, they too were surrounded. A furious struggle raged on into the afternoon.

By midday the 8th Division was reduced to two companies of the 2nd South Lancs and stragglers. Of their artillery, not a gun north of the river had escaped destruction or capture. Batteries which had been in action all night discovered the Germans almost upon them at 0600. The 5th Battery of the XLVth Brigade fought its 18-pounders until the enemy were within 200 yards and then, as a subaltern burned the maps and documents, its men took up rifles and Lewis guns and set upon their assailants. Hours later, a solitary gunner, still clutching his rifle, reached the British lines and reported that the battery had been wiped out. The major commanding the 32nd Battery succeeded in mounting his sole remaining field gun on a light railway wagon, and retreated down the track firing shrapnel while his men covered the flanks with their small arms. This 'self-propelled' weapon had to be abandoned in the end, but its gunners escaped.

At noon the mist had gone and the sun was blazing down on the scene. From the air, German squadrons returning from low-level attacks on the trenches could see dense columns of their own troops moving up and over Chemin des Dames, the spearheads marked by swaying observation balloons attached to lorries. Here and there in the churned up soil of the pulverized forward zone, mopping up parties wiped out the small stubborn pockets of resistance. Sulky pillars of oily smoke rose from knocked out tanks and burning ammunition dumps. Squads of pioneers in shirt sleeves were already repairing the torn roads and beyond the ridge German troops were making their way down the winding lanes to the glittering twin silver ribbons of the

Aisne and its attendant canal. Batteries cantered over the open fields and set up their guns.

On the far bank, tiny figures trailed across the green slopes looking for all the world like parties of hikers on a Sunday stroll. Near the villages on the menaced heights, chalky patches of fresh soil sprouted, showing where troops were urgently digging. In the distance solid columns of reserves were moving up. Isolated black and yellow smudges on the landscape indicated new ranging shots by the German heavy guns of the massive array of cannon which had been hauled forward.

Sweltering under their thick grey serge and heavy steel helmets, German machine gun companies heaved their clumsy sledge mountings up the hillside. Water cans for the cooling systems were filled in the shallows of the river. Other troops with entrenching tools dug sketchy weapon pits; ammunition boxes were stowed under cover and ranges taken. Behind them, traffic policemen directed heavy mortar teams to the remaining bridges and gave them preference over other troops. Like pack animals they strained at ropes and tugged their ugly weapons in the wake of the machine gunners.

An uneasy, unspoken, truce descended over the valley as the British dug in to defend the chain of hills between the Aisne and the Vesle – where they had originally wanted to site their defences – and the Germans regrouped and reorganized. Down the road towards Pontavert the regiments of the German 50th Division, a formation with a high reputation and the honour of capturing Fort Vaux at Verdun in 1916, tramped past trenches and broken walls where the red in the shoulder flash of the slaughtered Devons lent a tiny splash of colour to the dirty khaki uniforms of the dead. In Gernicourt wood harassed German battalion commanders had heated conversations over the newly laid field telephones as they tried to explain that although the fighting had ended, their formations were in complete confusion and needed time to sort themselves out.

Nevertheless, there were plenty of fresh units to take up the pursuit. Soon after 1600, with an ear-splitting crash, a minenwerfer raised a tall plume of black smoke near the makeshift British trenches. Another crashed down. And another. Machine guns chimed in before the smoke of the first bomb had cleared and the bucolic peace disintegrated as a new bombardment traced the defenders' line with drifting smoke and spurting soil. Sections of the assault platoons started to advance by short rushes and were met with a roar of small arms fire. All three brigades of the 25th Division had been detached from the parent formation – as they had been in March on the Somme and in Flanders in April – and put in the line. A British eyewitness of the afternoon attack recorded this tribute to the German infantry: 'The advance was made by trickling forward all along the front with small columns which wormed their way forward with great skill, and, what is perhaps more important, with great determination.'[59]

Companies and platoons formed from stragglers and training units thickened the British line. Those Germans who came up against 600 men from the 8th Division Lewis Gun School were singularly unfortunate. But fight as they might the weight of numbers gradually drove the British back to the crest of the hills and a bitter struggle took place to hold it. An NCO of the 1st Wiltshires suddenly dashed forward to an abandoned French machine gun, acquainted himself with its intricacies in the shortest instructional course on record, and started to blaze away with it. A startled friend suddenly found himself (against his better judgement) in the same gunpit helping him. For the next few days Lance-Corporal A. Asher and his Hotchkiss were inseparable.[59] One hundred veteran experts of the 74th Brigade Instructional Platoon exercised their deadly skills on masses of the enemy, but only an officer and two men escaped to pass on what new lessons they had learned on the afternoon of 27 May.

By early evening the 75th Brigade was running out of ammunition and sent an urgent call for cartridges and reinforcements. Heneker was able to provide the former at once, but officers had to comb the district for stragglers to supply the latter. Adding his own head-quarters guard, and its clerks and servants, he was able to dispatch 500 men; they arrived at the 75th Brigade headquarters about 1000 hours. The 7th Brigade had also been heavily hit and a lance-corporal with a charmed life had no difficulty in finding customers for a makeshift ambulance service he was operating with a captured German horse. As darkness fell it became obvious that the crest could not be held and the British fell back towards the Vesle, the Germans harrying them down the slopes and infiltrating through the many gaps in the line.

Stretcher bearers loading ambulances in the streets of Bouvancourt suddenly noticed German soldiers covering them from doors and windows. The whole of the 25th Field Ambulance was surrounded and captured, only the colonel and an American doctor escaping to report the event. Forty wagons of a column carrying small arms ammunition were cut off and although one or two skilful drivers fled across the fields, the rest fell into German hands.

Throughout that balmy night, soldiers of all branches of the service plodded wearily down the roads leading to the Vesle while the noise of sharp clashes with the thrusting Germans flared spasmodically behind them.

The 8th Border Regiment realized after a few exploratory patrols that it was isolated on the hill behind Roucy. Silently it formed up, and with a strong guard on each flank, marched off into the unknown. By dawn, after scattering a German attack on its right, it had reached safer quarters. Enthusiastic Germans who attempted a surprise push against the battered 7th Brigade at 0230 encountered instead a composite battalion of 300 men well-equipped with machine guns and were driven off with severe casualties.

By the evening of the first day, the British had been hurled back some eleven miles at the deepest point of penetration; the apex of the German thrust into the French front was twelve or thirteen miles. The Vesle had already been crossed at Bazoches. (It is worth noting that one of the unfortunate divisions crushed by the Germans *en route* to the Vesle was the French 21st Division which had protested against being sent in time and time again at Verdun and which had finally mutinied when ordered into action during the Nivelle offensive. On that occasion it was persuaded to submit itself to the machine guns once again after the ringleaders of the mutineers had been summarily shot. On 27 May, the fear of the firing squad was insignificant compared with the sledgehammer blows of the enemy and thousands of prisoners willingly streamed into the German cages safe, at last, from both sides.)

Broken in the centre, the French were able to pivot on the dour defence of the Bretons and the Pinon Forest. The German dead piled up as each assault was answered by the bright flames of the *mitrailleuses* stabbing out from the ugly black mouths of the pillboxes. Vauxillon and Laffaux villages were hammered to dust and yet repeatedly, when the German NCOs led the storm troops in, there were always men in shabby blue uniforms crouched behind rattling machine guns to mow them down.

CHAPTER TWENTY-ONE

BOCHE VERSUS BUTTERFLY

The stand on the left wing and the hinge formed by the French 45th and British 21st Divisions on the right, were the only bright spots in a day of unmitigated disaster. Everything the British commanders had forecast had come sadly and bloodily true. The divisions between the Aisne and the ridge had been destroyed. For Duchêne, the catastrophe came not so much as a surprise but a cruel revelation of his own fallibility. Frantically he committed a reserve division to throw the Germans back across the Aisne; it was engulfed with its fellows.

Only slightly less surprised than Duchêne was Ludendorff. He studied the reports of the day's fighting and travelled from Avesnes early the next day to the headquarters of the Seventh Army. He arrived at 0700 on the 28th (smugly beating the Crown Prince, commanding the Army Group, by a few minutes). In the conference that followed Von Boehn, the Seventh Army commander, revealed that he had already pushed on across the Vesle in preparation for seizing the heights. Ludendorff drove away in exultant but pensive mood. He had a big decision to make. When the hills fell, as they were certain to, he would have achieved his objective – and at relatively small cost. Should he then call a halt to the offensive and allow the Allies to rush reserves from the north? According to his original plan, the next step should be to strike with Von Hutier's army on the Somme and draw still more Allied troops to the south, before launching the true and final offensive against the British in Flanders. Nothing had happened to change his confident hopes for that project. If anything, it was a better prospect than ever.

On the other hand, the glowing vision of a march to Paris lay before him. The Marne was within easy striking distance

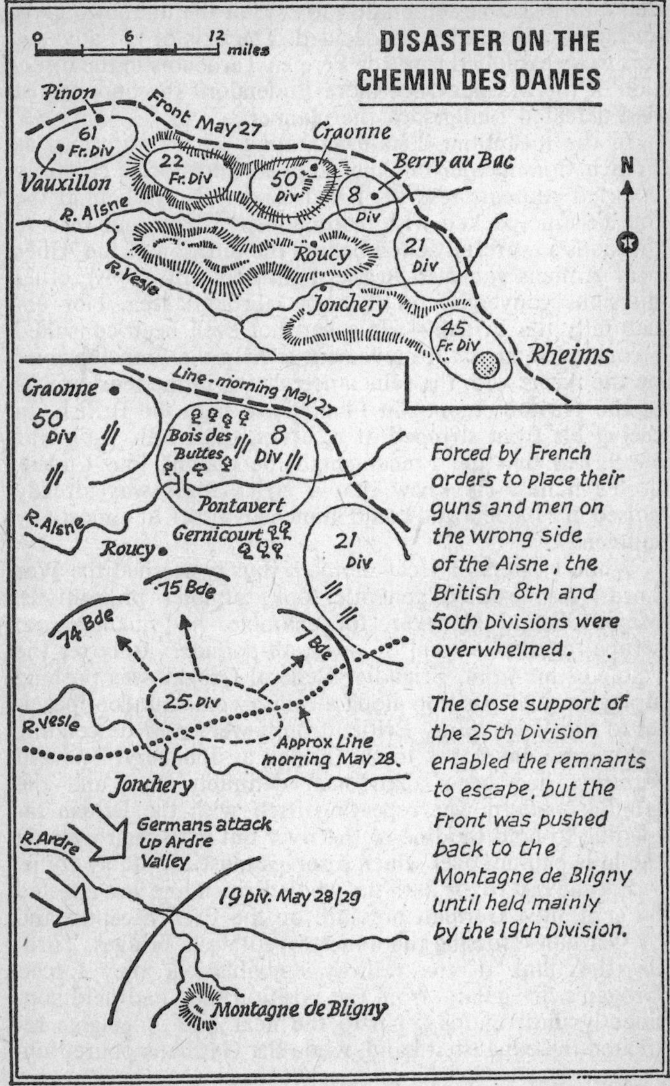
DISASTER ON THE CHEMIN DES DAMES
0
6
12
miles
N
Pinon
Front May 27
61 Fr. Div
Vauxillon
22 Fr. Div
Craonne
50 Div
Berry au Bac
8 Div
R. Aisne
Roucy
21 Div
R. Vesle
Jonchery
45 Fr. Div
Rheims
Line-morning May 27
Craonne
50 Div
Bois des Buttes
8 Div
Pontavert
R. Aisne
Gernicourt
Roucy
21 Div
75 Bde
74 Bde
7 Bde
25. Div
R. Vesle
Approx Line morning May 28.
Jonchery
Germans attack up Ardre Valley
R. Ardre
19 Div. May 28/29
Montagne de Bligny
Forced by French orders to place their guns and men on the wrong side of the Aisne, the British 8th and 50th Divisions were overwhelmed.
The close support of the 25th Division enabled the remnants to escape, but the Front was pushed back to the Montagne de Bligny until held mainly by the 19th Division.

and an irresistible temptation to exploit the unknown grew and grew. At midday he decided. The axis of the advance was to be exploited towards Fère en Tardenois in the direction of the Marne. Once more Ludendorff the opportunist had defeated Ludendorff the planner.

In the meantime, Pétain, counting on his authority as French Commander-in-Chief, dipped into Foch's carefully hoarded strategic reserve. Roads and railways behind the line became packed with troop convoys. The four reserve divisions so carefully sited behind the junction of the Allies near Amiens vanished in the night and with twelve other divisions converged on the breakthrough area. Not unnaturally the British – Haig had not even been consulted – contrasted the swift movement to help the French armies on the Aisne with the reluctance shown in the tense weeks of the previous month in Flanders to help the British. In seeing his front stripped of reserves, moreover, Haig was concerned that the French might be playing into Ludendorff's hands. He knew that a strike force was already poised in Flanders and could launch an attack at almost any moment.

While matters of great moment thus concerned the War Lords, less exalted generals took humbler precautions. Major-General Heneker, for example, had managed to scrape together a total of seven 18-pounders to cover the whole of his front. Brigadier-General Grogan was pushing stragglers into position along a railway embankment parallel to the Vesle. Stray British troops were now descending in swarms the slopes to the bridge at Jonchery. The hill top line had been abandoned definitely now and the familiar pattern was repeating itself with the British intending to hold the line of the river but with their eyes on the hills behind, over which reserves must inevitably come.

For the rest of the 28th the whole British line was affected by continued German pressure on the French centre and by Germans crossing the undestroyed Vesle bridges. Turning the flank of the railway embankment they forced Grogan's 'irregulars' from the position they had held confidently until midday. Up to the next line of heights retreated the exhausted band, while the Germans poured unscathed down the roads to the bridge at Jonchery, still spanning the river despite numerous attempts to destroy it. The arrival of a brigade of the French 154th Division, complete with supporting artillery brought some relief, but by evening a crisis again arose as the enemy seized a dominating hill. An inspired charge by 120 men of the 2nd Devons threw them back again.

After a comparatively quiet night the German pressure grew relentlessly on the 29th. Slowly the British and French, now completely intermixed, fell back to another ridge. The remnants of the 8th and 50th divisions were now all under the command of Major-General Heneker who sent out his officers to round up stragglers just as Coffin had done at Rosières. These he fed and armed and then hoarded at his headquarters, doling them out in miserly fashion for only the most acute crisis.

Grogan's force was now cunningly concealed just below the crest of a ridge and when the enemy appeared, it opened up a heavy fire which drove him to cover. Unable to locate the British posts, the enemy flailed the area blindly with small arms fire for a time and then tried again, only to run into yet another withering cross fire.

The Germans halted their abortive advance and soon the British troops saw stirring in the woods opposite, what looked like huge yellow eggs. Shortly afterwards, a line of fat observation balloons rose into the sky, the crews in the baskets searching diligently for the troublesome defenders; ugly aircraft with large black crosses droned overhead to help with the spotting. Obviously the Germans knew their job because soon mortar teams could be seen manhandling their weapons into position and at about 1500 a full-scale bombardment was opened. Although Heneker immediately directed the fire of his handful of guns on the valley where the enemy was concentrated, the rain of minenwerfer continued unabated. If the barrage was deadly it was also flattering for its attentions were directed on some 200 men, 'All hungry, sleepless, dirty; many bleeding from wounds of greater or less severity. A number of French colonial troops completed the toll. . . .' Grogan was fully aware that his little party could not hold out indefinitely and quietly sent a picked band to the next ridge to cover the withdrawal which was bound to come.

The bombardment continued for nearly three terrifying hours. Some of Grogan's men, who had only flimsy cover, were torn to shreds by the exploding minenwerfers; the little village of Treslon disappeared in a whirl of brickdust and flying tiles; worse still, the Allied artillery, obviously as mystified as the Germans as to the whereabouts of the British and French infantry, landed salvo after salvo in their midst. It was more than flesh and blood could stand and the line broke and fell back in confusion to Bouleuse Ridge, running as fast as their legs could carry them. Such exertions after days of battle were exhausting. One officer who reached the crest sat down to regain his breath, fell fast asleep, and could not be roused although the enemy were even then in the process of attacking the position. He was eventually thrown over a horse and led from the scene –still fast asleep.

Out of this band of frightened, strained, wild-eyed men, the ragged fragments of three complete divisions, Grogan once again created a firing line. In April the Australian officers who met at Grogan's headquarters before the night attack at Villers Bretonneux had considered him all in, yet on 29 May he was showing near superhuman reserves of energy. Energy was not enough Reinforcements were needed to stifle this calculated and full-scale attack which even the arrival of the 2nd Wiltshires, the vanguard of the 19th Division, could not be certain to contain. Reinforcements were needed everywhere. Even as the bombardment on Grogan's force reached its crescendo a battle-grimed French officer arrived at Heneker's headquarters bringing the news that the Germans had breached the line at Lhery, three miles away, with tanks. He had been sent by the commander of the French 154th Division with a personal request for help. Promptly, Heneker's latest collection of stragglers were ordered to their feet and marched off on the Lhery road only to learn a short time later (with unconcealed pleasure) that the breakthrough was a false alarm; the German tanks had turned out to be French armoured cars. In a somewhat less cheerful vein Heneker's scratch battalion then heard that instead they would be joining Grogan on the Bouleuse Ridge. They were received there with open arms as Grogan eyed covetously the seven Vickers guns the composite battalion had brought with them. But still more reinforcements were needed. All day the British had struggled against heavy odds and had been almost consumed. Many troops had become casualties covering the Vesle crossings during the morning including the 11th Lancashire Fusiliers who had been wiped out and four machine guns which had held on to the last, although surrounded.

Some German assaults were smashed by an unimpressed private named Thompson of the 4th Staffordshircs with his Lewis gun. The rest of the gun crew had been killed or wounded the previous day and all the drums except one had been lost. Somehow Private Thompson managed to reload the precious drum each time it was expended. Generally he re-emptied it just as the enemy were forming up from the last shattered assault and advancing under the impression they had silenced their baffling opponent. Private Thompson and his gun were still in action the following day, but by then he was able to find a more plentiful supply of drums.[59]

The rest of the 19th Division had followed the 2nd Wiltshires into the line and taken command of all the British troops remaining. Travelling from Chalons in buses, the 19th had the galling experience of being abused by French civilians, never slow to blame their Allies for the debacle.[70] On its arrival behind the Bouleuse Ridge during the night of the 29th, its battalions in full fighting order, the 19th Division found tattered scarecrows waiting to guide them into position. Youngsters in the 19th's full strength platoons stared wide-eyed at the small bands of ruffians strung about with a variety of British, French, and even German equipment, lying beside their weapons. It was obviously no time to be hesitant about digging in and the newcomers set about the job with a will but, before they had finished, the Germans laid down a resounding barrage from the same guns that had blasted Grogan's men the day before. Crouching in their half-dug holes the British troops heard whistles and put up their heads just as the German infantry rose to their feet. Apparently the local enemy commander did not expect serious resistance for instead of trickling forward in the latest approved fashion, the Germans swept forward in eight long waves. The target was too good to miss, but the numbers were overwhelming and the Wiltshires, 10th Worcesters, and 9th Royal Welch Fusiliers were slowly pushed back. Suddenly a tired French unit broke and the German infantry rushed into a gap between the Fusiliers and the next British battalion, the 9th Welch Regiment. Quickly setting up light machine guns they raked the Welchmen from both flanks and cut across their line of retreat; only one company of the 9th Welch survived the bomb-throwing, butt-swinging mêlée that followed.

Despite this disaster, the 19th Division, and the remnants of the other British divisions, lost only a mile or so of ground during the day. The 21st Division, still clinging grimly to the right of the French garrison at Rheims, lost hardly any at all. In the centre of the broken French front, however, the old enemies of the 8th Durhams, the 444th Infantry Regiment, created a sensation by reaching Jaulgonne on the Marne, a fact the Germans wasted no time in broadcasting over their embryo radio systems. Soissons had fallen the day before, when the French left wing had been pressed back and the stubborn Bretons silenced in their blockhouses. That had been shock enough, but to reach the Marne! The Germans had now penetrated nearly forty miles from the Chemin des Dames.

On this fateful day a small figure in a battered soft hat sat chewing his walrus moustache in the back of a car speeding along the roads towards the front. Clemenceau had decided to see the front for himself. One Tiger was about to come face to face with another.[10]

Abruptly Clemenceau's cavalcade was pulled up by a picket guarding the road; there was no point the Prime Minister was informed in driving to Belleu to see General Duchêne. The Germans were there. The convoy was redirected to the new 6th Army HQ at Oulchy le Chateau. It was an agonizing meeting for Duchêne, who knew that he alone must bear the responsibility for the greatest single advance made by the Germans in the whole war. Despite the half-hearted attempts of Clemenceau to cheer him up Duchêne remained 'Like a man who had been punched in the stomach'. Visits to the headquarters of the various corps commanders showed them to be no more optimistic than their chief. At 30th Corps HQ, General Chrétien bewailed his luck in holding a command that had sustained for the second time a massive surprise attack (the first occasion had been at Verdun). General de Maud'huy, who had commanded an army at the beginning of the war but had fallen from favour since, told Clemenceau frankly at XI Corps HQ that he blamed Duchêne for the debacle. This attack on Duchêne, coupled with the railing against Foch and Pétain which Clemenceau had heard elsewhere, must have depressed the normally resilient little man. He was warmly pleased, at any rate, to discover that Degoutte, commander of XXI Corps, was not at all dismayed by the prospect of facing the vanguard of victorious Germans, 'He may look like a little fat Chinese cook,' said Clemenceau later to Foch, 'but he knows his business and keeps calm.'

Within a matter of days, the Chinese Cook was to replace the Tyrannical Tiger. During that period Pétain was given more of the cherished French reserves including fresh American divisions behind the British line. As Haig was consulted only after the moves had been made, he was rightly indignant. Haig's own armies had been in action for six terrible weeks and were still facing the massed reserves of Prince Rupprecht's Army Group; Pétain was doubly ensuring the safety of his own front at the expense of the British. Pugnaciously, Haig (with the support of the British Government, who for once saw eye to eye with their Commander-in-Chief) extracted from Foch a promise that there would be no more 'stealing' of reserves. Haig kept to himself that 'Because of the doubtful condition of many French divisions,' he thought it a 'waste of good troops' to reinforce the French with Americans.[6]

This wrangling in high places was to have a far-reaching effect on the remaining months of the war; but it did nothing for the men staring with red-rimmed eyes over the white chalk parapets of the trenches near Rheims. On 31 May, parties of the 8th, 25th and 50th divisions were pulled back for rest and reorganization; the 21st Division was relieved and the 19th remained in the slowly stiffening line.

On 1 June, however, urgent orders sent composite battalions of the 8th, 50th, and 25th Divisions hurrying to the front again. By this time the 19th Division had dwindled to 2,000 troops although it still had thirty-five of its sixty-four Vickers guns dug into position. That afternoon, it was obvious that the guns would be needed. Enemy troops were reported concentrating in valleys and woods preparatory to an attack. At 1600 after the usual preliminary barrage, they moved forward, overran two companies of the 8th Gloucesters, and threatened to take the Wiltshires in the flank. Before they could effect this a counter-attack by all available British troops swept onto them; not to be outdone, Commandant A. de Lasbourde, of the 2/22 French Regiment, sharing the same sector, leaped over the parapet and waved his troops forward. Amid British yells, French cheers, and German oaths and shouts, the disputed trenches were recovered.

This blow, combined with stout French resistance in Rheims itself, kept the Germans quiet for days. Even Germans needed time to rest, count their dead, restock their ammunition dumps, and send convoys of ambulances to the railheads. Then at 0400 on the 6th, they struck again. Their objective was the hill of Bligny, 600 feet high and holding the key to the congested back area of Rheims just as the Mont des Cats ridge protected the rear of Ypres. Standing between the Germans and Bligny were the three brigades of the 19th division (the 58th had been reduced to a composite battalion) and the composite battalions of the 8th, 25th, and 50th divisions – still in the line after eleven days.

Any hopes of a walk-over were quickly dispelled. When the waves of the 86th and 23rd German Divisions were pressing forward over the torn ground on the 59th Brigade's front they were amazed to see a thin khaki line suddenly clamber out of the trenches, form up in no-man's-land, and come doubling towards them with their fourteen-inch bayonets fixed. The startled Germans faltered but the pace of the British quickened. With a howl of rage the charge was upon them. The battle-crazed soldiers of the Wiltshires, the Welch, and the Royal Welch Fusiliers, unleashed the frustrations that had been pent up ever since their battalions were cut to pieces a week earlier. The enemy ran for cover and the brigade officers had great difficulty in halting their men.[70]

The Germans advancing through the haze and dust against the 57th Brigade heard the uproar on their flank, but the trenches in front of them lay strangely silent. They were unaware that their silhouettes were growing sharper all the time in the sights of riflemen crouched behind the parapet, that fresh pans were ready to be slapped on poised Lewis guns, that the Vickers teams were waiting for them to reach the aiming points. The 10th Royal Warwicks, Worcesters, Gloucesters and the 50th Composite Battalion allowed the Germans to come within point-blank range before the fire order was given. The attack was scythed down. On the approaches to Bligny itself, held by the strongest of the 19th Division's brigades, the early morning attack failed to develop. At 1100, however, the French were driven back on the right and the forward companies of the 9th Cheshires were driven back over the crest. Working like men possessed the Germans mounted machine guns in time to stop the Cheshire support company when it came racing into the attack, but hardly had they recovered from this threat when yet another wave of cursing, shouting British were scrambling desperately up the hillside at them. One by one the German machine guns were knocked out and the 4th Shropshires, with the survivors of the Cheshires, carried the summit forcing the Germans back in tumbling disorder. The Germans did not come again while the British held this sector.[70]

Incredibly, the 19th Division, and the composite battalions attached to it, were kept in the line at the specific request of the general commanding the sector – a Frenchman who did not conceal his admiration for the fighting qualities of British troops. Not until 15 June were they relieved by the Italian 8th Division. The Italians entered the line, amid scenes of considerable confusion during which the 5th South Wales Borderers noted with amazement that every man of the incoming formation seemed to have brought his own dog with him.[1]

Elsewhere, the fragments of the departing divisions were collected and the kits of the dead were prepared for dispatch home. Parades were held to let the men know that, if nothing else, the sacrifice on the Chemin des Dames had served to warn French generals to heed the warnings of their Allies in the future. Nor were the French grudging in their amends. General Maistre referred to the stalwarts of the Aisne in glowing praise, and General Berthelot published two Orders of the Day announcing the award of the Croix de Guerre to the 2nd Devons and the 5th Battery RFA. The Shropshires got the medal too for their counter-attacks.

For the 8th and the 50th Divisions there was an honour peculiarly British. Since 21 March GHQ had kept a table showing the losses of each division. The 50th was at the top of the list with just under 17,000 casualties; the 8th Division were some 300 casualties short of that figure.

CHAPTER TWENTY-TWO

WE'RE HERE BECAUSE WE'RE HERE

The spring battles of 1918 were devastating, but both sides learned valuable lessons. For the British, the most important of these was that to retreat does not mean to be beaten; for the Germans, that to advance does not necessarily mean victory. One lesson all combatants learned was that the war need not have been fought below the surface of the ground; trenches were a thing of the past. Future conflicts, obviously, would be decided by quick movement on the ground and in the air. (The final irony is that only the Germans really remembered this, and that within twenty-two years of the Armistice Hitler accomplished what Ludendorff had failed.)

Today the battlefields of March, April and May, 1918 can be traversed in a few hours by car. Ypres is less than two hours from Dunkirk. The most eye-catching sights in the great square of Ypres are the advertisements for Whitbread's beer which festoon the restaurants – not that many British spend time there these days. In the visitors' books at the cemeteries the greatest number of signatures belong to Belgians. Entries in English, like that written by an old soldier from Ontario at the massive memorial to the Canadians at Poelcappelle, are rare: 'It is a lot better now than when I was here in 1915.' Looking at the trim gardens, the dignified yews, and the weedless lawns, one can believe him.

To drive still farther south, one wonders at the importance which a pleasant range of hills, including Mont Kemmel, once held. On a summer's morning at Arras, dozens of cars with GB plates can be seen scurrying determinedly toward sunnier spots; most of them travel a long way before stopping. Even today the Arras-Bapaume road makes grim travelling. There are few attractive lay-bys or picnic spots; undistinguished redbrick villages – Ervillers, Behagnies, and Sapignies – are passed without a glance. Beyond Bapaume, with its modern roadside garages, Le Transloy and Sailly-Saillisel flash by; good parking facilities in the pleasant irregular shaped square of Péronne are more likely to tempt the motorist to stop for a few minutes. A cold beer perhaps, a stroll down the street to catch a glimpse of the medieval castle, a glance at the crumbling ramparts, and then off again. At Athies no one would ever believe that the dull ordinary bridge across the canal had ever been important enough to fight over. And who would think of it anyway with a mind filled with thoughts of lunch at Soissons, or dinner at Rheims. No one wants to stop. The British rush past their history as if they were ashamed of it.

Even those who do turn aside from the main roads will find exploring difficult. There are few signposts for the idly curious. Only the odd wire-picket hedging marks the passing of a chilled, rain-soaked British working party many years ago in the fields below Southern Redoubt. Passchendaele itself is a dull, almost sullen village, with an ugly church and a dusty bus shelter. The grassy hummocks of Hill 60, unaltered since the last shell, now overlook a bungalow with a picture window; there is no memorial for the unrecovered bodies still entombed in the mine catacombs below. The pleasant land seems subdued as if ashamed of its violent past. In the Somme uplands the notices of the Imperial War Graves Commission are written in discreet letters on a dark green background, as if trying not to intrude their English words into the French countryside. One has to be alert to spot the small signpost leading to Regina Trench; the muted emblem carved on the gate which leads to the grass-covered ruins of Pozières windmill is weatherbeaten and worn, like the notice which points out almost diffidently that the Australian dead lay thicker here than anywhere else during the war. Few who visit the Tank Corps memorial nearby notice that the fence posts are six-pounder guns and that the driving chains of Mark Vs hang between them. The road which leads to Albert is peaceful and there is nothing to indicate to the tourist that these rolling fields of dun coloured corn once echoed for days on end the gasps, screams, and prayers of dying men; nothing recalls that the Third Army's broken divisions once trudged on weary legs past piles of bricks where those neat farms now stand. The winding country lanes are quiet. Poppies, small and delicate, decorate sunken roads and banks where once frightened human beings – khaki and grey alike – dug for their lives. Everywhere the countryside denies its past.

It is with surprise, then, that one suddenly comes face to face with a statue of a British soldier under the shade of tall trees in the hamlet of Flers – a monument recording the achievements of the 41st Division in 1916. Farther towards Albert the face of the monolith to the 20th Division is showing numerous cracks and appears to be leaning out of true. At Thiepval, French workmen bustle about the ungainly red-brick memorial commemorating thousands of missing. But there is no real hurry. The memorial will not run away and the missing and dead have been absent from the sight of man for more than fifty years now – often, even the regiments they served are no more.

To find the graves of the Fifth Army is not easy, but they are there, and in one of the most pleasant countrysides in France, a casual fisherman's dream – just as the glorious rolling woods and hills of Chemin des Dames offer a paradise for walkers. There, on a sunny hillside, the British regular soldiers who were killed in 1914 lie side by side with the amateurs and conscripts who died when the British returned in 1918. It is but two or three years ago that they found five of them still huddled in a Bruchmüller shellhole hidden in the thick undergrowth. They find Germans too. Ask the French workmen scything the grass in the big cemetery nearby what happens to them and he will nod to a corner where a passage through the hedge shows row upon row of black crosses. 'Les Boches,' he says, imitating the motion of a man spitting. 'Les Boches.' Yet it is spring again, and in the fertile soil of France the lush vegetation grows carelessly on the graves of the best and bravest young men of any nation; the workman scythes and weeds for them all. In this, perhaps, lies the real lesson. If there is one.

TABLE VI Main Infantry weapons in use during Spring 1918

	BRITISH		GERMAN		FRENCH
RIFLE	*Short Magazine Lee-Enfield*		*Mauser*		*Lebel*
Calibre	.303 in. (10 rds.)		.311 in. (5 rds.)		.315 in. (8 rds.)
Weight	8 lb. 2½ oz.		9 lb.		9 lb. 3½ oz.
Sights Max.	2,800 yds.		2,187 yds.		2,187 yds.
BAYONET	These averaged from 14 in. to 17 in. and weighed about 14 oz.				
LIGHT M.G.	*Lewis*	*Hotchkiss*	*Madsen*	*Bergmann*	*Chauchat*
Magazine	47 rd. drum	30 rd. strip	40 rd. box	Belt	20 rd. box
Weight	26 lb.	28 lb.	20 lb.	25 lb.	19 lb.
HEAVY M.G.*	*Vickers*		*Maxim*	*Erfurt*	*Hotchkiss*
Weight					
Gun	38 lb.		48 lb.	37 lb.	55 lb.
Mounting	48 lb. tripod		77 lb. sledge	52 lb. tripod	58 lb. tripod
Sights Max.	2,900 yds.		2,190 yds.		2,190 yds.

*The British and German guns were watercooled, and fired 250-round belts of rifle calibre ammunition. The French gun was air cooled and fired 30-round strips.

TABLE VII Artillery pieces and some statistics

BRITISH *Calibre*	*Shell*	*Range*	GERMAN *Calibre*	*Shell*	*Range*	FRENCH *Calibre*	*Shell*	*Range*
18 pdr.	18 lb.	6,500 yds.	77 mm. (3.1 in.)	15 lb.	7,500 yds.	75 mm. (3 in.)	15 lb.	9,300 yds*
4.5 in. (114 mm.)			120 mm. (4.7 in.)	46 lb.		150 mm. (6 in.)		
4.7 in. gun			130 mm. (5.2 in.)			155 mm. (6.2 in.)	95 lb.	7,000 yds.
(120 mm.)	50 lb.	1,500 yds.	150 mm. (5.9 in.)	88 lb.		370 mm. (14.6 in.)	8 cwt.	6 miles
60 pdr. (5 in.)		10,000 yds.	210 mm. (8.3 in.)	250 lb.		400 mm. (16 in.)		
6 in. gun			305 mm. (12 in.)	770 lb.		520 mm. (20 in.)	28 cwt.	12 miles
(150 mm.)	100 lb.		380 mm. (15 in.)	8 cwt.	28 miles			
6 in. how.			420 mm. (16.5 in.)	15.7 cwt.	6 miles			
(150 mm.)	100 lb.	7 miles						
8 in. how.								
(200 mm.)	290 lb.	7 miles						
8 in. gun								
9.2 in. (230 mm.)								
9.2 in. gun	380 lb.	14 miles						*1912 model
12 in. (300 mm.)	850 lb.							1897 model
15 in. (380 mm.)								7,400 yds.
Mortars			Mortars			Mortars		
Stokes 3 in.	10 lb.	1,200 yds.	Minenwerfer (2 in.)	50 lb.	450 yds.	Batignolles 240 mm. (9.5 in)		
Smoke mortar	25 lb.		1918 mortar	9 lb.	1,400 yds.		200 lb.	6 miles
			170 mm. (6.6 in.)	110 lb.	1,250 yds.	Dumezil	35 lb.	700 yds.

TABLE VIII

BATTLE ORDER OF THE THIRD ARMY, *General Sir Julian Byng.*

Front: 28 miles. Divisions: 14. Guns: 1,120 including 461 heavies.

XVII Corps (Lieutenant-General Sir Charles Fergusson).

15th (Scottish) Division, 4th Division.

VI Corps (Lieutenant-General Sir J. Haldane).

3rd Division, 34th Division, 59th (2nd North Midland) Division.

IV Corps (Lieutenant-General Sir George Harper).

6th Division, 51st (Highland) Division.

V Corps (Lieutenant-General Sir E. Fanshawe).

47th (2nd London) Division, 63rd (Royal Naval) Division, 17th (Northern) Division.

All the above divisions were in the line on March 21.

Reserves under Byng's command: Guards Division, near Arras; 25th Division at Bapaume; 19th and 2nd Divisions behind IV and V Corps.

Reserves under the command of G.H.Q. and placed behind Third Army: 40th Division in old Somme battle area and the 41st some twenty miles behind the line.

Additional reserves committed to aid of Third Army during March: 31st Division (from evening March 22); 42nd Division (March 24); 12th Division, 62nd Division (March 25); New Zealand Division and 4th Australian Division (March 25/26); 3rd Australian Division (March 27).

French reserves sent to the aid of the Fifth Army during the crisis: 125th Division (March 22); 9th, 10th and 1st Dismounted Cavalry (March 23); 55th (March 24); 1st, 56th and 35th (March 25); elements of two divisions (March 26).

The 22nd and 62nd French cavalry divisions also came into action in the area around March 24.

REFERENCES

1 Atkinson, *History of the South Wales Borderers, 1914–19*. Medici Society
2 Battalion War Diaries
3 Bean, *The A.I.F. in France, 1918*. Angus & Robertson, Sydney, 1937
4 Bean, *op cit*, and other sources
5 Binding, *A Fatalist in War*. Allen & Unwin, 1929
6 Blake, *The Private Papers of Douglas Haig*. Eyre & Spottiswoode, 1952
7 Boraston, *Sir Douglas Haig's Command*. Constable, 1922
8 Boraston, *The History of the Eighth Division*. Medici Society, 1926
9 Bruchmüller, *Die Artillerie beim Angriff im Stellungkreig*
10 Cartier, Raymond, *Histoire d'Une Victore*. Paris, 1968
11 Chapman, Guy, *A Passionate Prodigality*. MacGibbon & Kee, 1965
12 Churchill, W. S., *The World Crisis*. Butterworth, 1921
13 Edmonds, *Military Operations, France and Belgium, 1917*. H.M.S.O.
14 Edmonds, Official History, 1918*
15 Edmonds, Gough, Shaw-Sparrow, *op cit* and others
16 Essame, *Night Counter-Attack*. Macmillan, 1935
17 Essame: Paper
18 Essame: Personal recollections
19 Gale, *Call to Arms*. Hutchinson, 1968
20 German Regimental Histories
21 Gibbs, Philip, *From Bapaume to Passchendaele*. Heinemann, 1918
22 Gibbs, Philip, *The Pageant of the Years*. Gibbs and Phillips, 1964
23 Gibbs, Philip, War Dispatches
24 Gillon, *The Story of the 29th Division*. Nelson, 1925
25 Gladden, E. N., *Ypres, 1917*. Kimber, 1967
26 Goes, Capt G., *Der Grosse Schlacht im Frankreich*. Kolk, Berlin
27 Gordon, *The Unreturning Army*. Dent, 1968
28 Gough, *The Fifth Army*. Hodder & Stoughton, 1931
29 Haig, *Official Dispatches*. Dent, 1919
30 Harris, *The Other Half-Million*. Mercier Press, 1968
31 Headlam, *The Guards Division in the Great War*, Vol. II. Murray, 1924
32 Historical records of the 16th (Service) Battalion, Northumberland Fusiliers
33 History of the 33rd Division
34 The 47th (London) Division, 1914–19

35 History of the 49th Infantry Regiment
36 History of the 114th German Infantry Regiment
37 Horne, Alistair, *The Price of Glory*. Macmillan, 1962
38 Hutchison, Seton, *History and Memoirs of the 33rd Battalion, Machine Gun Corps*
39 Jerrold, *The Royal Naval Division*. Hutchinson, 1923
40 Junger, *Storm of Steel*. Chatto & Windus, 1929
41 Kuhl, Enstehung, *Durchfuhrung und Zussammenbruch der Offensive von 1918*. Deutsche, Berlin
42 Laffin, John, *Swifter Than Eagles*. Blackwood, 1964
43 Liddell Hart, *Foch, Man of Orleans*. Penguin, 1913
44 Lloyd George, *War Memoirs*. Odhams, 1937
45 Ludendorff, *My War Memoirs*. Hutchinson
46 Macpherson, Sir W. G. *et al, Medical Services – Diseases of the War*, Vol. II
47 Monash, *The Australian Victories in France, 1918*
48 Moody, R. S. H., *Historical Records of the Buffs, 1914–19*. Medici Society
49 Official History of the War in the Air
50 O'Neill, H. C., *The Royal Fusiliers in the Great War*. Heinemann, 1922
51 Pitt, Barrie, *1918, The Last Act*. Cassell, 1962
52 Records of the 35th Australian Infantry Battalion
53 Renn, Ludwig, *War*. Secker, 1929
54 Richards, Frank, *Old Soldiers Never Die*. Faber & Faber
55 Rogerson, *Twelve Days*. Arthur Barker, 1935
56 Sandilands, H. R., *The Twenty-Third Division 1914–19*. Nisbet, 1923
57 Scott & Brumwell, *The History of the 12th (Eastern) Division in the Great War*
58 Shaw-Sparrow, W., *The Fifth Army in March, 1918*. Bodley Head, 1921
59 Smith, Kincaid, *The 25th Division in France and Flanders*. Harrison, 1922
60 Smythe, *The Story of the Victoria Cross*. Muller, 1963
61 Carrington, *Soldier From the War Returning*. Hutchinson, 1965
62 Terraine, *Douglas Haig*. Hutchinson, 1965
63 War Diaries*
64 War Diary of the 6th Durham Light Infantry*
65 War Diary of the 8th Durham Light Infantry*
66 War Office documents, April, 1918*
67 Williams, John, *The Ides of May*
68 Wylly, *The Green Howards, 1914–19*
69 Wyrall, Everard, *The Duke of Cornwall's Light Infantry, 1914–19*. Methuen, 1932
70 Wyrall, Everard, *History of the 19th Division*. Arnold
71 Various personal recollections

INDEX